Praise for *Her Way*

"Kamen chronicles the complex ways young women understand and experience sexuality today…Kamen concludes, rather convincingly, that young women are finally beginning to make their own rules."

—*Ms.*

"Insightful…compelling…A provocative look at changing female sexuality."

—*Booklist*

"A bold new look at female sexuality in America today. Based on years of meticulous research, Paula Kamen has produced a fascinating, important study of how young women are redefining their roles and relationships in a post-boomer world."

—Iris Chang, author of *The Rape of Nanking*

"Paula Kamen succeeds where 'trends' fail, defining the sexual power of real women. Intellectual, political, and compassionate, *Her Way* shows that the freedom to live and love by our own standards—with men on our good side—is *the* way toward the social change that, truly, begins in our social lives."

—Lynn Harris, comedian/commentator, co-creator of the award-winning website breakupgirl.com and author of *Breakup Girl to the Rescue*

"Lively and entertaining, honoring the intimate voices of a diversity of women, *Her Way* is an authoritative study of our long slow journey toward sexual autonomy. Kamen is a savvy third-wave feminist who has done her homework. The book is a link between generations and a major stepping-stone toward fuller liberation. This is feminism for the twenty-first century!"

—Barbara Seaman, coeditor of *For Women Only:
Our Guide to Health Empowerment*
and *Ms.* contributing editor

"At last, a book about young women's sexual behavior that's actually written by a young woman! Paula Kamen documents women's sexual truths without judgment and—more important—without all the wrongheaded, double-standard-laden assumptions that all too often plague writing on this topic. Kamen brings the focus back where it should be: on women's own views, rather than others' views of them."

—Lisa Miya-Jervis, publisher, *Bitch* magazine

"*Her Way* gives women cause to celebrate! Paula Kamen's book shows how, for perhaps the first time in history, a generation of young women is truly defining sex on its own terms. Her nuanced analysis of this quiet but undeniable trend is optimistic while not shying away from the problems that remain, including the inertia of mainstream popular culture that insists on portraying women as sexy rather than as sexual beings in their own right."

—Lisa Douglass, Ph.D., coauthor of *Are We Having Fun Yet?*
The Intelligent Woman's Guide to Sex

"Extremely interesting . . . A well-written, optimistic portrait of a generation that doesn't usually get such good press!"

—Katha Pollitt, *Nation* columnist, author of *Subject to Debate:*
Sense and Dissents on Women, Politics and Culture

Her Way

Her Way

Young Women Remake the Sexual Revolution

PAULA KAMEN

BROADWAY BOOKS
New York

PRINTED IN THE UNITED STATES OF AMERICA

BROADWAY BOOKS and its logo, a letter B bisected on the di-
agonal, are trademarks of Broadway Books, a division of
Random House, Inc.

Visit our website at www.broadwaybooks.com

First Broadway Books trade paperback edition published
2002

Library of Congress Cataloging-in-Publication Data
Kamen, Paula.
Her way: Young women remake the sexual revolution /
Paula Kamen.
p.   cm.
Includes bibliographical references.
1. Young women—United States—Sexual behavior.
I. Title.

HQ29 .K35 2002
306.7'084'22—dc21   2001052695

ISBN 0-7679-1000-1

10   9   8   7   6   5   4   3   2   1

Contents

Acknowledgments

During the long and always challenging journey of researching and writing this book, I have been thankful for the many allies along the way. Making this book possible were all the women interviewed, my family, Dr. Ellen Berry, NYU Press editor Eric Zinner, and the dedicated editorial and marketing staff at NYU Press, including Asha Curran, Rachel Weiss, and Claire Griffin. John K. Wilson helped in all steps of this process. Josh Kilroy provided much appreciated editorial support. Cecilia Cancellero was also a much valued editor. My mother also regularly went above and beyond the call of duty, regularly giving me plastic grocery bags stuffed with articles (all having something to do with sex) that she had clipped from the half-dozen newspapers she regularly reads.

Helping with research, interview contacts, editorial suggestions (or just morale) were Daisy Hernandez, Bridget Brown, Marny Requa, Steve Rhodes, Felicia Kornbluh, Kristen Walsh, Jennifer Morris and friends, Clare Sullivan and family, Ellen Frank, Lisa Davis, Lisa Ormerod, Mary McCain, Pam Sourelis, Danny Postel, Melissa Sterne, Ann McCaffrey, Monica Sohn, Jason Schultz, Victoria Stagg Elliott, Anna Minkov, Elizabeth Austin, Wendy Bower, the National Writers Union, Janel Winter, Dick Detzner, Sasha Rubel, Helene Marcos, Vicki Weiss, Amy Keller, Adrienne Kneeland and Chris Jackiw, and Paul and Stephany Creamer. (Apologies to the roommates included in this group for the constant clutter from newspapers and magazines.) I also thank some of my most helpful interview sources, including Ilsa Lottes, Sarah Weddington, Florynce Kennedy, Judy Norsigian, Barbara Seaman, and the staff of the University Settlement of New York City. Helping me with transcription were Deidre Fuller, Becky Kamen, Tim Hegeman, and Transcription Professionals. Thanks to Kate Kirtz for coining the word *superrat* by accident over conversation.

For lodging and local contacts in various cities, I thank: Iris Chang and Brett Douglas, Jeanne Kim, Stephanie Wall, Laurel Carpenter, Mecca Carpenter and family, Jenai Lane, Dawn King and family, Amy Tague, Susan Hays, Dean Fiala, Mary Edwards, Pat Longoria and Mason Peck, and Ken and Becky Kurson.

I greatly appreciate the research support of the Ragdale Foundation and the Northwestern University Gender Studies Program, including the gracious Marena McPherson, Cathy Coppolillo, Rae Moses, and Fran Paden. I would also like to thank the Puffin Foundation and the City of Chicago

CAPS program for grants in 1994. For the paperback edition, I wish to thank editor Rebecca Cole for her support and enthusiasm.

Over the years, material from this book has appeared in different incarnations in other publications. The seeds were planted in a 1992 essay, "The Second Sexual Revolution," in Eric Liu's *Next Progressive* magazine. The section in chapter 8 on young feminist activism against acquaintance rape was printed in another form as three articles: "Erasing Rape: Media Hype an Attack on Sexual-Assault Research" in *EXTRA!* (A Publication of Fairness and Accuracy in Reporting), November/December 1993; "The Knotted Web of Sexual Relations," *Might Magazine* 1, 1994; and "Acquaintance Rape: Revolution and Reaction," in *"Bad Girls/Good Girls": Women, Sex, and Power in the Nineties*, Rutgers University Press, 1996. An early version of my introduction appeared in my commentary, "Clinton Failed to Recognize Sexual Generation Gap," *Chicago Tribune* "Womanews" sec., 11 October 1998.

Author's Note

I first decided to chronicle this sexual evolution nearly a decade ago after observing young women's increasing activism regarding sexual issues, along with my friends' greater number of choices in planning their lives. Today's young feminist activists have taken up where the boomers left off, addressing such tough sexual issues as acquaintance rape, safer sex, and lesbian and bisexual rights.

In the 1990s, while I visited campuses across the nation as a guest lecturer, I noticed that almost every college newspaper I picked up had banner headlines about rabble-rousers fighting for sexual rights. Articles about safer sex became as common as those about the new canned-food drive or updated library computer system. The bulletin boards also signaled the emerging issues. At Northwestern University, fliers were plastered around campus reading, "What is a dental dam?" and *"¿Que es un dental dam?"*—the result of a safer-sex group's activism. At conservative Christian schools such as Butler University in Indianapolis, a posting for the meeting of the gay and lesbian caucus was stapled near the notice of the Bible-study group. At the University of Texas at Austin, I heard about an "A-frame" set up during Rape Awareness Week in the spring, on which women post letters about their most private, formerly stigmatized experiences. At Mary Washington College in Virginia, a professor told me about her relief that a long string of women were at last coming forward to prosecute a male professor long suspected of sexual harassment.

The most common feminist activism I observed was against sexual violence, cutting across class and race and educational level. Almost every small campus I visited, such as the staid Lutheran Valparaiso University in Indiana, was holding a Take Back the Night March, which included speakers talking openly and honestly about a range of sexual experiences and breaking years of silence. Take Back the Night was conceived by radical antipornography feminists in 1978 in San Francisco and became popular at major universities in the 1980s. By 1993, the marches had become so common that even some of the carefully coiffed and often surgically reconstructed characters of *Beverly Hills 90210* were participating in one.

What was going on? I had been noticing for years the generational differences in sexual knowledge among my friends. I think back to when I was visiting my best friend in 1981 in her suburban all-the-houses-look-exactly-alike subdivision in south suburban Chicago. As we sat talking in her room, her voice suddenly became more serious. She told me that she had been sexually abused for years by a relative during her summer trips to Florida. But her real news was that she had finally stopped it. By chance, she had read an interesting article in the *Chicago Heights Star*, part of a three-part series about a newly named phenomenon called *sexual abuse*. For the first time, because of this openness in the media, she recognized her previously private experience being described by other women. The reporter clearly showed how wrong and intolerable these acts were, setting off what my friend called "an alarm" in her head. Finally she broke her silence and told her parents.

Boomers themselves have alerted me to often subtle differences. One older friend of mine who went to college at the height of the sexual revolution in the 1970s confided to me her shock at observing her twentysomething friend's shamelessness about sex. This Generation Xer had met a man at a party and told him up front that if they slept together that night, "it would just be sex" and she didn't want a relationship. Afterward, when he wanted to form a relationship with her, she sent him out the door, repeating the same warning. Right before she broke up with her boyfriend, this same woman told him that they should have sex one last time because she didn't know when she would have it again. The point is that when she was in her twenties, my boomer friend had observed women sleeping around indiscriminately, but she did not know any who were so sexually confident and deliberate about their own satisfaction. I most like to recount another revealing story about differences in generational knowledge about sex. While I was researching this book, my mother (now in her sixties) called to tell me about an article on new sexual trends she was reading in the *Ladies' Home Journal*. She wanted to make sure that I didn't miss the boat and covered this trend of "cunnunglus," which apparently now was very much in vogue.

My friends' individualistic, but also unextraordinary, paths have alerted me as well to changes that we now take for granted. Sexual freedom is an integral part of their individual life choices, and it hardly stands out as unusual. One of my best friends "lost" her virginity at 15, and another at 25, both without shame or earning a "reputation." Still another waited to have sex until she got married, but her sister has lived with a series of boyfriends. Friends talk openly about their sex lives and birth control and expect equal treatment from men. One friend even made her boyfried take a sugar pill every day, to remind him of her own commitment to birth control.

In addition, these women often observe traditional customs, but with a modern spin. One of my most conservative friends got married *after* buying a house in a Republican western suburb with her accountant boyfriend. Another friend married right out of college but wears no wedding ring, has kept her name, travels for her job half the year, and doesn't plan to have kids until she's in her late thirties. Although many women have bowed to tradition and taken their husbands' names, other couples have invented a new last name for both of them. One acquaintance took her "maiden name" as her first name and shares a last name with her husband. A few men I know, who feel a greater attachment to their wife's family than to their own, have taken her last name.

Instead of just reading and theorizing about why certain trends are happening, I have asked women themselves about their sexual identities and journeys and have also explored information—both from academics and from the popular media (which, of course, reflect and shape what women do)—that reveals women's attitudes. With what I discovered, I hope to fill the gap left by the existing literature on postboomer women's sexuality, which consists mostly of confessional essays based on little research beyond the author's Manhattan-based, Ivy League–educated circuit. Whereas most books on sex in general center on the flamboyant or fringe, I made a special effort to find the more "ordinary" voices, those without their own publicists, from the Hispanic telemarketer in Austin to the high school teacher in Florida. Most important, my background in journalism has helped me form a *qualitative* picture of young women's sexual struggles beyond the statistics concerning women's sex lives. There is more to sex in America than who is doing what to whom and how often.

Her Way is based primarily on my interviews with young women of the group known as "Generation X," who were born in the late 1960s through the very early 1980s. A majority were in their twenties during my main interview period, from 1993 to 1996. I unscientifically and loosely defined my sample age group as those who were too young to have used belts in their sanitary protection but who grew up before they could order stuff from the World Wide Web. All are of the generation more likely to have had their early sexual psyches shaped by Judy Blume than by Betty Friedan or Erica Jong. Even though my sample is not scientifically accurate, the core is indeed a diverse cross section of seventy-two American women, varying in marital status, religion, political views (from "anarchist" to right-wing fundamentalist Christian, with most falling between the extremes), education, income, and geographic region.

Apart from this core of young women, I interviewed more than ninety others, including researchers and activists, who offered important opinions from the sidelines. Several were women with whom I spoke either briefly or for long stretches on individual topics, such as a bartender commenting on how AIDS has affected her customers or a virgin I interviewed at a pro–sexual modesty Campus Crusade for Christ rally at Auburn University in Alabama. I also consulted a "control group" of eighteen young men, who made clearer the book's central variable of gender when discussing sexual behavior and attitudes. For a greater generational perspective, I interviewed older women, from regular mothers to those who have been high-profile fighters for women's sexual autonomy, including Sarah Weddington, who argued the landmark *Roe v. Wade* abortion-rights case in 1973; long-time women's health activist and author Barbara Seaman; Judy Norsigian, one of the editors of *Our Bodies, Ourselves*; and 1970s feminist leaders Gloria Steinem and Florynce Kennedy. My selection covered observers of sex in America from widely and sometimes wildly varying vantage points: I interviewed antiporn crusader Andrea Dworkin as well as the *Playboy* adviser. I found some of them at conferences and activist events, such as the 1993 antipornography "Speech, Equality and Harm" conference at the University of Chicago (from which I was almost ejected after a misunderstanding that I was a spy from the opposition) and the 1993 gay, lesbian, and bisexual rights march in Washington, D.C. I also reported from one of the country's largest consumerist tributes to American womanhood (and the only true orgy I have ever attended), a bridal expo near O'Hare Airport.

To make sure that I didn't determine the agenda of the discussions and would be open to new opinions and experiences, the interviews with the core group of women were open-ended, with questions both factual and personal. I started off asking general questions about the particular challenges facing this generation, their views of the sexual revolution, and their own sources of sexual information. I then explored their personal sexual influences, doubts, contradictions, obstacles, and goals. I had prepared additional questions to ask people who fit certain categories and experiences, such as married and single people, lesbians and bisexuals, and feminists. I also told everyone not to be "politically correct" with me or to tell me what they thought I wanted to hear. To create more complete and intimate profiles, I interviewed all the women from this core group in person.

In every case, I used a personal intermediary, a contact at a social service agency or workplace or school, so that the person had some connection to me and some accountability. As a result, I was able to talk with women who were very uncomfortable discussing sex but often had been "talked into" the interview by a mutual acquaintance, as well as those who were so open that I left with more details than requested or wanted to hear. Some of the most useful interviews were with people who were very uneasy talking to me, such as the conservative and highly introverted engineer cousin of a friend of a friend in Boston or a secretary in the office of an acquaintance in a small town in New Hampshire. While many offered to allow me to use their full names, for the sake of consistency, I use only the first names of my core sample of interview respondents. I didn't insist that everyone who talked to me be willing to be named, as I've done in the past, because of my need to get a variety of voices. Moreover, because of the personal nature of the material, I feared that only the bolder and the more beautiful would be willing to be identified in a book.

In revealing their new openness about sex, these women often shocked me by how comfortably they talked about the most personal aspects of their lives. This was a marked change from just thirty years ago, when researchers were breaking ground just getting women to talk *anonymously* about their experiences. One woman I interviewed explained to me why this was happening: "I think why people are open to talking to you when you ask questions, why they answer you so openly," said Cheryl, 31, a lawyer in Austin, "is because we're sick and tired of lies. We want to tell the truth, and the only truth that we know is our own."

I also based my analyses on a variety of other sources, from both high and low culture, to reflect the full range of women's influences and to give me some broader insights. For a scientific perspective, I used the most recent and best-established academic studies and journals, as well as large-scale government reports such as the 1995 National Survey of Family Growth (published in 1997), the principal and best source of detailed nationally representative information on women's sexual and contraceptive behavior. Another major source was the landmark 1994 University of Chicago National Health and Social Life Survey, which, despite its flaws, remains the most statistically accurate and comprehensive study ever of adult sexual behavior. To compare college students' evolving values and opinions on social issues since the 1970s, I used the UCLA report *The American Freshman: Thirty-Year Trends* and its subsequent single-year surveys. I relied on statistics from these larger-scale samples to describe the wider social changes instead of projecting the results of my much smaller one onto the larger population. While some of their results have been mentioned in the media, their often-buried findings about *women's* sexual evolutions have usually not been reported.

I had to look to other popular and qualitative studies to fill in some blanks left by the academic and government surveys, which are mainly concerned with health and pregnancy issues (not the nitty-gritty of what women feel or what happens in bed). To a lesser degree, I used some surveys sponsored by popular magazines, such as *Details'* 1996 Sex on Campus study of 1,752 college students (Elliot and Brantley 1997), which asked specialized and "human interest" questions. I also used less empirical but still enlightening feminist research from other sources, such as the reporting work of Shere Hite and Nancy Friday, which more closely examines specific patterns of women's experiences and expectations and uses women themselves as "experts." Even though their research has been criticized for not offering representative samples (using subjects who answered advertisements), they do show specific patterns of women's sexual experience. For example, Hite better describes women's mixed emotions about the sexual revolution than does any academic sociological graph. Both Hite and Friday also compared similar samples of boomer and postboomer women, spanning the decades of their research.

Her Way is a chronicle of women's continuing evolution toward conducting their sex lives on their own terms. The first chapter describes the emerging breed of sexually aggressive women, the superrats, as reflected in my interviews, in pop culture, and in the headlines. The second and third chapters examine the principal generational shift: young women's malelike sexual behavior, including having casual sex and challenging old sexual scripts in bed. The fourth chapter covers a less dramatic and more recent change that also revalues (but does not dictate) traditional female sexual restraint as part of young women's wider realm of choices. In chapters 5 and 6, young women redefine the family, including their concepts of marriage and the many options for remaining single. Chapter 7 expands on other types of male-free partnerships, those of bisexuals and lesbians. The next three chapters elaborate on the social movements behind all these shifts: Chapter 8 covers the fundamental movements of the 1960s and 1970s: careers and education, the sexual revolution, and the women's movement. Chapter 9 documents how, with these movements as a foundation, young women are defining morality as personal and are questioning organized religion, their most traditionally restrictive force. The final chapter analyzes one of our most newly empowering influences, the information age, and explores the radical nature of women's locker-room talk, safer-sex campaigns, and the informational media.

Why take all this time and trouble to document these intimate complexities? Too often, even the most independent among us trust outside authorities to describe, and possibly define, our roles and realities for us. Instead, we should recognize for ourselves what is happening.

Neat, prefabricated definitions only heap more shame, anxiety, and guilt on women's sexual experiences. We try to measure up to ideals that often don't exist or aren't possible, and we take for granted the gains of the women's movement, our educations, our jobs. But this is not a self-help book in the traditional sense. It won't teach you how to find that elusive G spot or put the spice back into your marriage. But it does investigate broader questions about what our choices are and why we even feel entitled to address women's sexual rights so openly—and so boldly—today.

Her Way

Introduction: The Sexual Evolution Toward Female Control

I want to be the girl with the most cake.
—Courtney Love and Hole, "Doll Parts," from *Live Through This*, 1994

And I made up my mind to find my own destiny. And deep in my heart the answer it was in me.
—Lauryn Hill, title song, "The Miseducation of Lauryn Hill," 1998

President William Jefferson Clinton will not be remembered as being naive about the ways of women. Yet he met more than his match in the 21-year-old White House intern Monica Lewinsky, whose ambition and audacity he disastrously underestimated. A few months before their relationship became public, a puzzled Clinton admitted to her, "If I had known what kind of person you really were, I wouldn't have gotten involved with you" (*Starr Report* 1998, B6). What Clinton did not realize was that Lewinsky's behavior was that of a new generation of women.

To understand Monica Lewinsky, you have to understand Monica Lewinsky's generation, which plays by rules entirely different from those of its predecessor. Lewinsky is one of the women born during and shaped by the sexual revolution, the women's movement, new education and work opportunities for women, new religious freedoms, and the information age. Sharing more of men's power, sense of entitlement, and social clout, Lewinsky and her peers generally feel more comfortable than did earlier generations in aggressively and unapologetically pursuing their own interests in sexual relationships, that is, doing it "her way." This highly individualistic generation is unpredictable and idiosyncratic in their behavior, not conforming to one neat and rigid mold, as women (and men) did in the past. Using their own taste as their barometer, they have a broad menu of choices at their finger-

3

tips (for instance, calculating, cold-blooded, noble, or romantic) and thus can end up with a distinctive sexual configuration on their plates.

Lewinsky, whose sexuality was powerful and puzzling enough to cause a constitutional crisis, embodies all these changes. In reality, her sexual profile—having many past sex partners, making the first move, indulging in diverse forms of play (oral sex in person and aural sex over the phone)—fits into the sexual mainstream of her generation (even though the Eisenhower administration–era white male journalists still dominating the nation's editorial pages constantly declared that she was an aberrant tramp) (Shreve 1998). One of the most surprising discoveries of the 1998 *Starr Report* was that Lewinsky was not a victimized schoolgirl, as had been previously reported. Rather, she was brazen, relentless, and self-centered in her quest for sex and power. In other words, she acted like a man. Instead of being innocent prey, the report revealed that she even initiated her affair with the president, as well as many of their sexual encounters.

As Barbara Walters pointed out in her March 3, 1999, TV interview on ABC, this affair wasn't a "one-way street." When Walters asked whether Lewinsky also "was gratified," Lewinsky said yes. Walters continued this line of inquiry: "And there were things that were done that made you as a woman happy and content?" Again her answer was affirmative, punctuated with a little laugh. Furthermore, when Clinton tried to break off their relationship, she did not leave quietly. The upwardly nubile intern instead demanded that the leader of the free world secure her a job, a powerful and lucrative one, "not [as] someone's administrative/executive assistant" and with a salary that "can provide me a comfortable living in NY" (*Starr Report* 1998, B6). As men have always done, Lewinsky indulged in locker-room talk and bragged about her conquest to at least ten friends.

At the same time, however, Lewinsky was a bundle of contradictions, not following a particular pattern of behavior. Indeed, some of her behavior was traditionally female. After all, she was the one servicing him sexually most of the time, as well as falling in love with him and entertaining fantasies of future wedded bliss.

Overall, Lewinsky, raised in the 1980s, acted entirely differently than the typical 21-year-old woman raised in the 1950s and 1960s would have done. Young women today feel entitled to conduct their sex lives on their own terms. Conversely, without access to quality information on female sexual desire, sexual health, and abortion, baby boomers in their early years were sexually ignorant. Even in the late 1960s, boomer women, lacking men's power and status, still weren't "liberated." They didn't yet have the education and career clout (which women claim today in unprecedented numbers) to become equal players in the game; consequently, even though the emerging sexual revolution permitted women to be sexually free, they still were supposed to follow men's orders and make their bodies unconditionally accessible.

The main reason that this shift has been overshadowed is because it is more an *evolution* than a revolution. A revolution is a sudden and dramatic (and often temporary) overthrow of an existing order. An evolution is less noticeable and more subtle: a gradual and slow but yet unstoppable, permanent process of change. The sexual evolution also involves more complex and less obvious power changes, which are in women's favor. The greatest change that the sexual revolution of the 1960s and 1970s produced was obtaining social permission for women to have sex outside marriage. This also was a boon for many men, who now had access to more women's bodies and made the rules about what exactly took place in bed. But in the 1980s and 1990s, continuing to assume more social and economic power and sexual knowledge, women took greater control of their sexual futures, decided when to say no as well as yes, discussed consequences, and challenged old sexual scripts based solely on men's physical pleasure. As a result, with women also in charge, the changes of today do not resemble the promiscuity and casualness of the 1970s. But while this may seem more conservative for this reason, the sexual evolution is really more radical because it is based on *women's* autonomy and choice, not just their sexual participation.

As a result, the images associated with women's sexual freedom often are entirely different. Whereas the sexual revolution catered to men's needs typified by *Playboy*, *Hustler*, *Risky Business* (1983), *Barbarella* (1968), sexy stewardess ads, singles bars, hot tubs, and "scoring," the competing sexual evolution is centered on women's getting what they need, such as Susie Bright's *Herotica* series, woman-centered porn films by Annie Sprinkle and Candida Royalle, *Our Bodies, Ourselves* (which was first widely published in the 1970s), the former sitcom *Ellen*, Madonna, the Lilith Fair, the Hitachi Magic Wand vibrator with the "G spot" attachment, sex-information web sites, Judy Blume's *Forever*, former Surgeon General Jocelyn Elders, rape hotlines, and Take Back the Night demonstrations.

I don't mean to glorify Monica Lewinsky or portray her as an ideal of the younger generation. But her example serves as a compelling one to bring many typical postboomer female sexual attitudes and behaviors to the surface for discussion. In her appetite for power and brazen threats and trading of sex for power, she does represent the darker side of this evolution. However, history might view others like her more positively. Other young women of her generation who share her strong sense of individuality, sexual entitlement, and quest for power made headlines throughout the 1990s for their roles in forging new rights for women. Demanding higher standards of treatment, women like Lieutenant Paula Coughlin, who exposed the assaults on women at the U.S. Navy's Tailhook Association convention, fought sexual harassment. Many, such as Patricia Bowman and Desiree Washington, who accused William Kennedy Smith and Mike Tyson, respectively, of rape, eventually were not afraid to show their faces when addressing the previously stigmatized issue of acquaintance rape. Young lesbians, such as Candace Gingrich and Chastity Bono (the respective sister and daughter of conservative heterosexual politicians), demonstrated the new generation's defiance of the closet and society's expectations. Likewise, following the lead of Shannon Faulkner, brave and resilient women are entering the Citadel and other military academies, the last strongholds of male power.

Outside the political arena, women are taking charge as well. High-profile postboomers from Ellen DeGeneres to Lauryn Hill have revolutionized pop culture. While I observed only a beginning trickle of such upstarts on the fringes ten years ago, today they occupy the mainstream. (I identify them as "the superrats," a superevolved subset of sexually assertive young women, who grow stronger and more common with every generation.)

Perhaps the ultimate pop-culture phenomenon to actually pay homage to this breed is the 2000 award-winning and box-office-record-trouncing Chinese-language feminist-fantasy film, *Crouching Tiger, Hidden Dragon*. This is a world-class action movie that is fundamentally charged by the upheaval of one unstoppable tidal force: the growing sense of sexual entitlement and expression of a very young woman, Jen, an aristocrat rebelling against an arranged marriage. The event that finally incites her to eventually run away from home (and beat up a lot of folks along the way) is a passionate sexual affair with a forbidden man, the bandit Lo.

Underscoring the action of the film are continuing dialogues about women's proper sexual roles. These conversations become increasingly heated and explicit between Jen and a slightly older more traditional woman, Shu Lien (finally ending in an elaborate sword-fight clash). At first, in the beginning of the film, Shu Lien gently defends the importance of duty, revealing that she never pursued her true love, Lu Mi Bai, because of questions of propriety. (He was the best friend of her slain fiancé.) Jen is not swayed: "To be free to live my own life, to choose whom I love. That is true happiness," she asserts, articulating a fundamental and newly prevailing generational conviction.

Television has also captured popular imagination—and high ratings—showcasing the trials and triumphs of this evolving breed. Wielding trendy designer heels and bags instead of swords and massive battle axes, the women of HBO's *Sex and the City*, starting its fourth season in 2001, have charted new ground in their level of sexual candor and support among friends, willingness to experiment, and assertiveness with partners. (As some critics have asserted, the show pictures straight women acting with the permissive sexual license traditionally reserved for gay men.) While *Sex and the City* has broken new ground for women over 30, a cluster of other programs has continued also in the past several years to reveal even younger women's evolutions. Upstarts from *Dawson's Creek, Charmed, the Gilmore Girls* (all on the WB), *Buffy the Vampire Slayer* (formerly on the WB, and recently moved to UPN), and *Dark Angel* (Fox) defiantly do sex on their own terms. As the entertainment president of the WB television network, Garth Ancier, explained in an article on this teen genre in *Entertainment Weekly*, "They've grown up in a world where women are more empowered. We're just reflecting that world" ("The Entertainers, 1999," 24).

Another member of the WB network sorority, *Felicity*, best embodies the complexities of this individualistic "her way" attitude. In episode 11 (January 19, 1999) of the show's first season, when the college freshman decides to have sex for the first time, she is unabashedly assertive, scheduling it in advance with her boyfriend in a date book, educating herself in the bookstore (with the book *Give Me an "O"*), getting protection at the school clinic, and consulting a myriad of friends. She ultimately decides not to go through with her plan, however, after she realizes that she was doing it mainly to fit in. Summing up this theme is a voice-over from a friend writing to her from another city, which could stand for the primary sexual mantra of the postboomers: "Our best decisions, the ones we never regret, come from listening to ourselves. And whatever you decide, you should be very proud." In another twist, later in the season (episode 16, March 21, 1999), Felicity does listen to herself and has her first sexual experience as a fling with a casual acquaintance, art student Eli, not her boyfriend.

These very public figures, often causing bewilderment to their elders, reveal a widespread yet largely unnamed and undocumented sexual movement, a sexual evolution. It is as though the 1970s sexual revolution never died but ever so slowly evolved from a male-defined movement into one in which women can now call the shots. For more women than ever before, this sexual evolution offers a different and enhanced type of sexual freedom than they had access to in the supposedly more free-wheeling 1960s and 1970s.

Whereas the sexual revolution of that era promised women sexual freedom on men's terms of promiscuity (always being available to satisfy their needs), the sexual evolution of the 1990s and beyond stresses the importance of women's taking charge. Young women's greater personal and social power has had a liberalizing effect on their sex lives (more than compensating for the conservative pull of the more visible AIDS crisis and "politically correct" feminist crusades against sexual harassment and date rape). Only recently, after thirty years of struggling for equal rights and financial independence, has women's power over their sexual lives become fully visible and documented.

To track these changes and explore how the sexual revolution became a sexual evolution, I interviewed dozens of postboomer women across the country and analyzed the latest national research. Among the people I interviewed, the most prominent generational sexual issues mentioned were their greater number of choices, control, and sense of entitlement to sex. Two major shifts since the 1970s characterize this sexual evolution, which set continuing sexual patterns for the future:

• As they gain more traditionally male power, young women's sexual profiles are becoming remarkably similar to men's in terms of age of first intercourse and number of sex partners and casual encounters. Now that women share male values, they are also more sexually aggressive, feel less guilt and shame, and are defiantly open about their behavior, from having a child out of marriage to coming out of the closet to cohabiting. This profile describes young American women in general, with the greatest changes taking place in the past twenty years among the white, middle class, and educated.

• At the same time, young women are not merely mimicking men but are beginning to redefine sex from their own distinct points of view. Control over their sex lives is their main goal. As women reevaluate traditional roles, male-defined scripts are being challenged, changing what actually goes on in bed. More women are granting new respect to traditionally female behavior that acknowledges the personal meaning of virginity and saying no (even for the sexually experienced). While the number of virgins has not increased, those who exist are coming proudly out of the closet, recognizing the power that comes from controlling their own sexuality, whatever they choose. In addition to discovering the pleasures of sex, young women are also exploring its dilemmas—ethics, morals, consequences, dangers, risks, responsibilities, rape, exploitation, spiritual integrity—and they are demanding better standards of treatment with more openness and communication.

Young women today, from the predatory Monica Lewinsky to the more down-to-earth heroine Felicity, have one thing in common: they are attempting to control their sex lives. Beyond that, their individual needs and desires are so diverse that they do not fit into neat categories. To the frustration of journalists (like me), the actual effects of the sexual evolution on the specific sexual habits of the North American female are difficult to describe. No other generation has encompassed more variety or included more individualistic behavior. This is not a complaint, as the power of the evolution is precisely that it has not resulted in one uniform set of actions and expectations but has given women a wider range of choices than ever.

In the 1950s and earlier, sexual-life scripts for middle-class women were more rigidly defined and easy to profile, with sex permitted only after marriage at an early age, typically right after high school. A "good girl" resisted a man's lustful urges, whereas a "bad girl" succumbed or even lured him into temptation. Sex was a male production, defined by the man's experience and requiring his direction and choreography. Today, however, young women's codes usually are not absolutely Puritan or wildly hedonistic, but are somewhere in between. Young women may often be aggressive in some ways but submissive in others. While exploring the politically incorrect, they don't classify themselves according to confining categories; they can be bisexual, not just hetero or homo; working moms, neither homemakers nor career women. One woman may want to wait to have intercourse until she is engaged but nevertheless has had oral sex with a dozen dates. Another woman may have many casual partners as long as she meets them during her college years on while on vacation. There are no ironclad rules or majority agreements about exactly when the appropriate time is to have sex (whether it should happen on the first date or at engagement) or how to define casual sex (as a one-night stand pick-up or a regular but casual relationship).

In a report on college students' sex lives for *Rolling Stone* in 1995, David Lipsky noted that a major change—necessary for such individualism—is tolerance, no matter what the choice. "Tolerance is generally the rule. Gay and lesbian groups are nowhere as strong and influential as they are on campus, and there is anecdotal evidence to suggest that experimentation—bisexuality, group sex and things even kinkier—is going on stronger than ever" (82). As men are discovering, postboomer women are more likely to use what is best for them as their standard of behavior. Over and over, reflecting

Felicity's friend's philosophy, young women have told me that all people are different and that the choices they make "depend on them." Fewer women give primary consideration to their main sexual rulers of the past, namely, shame, guilt, and the overwhelming desire to please others. Instead, they are more likely to question the limits suggested or imposed by their partners, their families, their old textbooks, their doctors, and their preachers.

This increase in women's sexual individualism has not led to complete satisfaction, however, and it probably never will. From a traditional point of view, this individualism sometimes clashes with duty and commitment, for when women are less aware of their own needs, they tend to cause fewer problems and upheavals for others, such as divorce (which is mostly initiated by women). At the other extreme, when women become too individualistic, the result is self-absorption, which can be just as misguided as women's traditional roles in the 1950s of pure self-abnegation, servitude to men, and masochism.

Indeed, even when not taken to an extreme, young women's individualism is limited in its power. No matter how they try, young women still face monumental external challenges to actually achieving control. After all, this is a world only half changed by feminism. No matter what their attitudes, young women still face some considerable challenges from those they know, and society in general. For one thing, men have not evolved to accept strong women at the same rate that these women have evolved. And, the playing field among women from different backgrounds—in this country and abroad—is still far from even. While the United States has the highest rates of teenage pregnancy and sexually transmitted diseases (across age groups) in the industrialized world, teenagers are denied accurate and complete sex education beyond pleas for abstinence. In regard to economic and cultural constraints, not every woman has the same choices available to her. Affluent, white, and straight women still have the highest expectations and the most freedom to behave as they wish, from being a stay-at-home mom to obtaining a safe abortion. Likewise, among women, AIDS is largely a problem of the poorest and most powerless minorities in the inner cities.

Despite some new expectations, the media and society at large still generally define beauty in narrow, traditionally male-defined terms. That is, you are deemed unattractive if you cannot fit gracefully into a size 6 Rayon tube top from the Delia's catalogue. Women entertainers such as Liz Phair or Salt 'n Pepa are allowed to swagger with sexual bravado as long as they don't deviate from the model aesthetic. And of course, even the waifs' sexual currency takes a nosedive as they age beyond their twenties. Already, at 32, I'm a full decade older than the average *Playboy* centerfold.

On a larger social scale, this postboomer individualism, along with a lack of history, leaves young women's rights vulnerable to political attack. As individualists, they are looking strictly to themselves for control and empowerment, seeing their sexual rights strictly as a matter of personal choice, not politics. They are less willing to subscribe to a larger political agenda, an ideological framework, which puts their sexual lives in a bigger context and emphasizes the importance of social consciousness and action. As I learned while researching my first book on young women's views of feminism, as a result, many women take their hard-won choices for granted and are not actively standing up for their rights. While activists are agitating for new sexual freedoms, the great majority of young women do not investigate women's rights beyond their own personal experiences and fail to understand the power of organizing to safeguard those rights they do have. And their lack of history also encourages self-absorption. They know nothing of even the most basic history of women's battles for sexual freedom; events as recent as those of the 1970s (such as the 1973 *Roe v. Wade* decision legalizing abortion) have faded completely from their collective memory. Polls reveal that even though most young women are pro-choice, a majority also believe that their access to abortion—or sex education or contraceptive choice, also under constant political attack—is guaranteed.

Personifying this lack of generational memory is a 30-year-old actress who appeared in a play I wrote, playing a part of a girl whose sister went to an unwed mothers' home in the early 1960s. During rehearsal, she turned to me and asked: "Unwed mothers' homes? What are they? I have some idea, but I'm not sure what they were all about." On one hand, I was thrilled that she was so unfamiliar with the world of shame that plagued our mothers' generation, which banished them to homes to hide and repent for their unwanted pregnancies. But later I realized that this typical ignorance of the past make us ill-equipped to defend future assaults on our mothers' hard-won and often tenuous freedoms.

Now specifically in the United States, with the new Bush administration even more actively and powerfully battling to restore an Old World Order, young women's general lack of political consciousness is especially troubling. In recent political elections, they have stood by silently and—as in the cases of Republican and conservative women—have actually actively voted in men who stand for issues contrary to their beliefs (as large numbers of them in polls claim to be pro-choice). As they celebrate and enjoy the empowering and entertaining personal (and consumer) "girl power" messages of recent films like *Charlie's Angels* and Angelina Jolie's action-hero romp *Tomb Raider*, and TV shows like *Sex and the City* and *Buffy*, young women generally fail to fully realize how their own personal sexual freedoms are in the very epicenter of heated cultural and political wars in this country (and around the world). The more gritty and less glamorous political battles raging outside of the airbrushed pop-culture realm are fundamentally about young women being able to control their sexuality, and hence, their lives.

In contrast, right-wing conservatives fully recognize the stakes. President Bush and his comrades feel a deep longing for the way things were in the past, as they have recently demonstrated early in his administration, such as by making moves in the direction of reviving a new Cold War with China and appointing officials from long-gone administrations (such as Defense Secretary Donald Rumsfeld). Their nostalgia also apparently extends to putting women in their place, such as they were in the "good old days" before the fuss of the women's movement. Far from representing a fringe group, these men in power reflect a large population in this country, those that are being forced to give up some of their control and genuinely fear the real radical gains that young women have made, especially in the area of sexual freedom. In the 1990s, three women specifically—Hillary Clinton, Anita Hill, and then Monica Lewinsky—stood as lightning rods of intense public debate and condemnation to illuminate these often beneath-the-surface and widening divisions, revealing the real clashes in this country around issues of women's sexual independence and control.

Conservatives have acted on these fears by raging more visible and direct battles against a wide range of reproductive rights. They have continued to impose a battery of abortion access restrictions that mainly affect teenage and poor women, express hostility to initiatives for emergency morning-after contraception that has the power to actually prevent hundreds of thousands of abortions in the first place, and limit government family-planning funding—on community, state, and federal levels, and in the Developing World. And once babies are born, these conservatives suddenly become indifferent to their plight, opposing initiatives for child care, health care, and a more flexible workplace for mothers.

In a less explosive, but also controversial arena, right-wingers continue to wipe out real sex education in schools, which women of my immediate age group, born in the 1960s and 1970s, appreciated at all-time-high levels in our adolescence. (When I was taking such classes in my mainstream all-American suburban junior high and high schools in the Reagan years, I had no idea that I was participating in a fleeting era of enlightened high-minded social progressivism.) Indeed, such real comprehensive education has been on the decline for those following; in 1988, pro-abstinence programs represented only 2 percent of sex education classes in school, but then rose to account for between a quarter and a third in 2001 (according to different published reports). Conservatives continue to blindly push through funding for these pro-abstinence programs, which are basically thinly veiled pleas for chastity that deny teenagers information about birth control and protection from disease, at a time when their rates of HIV and STDs are skyrocketing. This is also despite a lack of national studies proving the effectiveness of such programs to actually get teens to delay sex, as President Bush's own Surgeon General, David Satcher, asserted in his June 2001 "Call to Action" report on sexual health threats in the United States.

But as the threats become more visible and threatening, so has some resistance, offering some beginning hope. Women sent a clear public message on President's Day of 2001, when masses made donations to Planned Parenthood in the name of George W. Bush. Continuing a protest tradition from the past Bush administration, the National Organization for Women staged an April 2001 March on Washington for reproductive rights—which was primarily attended by young women, including those from more than 160 campuses (not a matter of public knowledge, since the rally was hardly covered in the media). Also, in numbers larger than ever before, more young women, imbued with a new sense of entitlement, are protesting for easier access to morning-after emergency contraception (as portrayed in a 2000 episode of *Felicity*), and for birth control coverage from their insurance plans and college clinics. On a deeper level, they reflect a heightened wave of public consciousness about discrepancies in women's health care, as ironically spurred by the introduction in 1998 of the male impotency drug, Viagra (which was greeted by instant widespread health-insurance coverage—as birth-control pills continued to be denied such treatment). Also spurring women's political consciousness about their bodies have been the widely publicized crusading young sisters Laura Berman, a psychotherapist, and Jennifer Berman, a urologist. Their 2000 book, *For Women Only: A Revolutionary Guide to Overcoming Sexual Dysfunction and Reclaiming Your Sex Life*, explicitly outlines how, in contrast to men, women's sexual dysfunction problems have been misunderstood, if not entirely ignored, by the medical establishment. (A student I met in Iowa City in 2001 told me she was inspired to start a feminist group at her high school after seeing them on *Oprah*.)

A major cultural movement of the past several years also stimulating newly candid popular dialogue about women's sexual control has been the play *The Vagina Monologues*. But the play, by longtime feminist activist and radical Eve Ensler, actually contains little that is new—as it basically repackages the same dialogues about women's sexual empowerment that the women's health movement (a separate branch of the women's movement) formulated way back in the 1970s. And I mean this as a compliment; the play functions to expose a whole new generation of women to these concepts in a fresh, non-heavy-handed, and even sexy way. It features interviews with a variety of women talking candidly about their most historically shamed body part— at times playfully, recognizing the pleasures of sexual discovery, and also then seriously, such as with a rape victim recounting her harrowing experience. Since 1998, hundreds of young feminist activist groups and women's centers around the world have made readings of the play a programming fixture on college campuses. These events typically attract massive sold-out audiences that rival the size of those seen at major sporting events, such as with the attendance of a thousand at Duke University and two thousand at Oregon State at Corvallis in February 2001. After a public reading of such material decrying shame and encouraging women's sexual pride, the climates for women on those campuses can no longer remain the same.

• • •

At the same time that I observe the progress necessary for the future, I also see a need to recognize women's gains. This counters the prevailing social commentary in the news media about young women's sexual choices, which ignores or even denies any progress, meanwhile generating fear and belittling the organized women's movement. Whereas I watch young women becoming more sexually empowered and assertive, conservative critics write, without challenge, that they are more sexually confused and misguided than ever. Indeed, of all the social revolutions of the 1960s and 1970s, none has been proclaimed to be more spent and doomed than the sexual one. The media line has been that the sexual revolution was stomped out for good in the 1980s with the advent of AIDS and in the 1990s when radical feminists supposedly delivered the final death blows with "sexual correctness."

Although these two issues have indeed had a chilling effect, the reports of their impact are often overstated. At the same time, some young writers complain about the restricting effects of AIDS, taking for granted their many lovers and entitlement to recreational sex. Reflecting other media refrains, recent college graduate Meghan Daum described in the *New York Times Magazine* the toll on the psyche of her generation:

> Our attitudes have been affected by the disease by leaving us scared, but our behavior has stayed largely the same. One result is a corrosion of the soul, a chronic dishonesty and fear that will most likely damage us more than the disease itself. In this world, peace of mind is a utopian concept. (Daum 1996, 33)

But meanwhile, throughout the article, she casually comments on her string of past lovers. The same is true of Katie Roiphe in her 1997 book *Last Night in Paradise*, in which she mourns AIDS as hampering sexual freedom at the same time that she reports on the atmosphere of promiscuity of her recent undergraduate years, when every weekend she would bump into various, ever-changing lovers of her roommates in the bathroom.

Critics have also united in blaming the women's movement for ruining sex. Instead of acknowledging the benefit of having more sexual choices and protections from assault, the media mainly mourn how "confused" and restricted young women have become. An example is the negative spin of an April 5, 1998, *New York Times Magazine* cover story about young mothers' increased options, whose headline is "Work or home? Breast or bottle? . . . No matter what they choose, they are made to feel bad. Mothers can't win." The authors of the best-selling man-trapping guide *The Rules* contend that feminism—not men's behavior and attitudes—has made women lonely and desperate. The authors confess their sad realization that they cannot have both feminist values and a personal life: "We didn't want to give up our liberation, but neither did we want to come home to empty apartments" (Fein and Schneider 1995, 2). Recent college graduate Wendy Shalit attracted a flurry of press coverage in 1999 with her book *A Return to Modesty*, which blamed the women's movement (and not men) for actually *causing* rape, stalking, and sexual harassment when it removed many gender-specific restrictions, including coed dorm floors. While Shalit calls feminists too permissive, at the same time conservative critics writing in the mainstream press—from Katie Roiphe to Camille Paglia to Christina Hoff Sommers— are berating feminists for *repressing* impressionable young women by brainwashing them with their sinister brand of "sexual correctness" (see Crichton 1993; Paglia 1992; Roiphe 1993b; and Sommers 1994). As proof, they point to highly publicized sex struggles over issues that were not widely recognized a few decades back, such as the 1991 U.S. Navy Tailhook scandal, the 1991 Clarence Thomas hearings, the 1995 Packwood revelations, the 1996 Mitsubishi reports, the 1997 U.S. Army sexual abuse trials, and the 1998 Paula Jones/Monica Lewinsky sex scandals.

Meanwhile, the critics have failed to see the more complex picture. Below the surface, young women's sexual power has grown slowly and widely, more than compensating for the cramping influence of AIDS and "sexual correctness." Many of these changes have not been recognized because most news and reports are biased in favor of the male perspective, for example, with newspaper articles in the late 1990s about the annual UCLA survey of college freshmen showing that young adults are less sexually permissive than the boomers. In fact, that was truer of the *men* surveyed, but in any case, it was a very small shift overall. Even the University of Chicago's 1994 National Health and Social Life Survey, the most comprehensive study of Americans' sexual behavior, is biased toward men—both the actual text and how it has been covered in the media. For example, the section on the effect of AIDS discusses how the disease curbed sexual behavior in the 1980s. But a closer look at the graphs reveals that AIDS led only to fewer overall partners *for men* (Laumann et al. 1994, 199). Nonetheless, the media widely reported the survey's results as marking a return to conservative values and behavior while ignoring the major changes in young American women's sexual practices and patterns.

Many men in the media do not view the sexual evolution positively because it imposes new limits on them, and so they dismiss this movement as oppressive "sexual correctness." For men, the resulting ethic of consent and communication may seem like an obstacle, whereas for women it is a measure of their rights. In reality, heterosexual relationships have always been politicized (he had the power, and she did not), but now the two sides have a more equal voice.

In articles about sexual politics and issues like date rape and sexual harassment, male writers tend to describe them as "confusing" without recognizing the positive power shifts taking place for women (see Baber 1995; Baker 1993; Edwards 1992; Madigan 1998). As testament to this difference in perception, women's magazines have almost ignored the issue of "sexual correctness," but men's are obsessed with it. And when men's publications report on "sexual correctness," the complaints mainly come from males.

A more positive, and overlooked, perspective on this "war of the sexes" is that women are generally less tolerant of abuse in their public and personal lives, tackling difficult issues with new resolve. Even though, as conservatives contend, some women have taken date rape and harassment too far, the greater reality of women gaining power in their sex lives is a far more pro-found, pervasive, and positive change to report. In reality, I have not noticed women actually complain about how confusing and burdensome it is to have more communication about and consent for sex.

The media overlook the sexual evolution because it mainly involves peo-ple in the mainstream and not on the more colorful fringes. The media are naturally more attracted to the theatrical and extreme instead of the more mundane lives of ordinary people. Some of the most famous accounts of the sexual revolution of the 1970s, such as Gay Talese's *Thy Neighbor's Wife*, center on the exploits of the most self-promoting and flamboyant men, such as Hugh Hefner, founder of *Playboy*; Al Goldstein, publisher of the less ven-erated *Screw* magazine; and John Williamson, the force behind Sandstone, the legendary wife-swapping center in California.

The sexual evolution also is not obvious, to either the media or even those women taking part in it, because it is the result of many slowly grow-ing, large-scale social movements that we now, more widely, take for granted. The once radical values of the women's movement for more equal-ity and education and those of the sexual revolution for sexual permission have now become fully absorbed into the mainstream's consciousness. In public discussions about sex, the more inflammatory and dramatic issues of AIDS and sexual correctness naturally overshadow these slow-moving and more subtle social changes. Furthermore, as religion has evolved to become a more private issue, it exerts less formal authority to limit women's sexual behavior. The individualistic, self-oriented ideologies of psychotherapy and New Age spirituality, emphasizing personal growth and freedom, have also slowly pervaded the media. Consequently, the media have become more open about sex, giving women better and more information about their bodies and sexual rights. This evolution toward women's sexual control is the natural product of living in a modern industrialized society, and Ameri-can women's new view of sex reflects that of other Western nations (Smith 1994b, 19).

But a societal change of the magnitude of the sexual evolution demands some serious public in-depth discussion and analysis—along with some lighter moments of appreciation. This book is a beginning point. In recent years, groups of individual young women discussed here, from Monica to Buffy, have stimulated some national dialogue, revealing the iceberg of sex-ual change developing beneath the surface for their generation. This book picks up with and expands that dialogue. On a basic level, it documents general social changes with many specific overlooked statistics, culled from a growing body of knowledge in many fields, from public health to sexology. But most important, it reports the real story of the sexual evolution by transmitting the voices of the least consulted experts of all, those on the front lines: young women themselves.

I
Doing It "His Way"

1. Superrats: The New Breed of Sexual Individualists

She was aggressive and vulnerable, petulant and infatuated, easy and catty, and ultimately, a young woman scorned.
> —*Chicago Tribune* story about Monica Lewinsky at the release of the *Starr Report*, September 13, 1998

I've been a bad, bad girl
I've been careless with a delicate man
And it's a sad, sad world
When a girl will break a boy just because she can.
> —Fiona Apple, "Criminal," from *Tidal*, 1996

When Nancy Friday interviewed Generation-X women for her book *Women on Top*, she noted that "their voices sound like a new race of women." That is, in describing their sexual fantasies, the young women she sampled felt much less guilt than did their boomer counterparts in her 1973 book, *My Secret Garden*. Friday calls them "a new race," and I describe them as "a new breed" or, more specifically, "superrats." Although this label may seem insulting at first, I use it with all due respect to refer to an often confounding, sexually savvy breed of young women, who have evolved to become more unstoppable and more prevalent with every generation. Imbued with a large streak of traditionally male (aggressive, self-gratifying) attitudes and behavior, these women illustrate some of the most dramatic sexual changes of the past three decades. These superrats may look different, want a variety of things, come from different backgrounds, have libidos of varying capacities and demands, and confront different obstacles, but they are united by one common trait: the expectation of and insistence on conducting their sex lives on their own terms and with a new degree of openness. When it comes to sharing information about sex and what goes on in their lives, they do ask, and they do tell.

As a result, these women are not popular with traditional authority figures. The unromantic label *rat* indicates that they are widely considered noisome and disruptive, often condemned as pests or even as a social menace, reflecting the gap between their expectations and those of society. The prefix *super* characterizes the development and pattern of future generations of women. It also describes their evolution toward unprecedented levels of self-preservation and survival despite an often hostile environment and repeated attempts by governing authorities (Republicans, fundamentalists, and the like) to shame and curb them. A greater number than ever before are protected by their imperviousness to excessive self-blame, a time-honored means of keeping previous generations of "rats" under control.

This state of "super" evolution, however, is possible only because it builds on the work of other generations, which had progressively higher expectations. In one generation, these superrats have undergone a swifter and more dramatic evolution than anything that Darwin observed on the Galápagos. While not always representing the majority, the superrats are a substantial mainstream force whose influence extends beyond feminist or campus enclaves; they are breaking ranks in the military, the suburbs, housing projects, college campuses, and churches. Yet they commonly are not distinguished by any particular color scheme or style of clothes. They may or may not like jazz, wear clothes made of natural fibers, or speak with an alluring foreign accent. Instead of distracting you with their sexiness like a costumed Anaïs Nin or a Salome discarding seven veils or a lude-popping Diane Keaton looking for Mr. Goodbar, they are more likely to look like (and be) you or your stepsister or daughter or girlfriend or administrative assistant. And thus they are often difficult to classify. Indeed, much of what makes a superrat is in the eye of the beholder. Most superrats aren't interested in rigid classifications and ironclad ideologies but are more concerned about what they do than how they label themselves. As individualists, they also insist on making their own choices, which do not conform to any one particular ideological scheme. But superrats shouldn't be confused with feminists. While they may be similar to feminists because of their desire to take control of their own lives, superrats are not necessarily *political* about their sexual freedom. Although superrats have absorbed the individualistic advances of feminism, such as sexual self-determination and control, they have left aside the parts about political awareness, organizing, and making a connection to other women.

Most of the women I interviewed could be classified in some manner as superrats because they have taken control of their lives. But in other aspects of their lives, they may express contradictions or inconsistencies, be assertive in some ways but not in others, and feel guilt about sex in some situations but not all. For this reason, "superrat" is probably most appropriate as an adjective describing the sexual assertiveness of this new generation, instead of as a rigid academic category describing their complete personhood. A common link is the trouble and confusion that they cause. Some superrats, such as the sexually aggressive Monica Lewinsky, caused notable political upsets. Other superrats have also raised eyebrows: Princess Diana, who incurred the wrath of her elders by divorcing her husband instead of living in an empty marriage, as she would have been required to do not many years earlier, was a royal superrat. Roseanne, who broke new ground in sitcoms exploring the tensions created by clashes of gender, class, and sexual orientation, is a superrat role model. The protagonist of Judy Blume's much banned and much dog-eared 1975 book *Forever*, teenaged Kath, inspired this generation of superrats by going to Planned Parenthood to get the Pill and openly discussing her conflicts and experiences. Worst of all, she had sex with her boyfriend without getting punished for it.

Throughout history, isolated and solitary women signaled the superrat tradition. Mary McCarthy's 1963 novel *The Group*, which explicitly details a first sexual experience and a visit to a birth control clinic, was the *Forever* of the boomer generation. Simone de Beauvoir, who wrote about women's sexual equality in the 1950s, is a superrat emerita. So is anarchist Emma Goldman, who in the early twentieth century made the first theoretical link between women's liberation and contraception—thereby inspiring Margaret Sanger, the founder of Planned Parenthood, another of her breed. The very first superrat can be found in the Old Testament: Eve, who by bringing the wrath of God down on all humankind, also caused some headaches. The point is that superrats have always existed but in much smaller numbers than today.

Profiles of Attitude: Five Superrats

A white, middle-class, educated woman, Megan, 22, represents one breed of superrat. She doesn't appear to be a rebel and is traditional in many ways. We met at an upscale pizza place in Brookline, a suburb of Boston, near the insurance company where she works. A recent graduate of the College of the Holy Cross in Wooster, Massachusetts, Megan was raised in a strict, traditional Catholic family and is engaged to an aspiring Republican businessman. Beneath the surface is an individual who is constantly challenging roles that don't fit her. She has never suppressed her natural assertiveness. "When I was in high school, I was always very energetic, but when I went to college, I became *very* outgoing," she explained. " I remember there was this dance junior year. And [my sister] called me up and she was like: 'Can you get me a date?' And so I started calling up all these guys I had never met in my life but they looked cute. I was like, 'Hi, I'm so and so. I'm calling for a friend of mine. Do you want to go to a dance with her?' And people were like, 'I can't believe you're doing this.' And I didn't think anything about it."

Megan also defied traditional female courting procedures on the night she met her fiancé, when they met at a campus bar and then slept together. While she regrets the experience for going too far too soon, she doesn't blame herself. Less religious than her mother and defining religion as a personal matter, Megan maintains that premarital sex is not "a mortal sin" as long as she is "conscious" about doing it. "In my book, it's wrong. . . . But that doesn't mean I'm not going to do it. It's part of nature I guess. If it's going to happen, it's going to happen. I'm not going to beat myself up about it." Also unlike her mother (and despite some ambivalence about premarital sex), Megan had no doubts about living with her boyfriend in college. "I had my own dorm room, but I lived with him the entire semester, all except two nights when I stayed in my room. We were happy together." This arrangement was possible, she explained, because of loopholes in security. "The girls have these metal security codes. You have this code and a magnetic strip, and that opens the door. But the guys don't have anything. You could just walk onto the guys' floor."

Nonetheless, Megan is starting to notice that some of her assertive attitudes are causing trouble in her relationship with her fiancé, who just informed her that he expects her to quit her job when they have kids. "Even now, we'll go shopping and he'll see a mother with her two kids at the store, and he'll be like, 'That will be you in ten years.' I'll be like, 'Yeah, and you'll be right there with me.' And he's like, 'No I won't.' And I'm like, 'Yes you will, or I'm not going to be there.' I refuse to let him shirk his responsibilities with raising a family. . . . The kids feel it as much if the father isn't there than if the mother isn't there. You need that pair to make it complete."

Describing her superrat philosophies with evident satisfaction was Stacie

S., a 27-year-old black social worker in Forest Park, Illinois. We met at her one-bedroom condo that she had bought two months earlier in this working-class, racially integrated western Chicago suburb. Stacie calls herself a "serial monogamist," usually meeting boyfriends through her elaborate network of friends. Her ultimate goals are marriage and a large family, although she stated that she wouldn't be averse to having a child on her own if she hadn't gotten married by her mid-thirties. She has always been dating someone or been in a committed relationship, never "super single, as in not seeing anybody for more than two weeks." When she spoke, she smiled widely and brightly. "I get a lot of guys who think that I probably have self-esteem problems because I'm overweight," she said. "But I never had a problem getting a man and keeping one." Often her dates are surprised at how well Stacie has managed her life. The daughter of postal workers, she put herself through college and graduate school with the help of academic scholarships, and with a friend, she started a small sales business of sorority merchandise. She is especially proud of her investment portfolio—and appreciates her single status without dependents.

Stacie's sexual attitudes have changed since she was a student at Immaculate Heart of Mary High School, when she was too burdened by guilt to have sex. "It's like if it feels good, do it. Just protect yourself. You know, the whole AIDS epidemic and everything, I'm sorry, it has not changed the sexual patterns of the twentysomethings or Generation X. My friends, we're still having the same amount of sex as we had before AIDS, if not more. Now we're smarter, older, and now we're protecting ourselves in ways that we weren't before."

I asked her if she thought women of this generation were more aggressive, and she said yes, keeping her own behavior in mind. "It's like the person I'm dating, I wanted him so bad. I mean, it was like . . . I don't know. I just thought about him all the time. And, you know, I wanted to get to know him—*in the biblical sense*. I didn't want to know what he thought about or anything. I didn't want to know what was his favorite color," she sighs. "He's just . . . [a] man. . . . So, the night that I decided I wanted to, I called him up, asked him what he was doing. . . . I had never been over to his house before. 'I'm going to come by.' And he was like, 'Yeah, I want to see you.'. . . I put on the sexy underwear and put some condoms in my purse, and I went over there. And I don't consider myself very aggressive, but as I laid across the bed and batted my eyes a couple times, I was pretty sure it was pretty obvious what I wanted. And he gave it to me. And we've been together."

I asked her for more details, for instance, whether she thinks women of this age group are more demanding in bed. "You know, here's the thing. I don't demand that I have an orgasm, but if I don't have one, nobody's going to sleep that night." I asked her to elaborate. "'No, you can't go to sleep until I come.' And I will talk to you. I will poke you. Because then it's like you're not trying to please me. Because I really feel that it doesn't take much to have an orgasm. The least you could do is spend a little time on me and my body and trying to find out what makes me tick. . . . Because it's like, I can have a good time without having an orgasm, but that says a lot about the man. Is he taking the time? Is he talking to me? Is he trying to find out what I like? Did he even do that before we went there? You know, were we talking about sex before that? Did we talk about what we liked? Did we talk about what does it for us? . . . You know, if I don't feel good about what's going on, nothing is going to happen. And it's like, it's not going to happen again. I don't have time for this. 'Whack sex,' as me and my friends call it. Because I have needs, too. I have needs. Sex is supposed to be enjoyable for the both of us. That's an outdated idea that, you know, it's just a function, and men have all the fun. I think we ought to be having some fun. You know, then what's the purpose?"

A much more "socially contemptible" superrat I interviewed is someone with a predatory name, Cat. Like minority and teenaged superrats, as a poor woman on welfare, she is feared most by society as an affront to the middle-class way of life. She is a white single mother living on the outskirts of Austin, Texas, with a criminal record for selling cocaine to an undercover FBI agent. Also, like a surprisingly large proportion of the country's poorest women, she has been a "sex worker," earning money as a stripper. Although Cat, 26, has fewer options than do middle-class women to conduct her life "her way," she is a superrat in attitude, as she expressed a desire to take care of her own needs, which have developed slowly during years of abuse.

I drove down dusty, rural roads to reach her government housing development, a sprawling and strangely quiet subdivision of two-story apartments, which contradicted my Chicago-born image of "the projects" as menacing urban high-rises. Cat answered the door wearing an oversized T-shirt and biking shorts, resembling the all-American ideal of a slim blonde. If not for her imperfect teeth, she could be the double of the character Shelly on the 1990s CBS television show *Northern Exposure*. While we talked, I gave her son, 8, and daughter, 7, a spare tape recorder to play with, to distract them. "These kids are starved for attention," she explained. From time to time, they listened to our conversation and filled in gaps in their mother's story.

"I haven't had a real pretty life," she said. "So, what in particular, would you like to know?" I asked her to give a short summary. "I was three when my parents got divorced," she said. "My mom remarried. I had a stepfather that beat me up for twelve years. I was raped when I was fifteen. I married the first man I had sex with. I was married five and a half years. He was abusive. So I left him. He was an active alcoholic drug addict. Whenever he and I split up, I went nutzoid. I was very active in drugs and such for about three years. I was a topless dancer. And then I was put in a psychiatric hospital twice. I went through treatment three times. I finally decided to get my life together, and I got my kids back about two years ago. They were with their father. . . . I was in a relationship at the time with a man who was a drug counselor. He relapsed, started shooting heroine, tried to kill me, literally, and I had left. I fled Corpus Christi. . . . When I got to Austin, I was staying at a center for battered women. I was considered homeless, so I got into this apartment complex. The center for battered women has a thrift store called SAC. They gave me the mattress and box springs for all three of us, the two couches, and some dishes. The rest of it, my mom gave me the TV, and this stuff belongs to a guy I let stay here for a little while."

Cat has planned her life. Now on public aid, she will use government Pell grants and scholarships to pay for her associate's degree in human services from Austin Community College, which will help qualify her to work as a drug counselor.

The conversation naturally kept switching to sex, which has been a major defining theme in her life. Cat told me that she had slept with seventy-five men, all but nine during a two-year period when she "went bonkers" on drugs and stripped for a living. Since that time, she has been learning about maturity and independence, taking control of her life as best she can. Major influences in her life have been therapy and television talk shows, which have taught her the importance of self-esteem in making sexual decisions.

I asked her if this new attitude now causes conflicts with men. "It has, because if I go to sleep with some guy and he lies there and tells me what to do, I kick him out. I have. This one guy, he told me to give him head and I wouldn't do it. And he was trying to make me. So I did, but I stopped right before he came and I threw him out. I threw his clothes out the window. I wanted to humiliate him, and I knew that would humiliate him. I wanted him to feel like I felt, completely degraded. That's how I felt. He obviously didn't see me as a person but as an object to fulfill his pleasure. I didn't appreciate it much. He never told nobody about that. That was a long time ago. I wouldn't do that now. My morals have grown a little bit."

But this new assertiveness has come slowly. Cat's saying no to whatever men tell her to do goes against everything she was taught. "I've been treated like an object for a living. It took me a long time to develop enough self-respect and enough self-esteem. It took me until probably a year and a half ago to finally learn that it's OK to say no, and I don't have to. I would go out with a guy, and I would think I had to have sex with him. . . . That had been reinforced so much throughout my life that I thought that my purpose in life was to be some guy's piece of ass. . . . I'll tell you what. I haven't ever really ever enjoyed sex for sex, not until recently. Because I had never realized that having sex was there for my pleasure too. I would use sex as a power thing. I would use sex for love, in my mind. It was never just for pleasure."

Now this new pleasure is possible only with constant communication with her new boyfriend. "I went into this relationship very open. And I talked to him about everything, right down to sex. Most guys aren't comfortable talking about it. I wouldn't have had sex with him if he wasn't comfortable talking about it. I have issues. I was raped. And I have issues. And I have to deal with them, or I'm not going to be able to respond. . . . It's just because I'm so much more aware of everything and I've worked on stuff."

The two youngest subjects that I interviewed, high school students, are perhaps the most "fearsome" superrats, even to only slightly older women. These two friends, who attend Wheeling High School (in a working- and middle-class suburb northwest of Chicago), were so experienced with sex and relationships that they were almost jaded. Both are leaders in their high school ROTC program, plan to enter the military, and have already had at least a few long-term relationships with older men. They also stood out from the rest of the interview sample as having more regrets and confusion about their recent behavior.

The youngest, Bridget, 16 (but almost 17, she said), went all the way with her boyfriend when she was 14 (but almost 15, she said). "I did it because I was curious." Bridget said that the sex soon took over and ruined the relationship. "I was just curious. I kept saying, 'Yeah, I'm totally sure I'm ready.' And then when it was all over, it was like, 'I can't believe I did this.' We just sat in the car on the way home in silence. I didn't want to make him feel guilty. We were really close at that point, and I didn't want to put pressure on him like, 'Oh, you know, it was your fault.' Because it wasn't. I mean he totally asked."

Yet Bridget feels more regretful than guilty about the experience, but as a believer in sexual openness, she said she also feels no shame in telling me about the intimate details of her life. "I think that talking about your problems and your situations, it cleanses the soul. To keep things in, that builds things up until you can't take it anymore. So you go a little crazy. So I don't have a real problem talking about my relationships and stuff. It doesn't bother me. Because I want other people to learn what I've learned." Since then, after that first relationship ended, she said she has become like the boys in her class, treating sex "like a game." "When I want something, and I'm talking about sexually, if I want a guy, then I'm going to go for it. I'm going to be the aggressor. I don't care. It doesn't bother me." Recently, though, a 22-year-old male friend turned her down. "He was a military guy. He was medically discharged from the army. He had like these little tattoos that said 'scandalous.' It was this thing that him and these three guys had. They all had 'scandalous' tattooed on their arm. It was a group thing."

At the age of 17 (almost 18, she said), her friend Kamilla has already had two emotionally intense two-year relationships. Also first having sex at 15, Kamilla, too, now dates only older men. Her current boyfriend, in his early twenties, is a friend of her older brother. "I want to see someone who knows what they're doing, has a job, goes to college," she explained. Both she and Bridget, dressed fashionably in sleek hipster garb, often hang out in college coffee houses in Evanston, as well as with older military and working men. They repeatedly compared these older men with males their own age, whom they dismissed as still acting like children. They cited the example of a group of male friends their own age recently going out on "a mission" to ring doorbells and play "ding dong ditch." "They're jerks. Really immature," said Kamilla, smoking a thin cigarette in the booth of a suburban diner. "You look at them and you laugh."

But Kamilla said that she had reached a different stage of her life in which she takes males less seriously. Her greatest ambitions are reserved for her anticipated career in the marines; she was ranked the best female on her rifle team in high school. When she talks about the military, her eyes light up in the same way as they did when she described the love she felt for her first boyfriend at the age of 15. "I'm a very passionate kind of person, so when I thought I found the person to share that with me and return the same affection I felt for him, I felt that I was in paradise. I hoped that it would go on for years." But letdowns from him proved to her that she had to become independent and derive her value from her own achievements. "That's why I was saying you should be content with yourself first. So even if you don't have that person, you are still going to be in your own paradise in a way, because you are going to be doing what you want to do. And you won't be dependent on that other person to bring happiness into your life."

Entertainment and the Media

These women's sexually independent and antivictim sensibilities are also becoming more and more visible in the entertainment and news media. You have probably seen them. The first generation of openly lesbian entertainers and sports figures, who most vividly illustrate young women's desire to live on their own terms, are superrats. Their work reflects their lack of shame and even pride: Melissa Etheridge went so far as to call an album *Yes, I Am* (1993), and k. d. lang entitled hers *All You Can Eat* (1995) and *Drag* (1997). On the 1997 album *Shaming of the Sun*, the Indigo Girls make no apologies for themselves, singing, "It's all right if you hate that way, hate me 'cause I'm different, hate me 'cause I'm gay." One of the most fearless athletes in America, punk professional bicyclist Missy Giove, was sponsored in 1996 by such corporate heavyweight sponsors as Reebok and Volvo-Cannondale, despite being a lesbian. In 1997, riding a wave of media buzz, Ellen DeGeneres came out on the cover of *Time* magazine, weeks before her alter ego sitcom character took the well-publicized and high-rated plunge.

In music, Sarah McLachlan, Erykah Badu, Bjork, Sinead O'Connor, Lauryn Hill, Alanis Morissette, Fiona Apple, P. J. Harvey, Tori Amos, rappers TLC, Lil' Kim, and Salt 'n Pepa, and Missy Elliot all are superrats, singing with the bravado formerly reserved for men about both the pleasures and the really painful parts of sex and love. They each express superrat messages in styles as individualistic as themselves. Perhaps Liz Phair's "Fuck and Run," from her 1993 album *Exile in Guyville*, could be a superrat anthem, lamenting her emptiness after a one-night stand. She is critical of men, reveals a wide range of emotions about sex, yet makes no apologies for her lust.

While such performers, singing authentically and assertively about their desires, have always been around, they now have become a full-fledged powerful sisterhood, with enough muscle to create the Lilith Tour, one of the major music events of the late 1990s. The Grammy Awards show that women now dominate popular music, having taken over most of the main categories in the 1990s. These women stand out from female musicians of the past in many ways, including the fact that they often produce their own recordings, thereby preserving more of the integrity of their sound and message.

In country music, young singers such as Wynona Judd, Patty Loveless, Faith Hill, Tricia Yearwood, and Pam Tillis now rule the genre. They direct their careers themselves and sing about women's independence with new spirit. Over the past fifteen years, this mind-set changed dramatically from Reba McEntire's 1986 song "Whoever's in New England," about a dutiful wife waiting out her husband's philandering period. Now the songs are more sexually independent, such as the 1995 "Independence Day" by Martina McBride, which is about a battered wife fighting back, and Shania Twain's 1995 "Any Man of Mine," which refuses to tolerate any betrayals by her man.

The most super of the superrats, Madonna, influenced a whole generation in the 1980s. When I was in high school in the early to mid-1980s, I first observed her influence when many of my classmates started to imitate her look by wearing clusters of rubber bracelets and externally visible lacy lingerie. I slowly learned to appreciate her effect on these young women, leading them to a new self-assurance and awareness. More effectively than any honors-level graduate symposium ever could, her videos illustrated the shifting and socially defined character of female sexuality. As if she were trying on costumes, Madonna easily moved from one female sexual pose to another—from a pouty Marilyn Monroe to a futuristic singer wearing a pointed cone-shaped bra—demonstrating how many of women's outer trappings are just masquerades. She made female sexuality an object of public discussion, as something separate and distinct from male sexuality, and introduced themes reflecting women's sexual diversity.

Courtney Love of Hole, named one of the top twenty-five influential Americans by *Time* in 1996, went a step further by yelling in rage while wearing an overly frilly, docile, feminine baby-doll dress. Her albums, *Pretty on the Inside* (1991) and *Live through This* (1994), lampoon outmoded female roles, with the cover of the latter one featuring an overly emotional Miss America with her mascara smeared in undignified glops.

Meanwhile, young male music groups have expressed bemusement at this sexually aggressive breed. In their song "Crazy," the group James ruminates about an out-of-control girlfriend making outrageous demands. Even the neighbors complain about the noise she makes in bed; the song explains, "She only comes when she's on top." One popular heavy rocker of the mid- to late 1990s, the Offspring, gained popularity with the single "Self-Esteem," which chronicles a man's helplessness to stand up to his domineering girlfriend.

Teen superrats in movies also came of age in the late 1990s, refuting the double standard. According to *New York Times* movie critic Stephen Holden,

> More than 40 years after he was invented by James Dean in "A Rebel without a Cause," the stock image of the teen-age rebel hero—the sexy mixed-up kid searching for his identity—has begun to fade from the center of teen mythology. In movies as in pop music, the focus has shifted from boy power to girl power.

This is a change even from the early 1980s when, desperate for information on sex, young women had to rely on films about sexual initiation that were told through boys' eyes. Postboomer women were thus forced to follow the exploits of the heroes of *Spring Break* (1983) and *Losin' It* (1982). In *Risky Business* (1983), the main character, Tom Cruise, actually trades women as business commodities, setting up a prostitution service for his friends and wowing a horny Princeton recruiter in the process. During this decade, girls expressed mainly romantic yearnings, an example being Molly Ringwald in *Sixteen Candles*, which ends with the protagonist innocently sharing birthday cake with the now-chaste popular guy, who has renounced the meaningless sex he had with his "easy" ex-girlfriend.

In film, superrats slowly began to emerge in the late 1980s. In the 1987 *River's Edge*, Ione Skye aggressively goes after her man. In 1992, teen videomaker Sadie Benning produced a short, *It Wasn't Love*, which attacks stereotypes by depicting a female couple's explicit adventures in a fast-food parking lot. In *Just Another Girl on the IRT* (1993), black filmmaker Leslie Harris portrayed a realistic young woman's life in the projects and her sexually curious and outspoken character. Finally, in 1996 and 1997, this genre of films became noticeable as a movement. With *Manny and Lo* and *Girls Town* (1996), streetwise teenage girls take charge of their lives and challenge views of women as sexually passive. The entire hit 1997 movie *Chasing Amy* was about a young man coming to grips with the adventurous sexual history of his bisexual girlfriend. The 1997 independent features, *Wedding Bell Blues*, *Ripe*, *Female Perversions*, and *Cadillac Ranch* and the 1998 *High Art* portray women's complex quests for sexual and personal fulfillment. Christina Ricci's character in 1998's *The Opposite Sex* attracted widespread attention with her rampage of stealing and then dumping others' boyfriends (including that of her stepbrother).

Following this trend, superrats began to appear as well in the late 1990s on television. One of the top-rated shows of the 1990s, *Melrose Place*, was based on superrat sexual power. Heather Locklear, then 33, who played the savvy and sexually experienced advertising executive (and landlord) Amanda Woodward, explained the show's appeal to *Playboy* editor David Rensin:

> They [viewers] like it because the women hold all the power—which is as it should be—and the men very often have no balls. So often women are on the other side of the coin. It is also great to see men take off their shirts for a change. It's great to see the men get beat up a little bit in relationships. We don't want to make it like the guys are just dumb, of course. They are smart, but the women are just smarter. Also, the women get to have as much sex as they want and jump from bed to bed. No one's giving them shit for it. (1994, 137)

But no television show better epitomized superrats on the loose than the successor to *Melrose Place,* HBO's hit *Sex and the City,* by the same creator, Darren Star. The show featured four hip alpha females: powerful professional women over thirty who often pursue men just for sex. "I just had sex like a man," declared Sarah Jessica Parker's character after an afternoon tryst. "I left feeling powerful, potent, and incredibly alive" (Tharps 1999, 70). Also in the late 1990s, TV teens followed in these older women's self-gratifying footsteps. Actress Michelle Williams was assertive to the extreme when she broke hearts on the adult-rated teen sex drama *Dawson's Creek.* On the long-running *Beverly Hills 90210,* Tiffany Amber Thiessen's character bed-hopped with evident relish between her plots to annihilate the other characters.

At the same time, superrats have become visible as advisers. Cautioning women to be wary of the advice of the 1996 best seller *The Rules,* a guide to traditional female scripts, two of the most talked-about dating guides of 2000 are *Date like a Man: To Get the Man You Want and Have Fun Doing It!* (2000) by Myreah Moore and Jodie Gould, and *Get a Life Then Get a Man: A Single Woman's Guide* (2000), by Jennifer Bawden. When she was 25, Sari Locker wrote the very frank *Mindblowing Sex in the Nineties* (1995) and hosted the cable sex talkfest "Late Date with Sari," a forerunner to MTV's longer-lasting *Loveline.* For much of the 1990s, the sex columnist for *Details* magazine, which was targeted to men in their twenties, was Anka Radakovich, in her late thirties. These Generation-X women gave advice without apologies. In contrast, in 1969, when Joan Terry Garrity shared personal tidbits about her sex life in her best-selling graphic sex guide, *The Sensuous Woman,* she used a pen name, "J," to protect her mother. Today, not only do Locker and Radakovich use their real names, they even appear on the cover of their book jackets wearing tight red halter tops (Anka's has black stripes).

At the same time, real-life superrats have made themselves seen and heard in the news media, exposing old skeletons of sexism that they inherited from another era. Demanding better standards of treatment, they have tackled the most private and thorny issues, such as sexual harassment. Unlike many of the superrats of the entertainment world, they often act directly as agents of change, with specific political agendas and influence and not necessarily conforming to shallow male-defined standards of beauty (often, however, like Monica Lewinsky, they are subject to immense public ridicule when they don't).

In 1991, Anita Hill created furor in the U.S. Senate when she testified against a nominee for the U.S. Supreme Court, Clarence Thomas, accusing him of sexual harassment. Several years later, prompted by *Washington Post* reporter Florence Graves, twenty women came forward and demanded the resignation of Senator Bob Packwood for what Senator Barbara Mikulski called "a systematic abuse of women, power and this Senate" (Goodman 1995, 15). Not even the U.S. Navy is immune to the superrats. In 1991, an admiral's aide, superrat Lieutenant Paula Coughlin, reported the numerous assaults on women at the Tailhook Association convention in Las Vegas. In 1992, Christine Franklin, a high school student in Gwinnett County, Georgia, sued—and won—her high school for failing to stop a teacher who forced unwanted sexual attention on her. That case has encouraged a growing number of high school students to take action under this broad interpretation of Title IX of the 1972 Education Act.

Even just a few years ago, victims of acquaintance rape would have never come forward or been taken seriously. But in 1992, Patricia Bowman, accusing a young Kennedy relative, appeared on national television to show her face and assert her credibility. Shortly thereafter, Desiree Washington, an 18-year-old, 105-pound beauty-pageant contestant, helped convict the heavyweight boxing champion Mike Tyson. At the Virginia Polytechnic State University in 1996, a less famous young woman, Christy Brzonkala, 18, made front-page headlines in the *New York Times* because she felt her case against the two football players who raped her had not been adequately prosecuted. "[Brzonkala], who was once too ashamed and traumatized to confide even in her parents, is now willing to publicize her case not only in print, but on television" (February 11, 1996).

With similar spirit, young superrats have fought publicly against being judged for being unwed mothers, which not too long ago was one of the worst possible transgressions. In 1998, three teenage mothers made national news fighting their high schools' National Honors Society chapters. The schools had cited the evidence of their sexual activity (their children) as revealing the girls' poor characters. Outraged, Amanda Lemon filed a grievance against Xenia (Ohio) High School. "If they've discriminated against me," she told *People* magazine, "They'll do it to others" (Jewel 1998, 150). Also that year, the ACLU filed suit against the high school of teenage mothers Somer Chipman and Chastity Glass, also denied entry into their school's National Honors Society chapter in Williamstown, Kentucky. "I understand their point," Chipman told the *Cincinnati Post*. "But they are sexually discriminating against women because they cannot make sure that males have not had sex." In the high school honors ceremony, when their names were not called out, Chipman and Glass defiantly walked out on to the gym floor. "Students, some teachers, and all the inductees applauded them before they were whisked off by counselors," the *Post* reported (Vance 1998).

Superrats making the news have come from the most traditionally chaste institutions, even the Miss America Pageant. In 1998, Kate Shindle became a controversial Miss America for her widespread, tireless public campaigning for AIDS awareness across the world, from conservative high schools to an international AIDS conference in Geneva, Switzerland. A Chicago neighborhood newspaper reported her boldness:

> Shindle has described herself as an anti-abortion/Republican/Catholic school alumna who never made any secret of her intention to focus on this once-taboo topic. In fact, she promised to make AIDS education her top priority as early as when the judges were asking her what she would do if she were crowned Miss America. (Butler 1998, 5)

Others with Republican associations have made headlines. As a gay and lesbian rights activist, superrat Candace Gingrich went beyond her brother's call for "tolerance" of homosexuals: "For him to say we should be tolerated," she told the *New York Times*, "that still allows for us to be fired merely for being gay or lesbian, and that's not tolerance, that's discrimination. I want him to understand that discrimination is wrong" (Seelye 1995, A9). Many young lesbians have made headlines demanding new openness. Lieutenant Commander Zoe Dunning, 31, a lesbian reserve officer, won the navy's acceptance when it dropped its efforts in 1995 to discharge her. Attorney Robin Joy Shahar, 28, sued Georgia attorney general Michael Bowers, who denied her a position in the Georgia Department of Law after he discovered that she was planning to marry another woman. Bowers (who won the case in 1997) is famous for his role in the 1986 landmark Supreme Court case, *Bowers v. Hardwick*, which limited privacy rights for gays and banned sodomy in Georgia. In 1998, Los Angeles artist and performance artist Jill Abrams stopped traffic in West Los Angeles with her billboard of two giddy brides on a motorcycle celebrating their "freedom to marry," protesting the 1996 passage of the Defense of Marriage Act.

Like the unwed superrats trying to get into the National Honors Society, teenage lesbians also have made news suing their schools. In 1996, in Salt Lake City, 17-year-old high school senior Kelli Peterson found herself embroiled in a national battle after she started an extracurricular club, the Gay/Straight Alliance. In response, her school, fearing lawsuits for specifically targeting gays, banned all clubs from the school, provoking a national debate about schools' right to restrict such clubs. (Her story was the topic of a 1998 documentary, *Out of the Past*, which won the Audience Award for best documentary at that year's Sundance Film Festival.) In 1998, tenth grader Alana Flores brought suit against a school district in *Flores vs. Morgan Hill*. She and five other classmates (four girls and one boy) sued Live Oak High School and the Morgan Hill (California) school districts for failing to protect them from constant sexual harassment. "I could have graduated from Live Oak, moved on with my life, and never looked back," she told *Curve* magazine. "But there was always something in me that said that's not the right thing to do, because it could happen to somebody else, over and over again" (Clair 1999, 19).

To the public, the most amazing aspect of these cases was not that these women may have suffered the alleged injustices. "The remarkable fact," said Ellen Goodman in her September 12, 1995, syndicated *Boston Globe* column describing Packwood's ouster, "is that for the first time, a Senate Committee defined sexual misconduct toward women as an abuse of power." A decade earlier, these claims would never have even prompted a hearing. But the most unbelievable part was that *these women stood up at all*. In the past, they would have blamed themselves. Instead, they shifted the blame to men, and not just any men. In the harassment and date rape cases, the men accused were powerful and established. In addition, these incidents took place while these women were on dates, whereas in the past, just the fact that they allowed themselves to be alone with the man would have been enough to invalidate their case. Now, however, such women believe that they are entitled to sexual control, even on a date.

The fear of superrats is not new. In 1942, Philip Wylie warned the world about them in his *Generation of Vipers*, noting that the rising number of women having children outside marriage served as

> proof that young men were eventually ensnared in their gynocracy. . . .
> Young men . . . bounce anxiously away from their first few brutal contacts
> with modern young women, frightened to find that their shining hair is vul-
> canized, their agate eyes are embedded in cement, and their ruby lips case-
> hardened into pliers for the bending of males like wire. (195)

Continuing this line of reasoning, a 1959 *New York Times* story about a report by the North Carolina Conference for Social Service "suggested that a new spirit of female boldness might be . . . responsible for the rise in illegitimate relationships" (Solinger 1992, 35).

Now with superrats becoming more numerous and unapologetic, society's fear of them has become even more evident. Playwright David Mamet drew crowds to the theater and screen with his 1992 play *Oleanna*, about a crazed college student who is brainwashed by radical feminists to accuse a professor unfairly of sexual harassment and thereby destroy his career. A wave of films in the early 1990s played to these fears, with sexually aggressive women fated to suffer tragic, violent deaths: Sharon Stone in *Basic Instinct*, Rebecca de Mornay in *The Hand That Rocks the Cradle*, and Jennifer Jason Leigh in *Single White Female*. Often the critics' views of such sexually aggressive women are revealing. In reviewing a crop of teen movies in the late 1990s, male writers took the greatest pains to single out the sexually brazen female characters as troubling. In 1999, *New York Times* movie critic Stephen Holden wrote that "the ruthless female leading characters are downright scary in *Jawbreaker* and *Cruel Intentions* in the way they view boys as trophies" (A13). When decrying the sexual explicitness of teen films, another *New York Times* critic, Rick Marin, recommended that "some of these young women . . . take up a new provirginity book by Wendy Shalit, *A Return to Modesty,* out of sheer performance anxiety" (1999, B9).

In a recent article about sex on the Vassar College campus, where women outnumber men and commonly take the role of the aggressor, the male reporter mourned the emptiness of sex when women don't at least feign some resistance. "Perhaps there are college campuses somewhere in America where the vestiges of sexual repression and denial still maintain, but not here, that's for sure. Here, the fraternity boy of the soul is dead," writes Eric Konigsberg (1998, 99). These critics are not concerned, however, with the threat of sexually aggressive males.

Scholars have joined in as well, blaming young women and women's rights for all our current social problems. In his 1993 book, *Love and Friendship*, the late conservative cultural critic Allan Bloom blamed young feminists for ruining eroticism with their politics. Reflecting this thinking, another University of Chicago professor, Leon R. Kass, condemned young single women in his essay "Courtship's End," printed in the February 9, 1997, *Chicago Tribune Magazine* (reprinted from the neoconservative journal *The Public Interest*). He described the new breed of predatory female who "enfeeble men" and have ruined the sanctity of courtship:

> [Men] are now matched by some female trophy hunters. But most young women strike me as sad, lonely and confused; hoping for something more, they are not enjoying their hard-won sexual liberation as much as liberation theory says they should. . . . For the first time in human history, mature women by the tens of thousands live the entire decade of their 20s—their most fertile years—neither in the homes of their fathers nor in the homes of their husbands, unprotected, lonely and out of sync with their inborn natures. (20)

Superrats may also trouble another, less obvious contingent: feminists. Some feminists take issue with them for embracing traditionally male sexual values of aggression and self-gratification and overlooking traditional female ways of sharing and connection. For many superrats, especially those in entertainment, this rebellion may be superficial. They often aren't as revolutionary as they sound and still are tied to male-defined standards of beauty. Indeed, our popular culture tolerates superrats only if they look like they just stepped out of the pages of *Cosmo*, armed with an arsenal of beauty products and dieting maneuvers. As long as she can turn men on, a sexually aggressive woman is allowed to assert herself at will. Almost all the entertainers mentioned here and others—from Britney Spears to the cast of *Sex and the City*—would not have attracted such a public forum (and array of corporate sponsors) to broadcast their sexual rebellions if they didn't look the way they do. In addition, many of these feminists deplore the current lack of superrat politics. Ironically, even though feminism directly shaped most of these young women, securing their expectations and rights to be sexually independent, superrats often do not identify as feminists and may actually reject the label. But love them or fear them, superrats are here to stay, and the best way of coping with them is to understand that they are changing the rules of sex and relationships. They provide powerful testimony that despite some longings to the contrary, the sexual revolution did indeed happen and they are its greatest legacy.

2. Portrait of a Generation: Male and Female Sex Patterns Converge

My fiancé and I have had sex before, but now he wants to wait until we're married to do it again. This seems unfair. How should I handle it?
— G. F., 27, in "Sex Q&A" column, *Mademoiselle,* June 1998

I think every woman should have at least two lovers. If she doesn't, something is wrong. Men do it all the time.
— Aisha, on *Jerry Springer,* exploring the theme of "girlfriends who cheat,"
October 8, 1997

I "In college, before I had a boyfriend, I was what you would say promiscuous," said Shelly, 24, a Miami high school teacher with a soft Georgia accent. "I would have more casual relationships. Like I didn't want a boyfriend and I had a couple of different guys for two and a half years that I hung out with. And neither one of us wanted a commitment or anything." Like the other women that I interviewed, Shelly has had a sex life that is far from traditionally female. Actually, it is better described as traditionally male. As men have done more freely through history, Shelly formed sexual relationships on a variety of levels, from casual to committed, separating sex from love. "I never really thought about it until I started dating my boyfriend," said Shelly, "and he would always bring it up. . . . But even though he would always try to make me feel guilty about it, I never felt guilty about it. . . . I'm glad that I did it. I definitely think that people should have sex before they get married. I think it's unrealistic—if that's supposed to be such a big aspect of a relationship, then it needs to be experienced before you get married. If you're not sexually happy with the person you're married to, then you've got a problem."

Shelly and her friends Janine and Tammy, also high school teachers of the same age, are not ashamed of their unwed sex lives, for they know they will avoid committing themselves to a husband for life just to satisfy their repressed lust (as Shelly and Janine saw their now-divorced mothers do). Tammy noted that if they had married the first men they had sex with, those ex-boyfriends would now be their ex-husbands. In fact, Janine was so determined to avoid confusing sex and love that after she had sex with her high school boyfriend, she deliberately experimented with a male friend because "I didn't want to be fooled." When I asked her to explain, she said, "You don't want to be fooled by what society says is the right thing to do. I mean society says you wait, you have sex with one person and you marry that person. My mom got married when she was 19 and had me when she was 20. And from what she tells me, that was her first sexual experience. And that's why the second person was a good friend of mine, and afterwards it was like sex is no big deal. Sex is sex. And I think after that I started to separate the two."

Besides, waiting to have sex within the bounds of matrimony just isn't as practical as it was for their mothers. These women's single years last much longer, from just after high school to several years past college, and that period is just too long to wait. Also unlike their mothers, all three of these women are pursuing master's degrees, as part of the first generation of women to outnumber men doing so. Now, before they become tethered to another human as a wife, they see this as time to work on themselves.

As young women have grown to mirror men in public in areas like education and career aspirations, they also have shifted to resemble them in private, in the bedroom (Smith 1994b, xii; also see Fillion 1996). Indeed, as my research reveals, in the thirty years in which they have gained new social status, young American women have undergone an almost invisible evolution in attitude, number of sex partners, and what they specifically do in bed. Despite some chipping away by AIDS, the levels of their permissiveness and assertiveness have gradually risen since the 1970s, generally leveling off in the 1990s. Even though most women still associate sex with love more than men do, the two genders' sexual attitudes and behaviors have never been more similar. As the superrats profiled earlier illustrate, they are following the patterns established by the baby boomers to become more sexually independent and individualistic. As a result, the generation gap is smaller; that is, young women with boomer parents have much more in common than the boomers did with their parents. This is evident in the most comprehensive sex survey to date, the 1994 University of Chicago National Health and Social Life Survey (NHSLS, discussed in greater detail later in this chapter). One of its major findings is that young women account for the greatest sexual changes in the American population. Young women now share men's unpredictable patterns of earlier sexual experimentation with many sexual partners, followed by cohabitation and breakups. Even though most women eventually settle down with one partner when they get married, their road to that point is often long and indirect, with many detours along the way. "A more general pattern of young women's sexual experiences becoming somewhat more like men's seems to be emerging in terms of both same- and opposite-gender activity," the authors concluded in *The Social Organization of Sexuality*, in which the Chicago study's results are published and analyzed (Laumann et al. 1994, 310).

An exhaustive study of college and university students' sexual behavior, *Details* magazine's Sex on Campus survey, also reveals such a radical evolution. According to this 1996 survey, women's sexual behavior is now almost identical to that of men and is sometimes even more permissive. Although the percentages were almost identical, more females (81 percent) than males (80 percent) surveyed said they were not virgins. Women also surpassed men in frequency of sex, with 36 percent reporting that they had sex two or three times a week, compared with only 25 percent of the men. What they do in bed has also changed. The study also asserted, symbolic of this change, that the students' overall preference had shifted to the woman-on-top position. (However, it was mainly male preferences that accounted for this, as the plurality of women, 48 percent, still preferred the "man on top.") Still, this change shows that men are beginning to view sex as not necessarily defined by their dominance, physically or otherwise (Elliott and Brantley 1997, 5, 136, 138).

Smaller academic studies also back up this trend. University of Maryland Professor Ilsa L. Lottes wrote in the journal *Sex Roles* that compared with the men in her sample, the women reported similar percentages of age of first intercourse, oral and anal sex participation, satisfaction of their sex needs and desires by their sexual partners, and reactions to recent intercourse. Although the women were, on the whole, less promiscuous than men, many acknowledged that they had had multiple sex partners and sex without emotional involvement.

White, Educated, and Middle Class

When discussing women who act like men, it is important to state just which women we are talking about. In fact, almost all women have changed since the 1950s, with different classes and races of women acting more alike—and more like men. In the past, very generally speaking and according to available data, black women and women from poorer backgrounds acted more like men, whereas today, all women act more like men. In addition, the sexual behavior of American adults in general is strikingly similar. Indeed, one of the most dramatic findings of the University of Chicago's National Health and Social Life survey is how alike the sexual behavior of Americans of different age groups was.

In the past thirty years, the group that changed the most in terms of acting more like men was white women, who have caught up with their black counterparts. This is the central finding of the "big picture" report, *The Demography of Sexual Behavior*, by University of Chicago researcher Tom Smith. In 1970, 26 percent of white teens had had premarital sex, versus 46 percent of African American teenage girls. By 1988, that gap had nearly closed: 50 percent of white girls aged 15 to 19 reported having premarital sex, compared with 58 percent of African American girls the same age (Smith 1994b, xiii). In fact, white, middle-class, college-educated women in their twenties have had more sex partners than any other group of women. The 1995 National Survey of Family Growth reports that the highest percentages of women having four or more partners over their lifetimes were women in these three categories of race, income, and education (39).

Class is also less of a factor for the postboomers than for their predecessors. The old stereotype of the "slut" from a poor or working-class background who gets more than her share of the action as the "good girl" from the middle class looks on disapprovingly and chastely from the wings has been largely discredited. In fact, the authors of a 1997 study published in the *Archives of Sexual Behavior* observed the interesting phenomenon of educated women's evolving to act more like the "lower classes." Among young adults, "the lower level norms are becoming the predominant cultural norms," wrote Martin S. Weinberg and his colleagues (1997). Their sample of a college population found that women of all classes had very similar sexual profiles, including number of sexual partners and sexual initiation, regardless of their parents' level of achievement. (Class was a slightly more important variable for the men; for example, men of the "lower classes" had sex earlier and with more partners.) The 1994 University of Chicago NHSLS also revealed few differences across educational levels. In contrast, class— measured by levels of education or achievement—was a greater variable for the baby boomers. A 1969/70 sample of college students found that women and men with less education had more partners and started having sex earlier. Before that date, women of all backgrounds acted more "traditionally female." Unlike men, these women, such as those studied by Alfred Kinsey in the 1950s, uniformly reported being restrained and modest, their sexual activity confined almost exclusively to marriage (Weinberg, Lottes, and Gordon 1997).

Among women, however, some differences still remain. Of all the social forces influencing this new breed of women, *education* is the strongest variable shaping individual behavior. Education liberalizes sexual behavior for women, transforming values to become more "masculine" and to challenge double standards. In addition, education gives women more financial muscle to even the balance of power in their relationships and to be more selective about when they form them. Educated women are more likely to delay marriage, initiate sex, and experiment with more "adventurous" practices. Most notably, their sexual activity is less confined to goals of procreation and includes sex for recreation, with a higher incidence of masturbation, sexual satisfaction, lesbian sex, and oral and anal sex.

In addition to education, those women most likely to break free of traditionally restrictive sexual scripts share some other related characteristics. As the truest "superrats," unconventional, assertive, feminist-oriented, and sexually liberal women are more likely to initiate sex than are their conservative counterparts. Many studies identify more sexually aggressive women as those who are more willing to masturbate, who show their lovers how to arouse them, and who have had more sex partners (McCormick 1994, 23; also see Grauerhotz and Serpe 1985; Jesser 1978).

Although education and liberal views shape women's behavior most consistently, other variables affect individual practices. For example, whites and blacks have similar numbers of sexual partners over their lifetimes, more than Asians, Hispanics, and Native Americans have (Laumann et al. 1994, 187). Black women have sex earlier and are less likely to marry than are women of other racial and ethnic groups. Women in rural areas and those who attend church regularly marry earlier and have sex later than do women in large cities (Smith 1994b, xiii). Another important distinction is that some differences among women do not show up in empirical studies or in statistical graphs. Just using common sense, we know that poor women do not have the same quality of life. Poor women with less education and fewer resources accordingly have fewer choices and less control over their lives. Instead of being able to celebrate their sex lives, they are often trapped by them. With less sex education and access to birth control and abortion, they are much more vulnerable to unplanned pregnancies. In contrast, more affluent women can manage their sex lives with a Visa card, purchasing child care and health care services.

My interviews highlighted the often subtle differences in quality of life that are not documented by the major surveys. Women from lower-income backgrounds had many fewer options and hopes for directing their lives in their teen years. Nonetheless, they shared the "I'm-doing-it-on-my-terms" views of the other women. After learning lessons as teens, these mostly twentysomething poor and uneducated women had definite goals and the expectation of taking sexual control of their lives, generally to become independent. Cat, 26, a single mother on welfare in Austin, Texas (see chapter 1), had enrolled in a community college on a path toward a career, and she had also vowed to be more assertive with men and in her sex life. In regard to race, black women in particular, such as Stacie S., also profiled in the previous chapter, seemed to express stronger attitudes of independence. This mind-set, a result of cultural and economic influences, is difficult to explain. Perhaps it is a response to lower marriage rates, often attributed to the high unemployment of young black men and increased discrimination, both of which mean that black women must expect to look after themselves. The black women I interviewed strongly believed that they did not expect, as Stacie said, "a man on white horse" to direct their personal lives and rescue them. Instead, they planned to rescue themselves.

Thinking "His Way"

The greatest sexual evolution has taken place inside women's heads. Young women of all backgrounds share men's sexual expectations for control, which differs from the baby boomers at their age, even the more promiscuous among them. In fact, young women's sexual attitudes and behavior today are more in sync than they were with the boomers. The behavior of the women who came of age in the 1960s and 1970s was much more permissive than their attitudes were. For example, they often participated in premarital sex but then condemned it, whereas contemporary young women are less likely to suffer from this contradiction. This generational pattern proves sex researchers' theory that our psyche takes a while to catch up with our behavior (Lottes 1993, 660).

Young women's overall values today have greatly influenced their sexual attitudes, which now closely resemble those of men. These values have, furthermore, made them more permissive overall, despite the restraining effect of AIDS. Studies clearly demonstrate that a more "instrumental" or masculine personality is associated with greater sexual experience, including the frequency of sexual intercourse and oral sex, the number of sexual partners, the age at which the respondents first had sex, and more relaxed feelings about having sex (Leary and Snell 1988; Whitley 1988). The Roper Virginia Slims 2000 survey reported that men and women define themselves according to almost identical values. From a list of twenty-four traits—ranging from having children to valuing religion—both men and women most often (about 60 percent) chose their independence as being most important. The fact that young women's values are evolving to become more "male" was the principal conclusion of *The American Freshman: Thirty Year Trends,* an annual survey by the Higher Research Institute at the University of California at Los Angeles. The main finding of its summary of college freshmen's attitudes from 1966 to 1996 was a "gender convergence" in values, with men's and women's educational aspirations nearly identical in the latest surveys. The authors attribute the change to a shift in women's values, not men's.

This overall convergence of male and female attitudes also was the finding of researcher Jean M. Twenge. Observing her own classmates at the University of Michigan, she noted in the journal *Sex Roles* in 1997 that women were adopting more "male" values while men were still rejecting the traditionally female. She then confirmed this hypothesis by surveying students according to the two most common statistical measures of traditional male and female personality traits, the Bem Sex-Role Inventory and the Personal Attributes Questionnaire, which measure traits according to the masculine "instrumental" scales of being "assertive" and "independent" and the feminine range of "expressive" traits such as "understanding of others" and "gentle." Twenge compared these results with those of similar samples taken by others over a twenty-year period until 1995 and found that the prevalence of male traits rose steadily for each female group. "The generational effect is really, really strong," she noted. Twenge explained women's more "masculine" and egalitarian" values as the result of women's career goals, which demand more male standards of behavior. Young women today also are more likely to have working mothers, and studies have shown that such daughters have more androgynous or masculine traits. Finally, Twenge discussed the impact of women's sports, which have become standard since the 1972 ratification of Title IX, mandating equal treatment of girls' sports.

The Double Standard

When women think more like men, they challenge many old societal judgments about women's sexuality. Most notably, they question the "double standard," a primary force in the past that limited women's promiscuity. Today, even though the double standard still certainly exists, especially during the teenage years, society takes gender into account less often when judging whether a person's sexual behavior is right or wrong. Some of the strongest evidence that the double standard is taking a beating is the high number of women's partners and their early first sexual experiences. In the past, more women specifically limited their sexual activity for fear of getting "a bad reputation," a concern that seems less important today. Now, especially as women move past high school, the label *slut* has less influence on their behavior or psyches. Women are less often defined, negatively or positively, by what they do or don't do in bed. In most circles, virginity is not elevated on a pedestal as it was before the 1960s. In turn, promiscuity is no longer glorified, as it was during the sexual revolution when it defined someone as "liberated."

Surveys show that both young men and women have slowly established similar sexual standards. Of the women questioned by the Roper Organization for the Virginia Slims Opinion Poll in 1970, 30 percent agreed that "single women should not enjoy the same kind of freedom as single men," whereas in 1990, about half that number, 16 percent, held that attitude. After questioning two groups of college students about a variety of sexual acts, Susan Sprecher of Illinois State University found that "sexual standards endorsed for a male are the same as the sexual standards endorsed for a female" (Sprecher 1989, 245). The two thousand male and female respondents of the 1996 *Details* Sex on Campus survey also shared the same sexual standards, although men reported having more actual partners. Of the men surveyed, nearly the same number agreed that "it's fine for women to have multiple sex partners" (22 percent) as agreed that "it's fine for men to have multiple sex partners" (27 percent). Women also set the same standards for themselves as for men: 13 percent supported this behavior from men, and 14 percent for women (15).

Surveys of popular culture, including women's magazines, reflect these changes. The article, "Should You Reveal How Many People You've Slept With?" in the March 1999 *Cosmopolitan* described some of the changes. One respondent, Cynthia, 28, a lab technician, summed up the current norms: "Definitely tell your partner, but if the number is more than 10, lie.

That seems to be the magic number in men's heads that turns fabulous girl-friends into trampy ho-bags." The number she cited was large for middle-class boomers of the past and still has some restrictions (68). Both sexes also deny the old myths about women's sexuality that supported the double standard. Young people are more likely to believe that girls' sexual desires are real, normal, and widespread, a belief that makes young women more likely to pursue sex as something that they need, and not as something that just happens to them, "sweeping them away." In her 1993 report on college students, University of Maryland professor Ilsa Lottes noted that challenging traditional views, a majority of her male sample (65 percent) reported that marrying a virgin was not important at all. Only about half of both the males (50 percent) and the females (45 percent) reported that men have a greater sex drive than women do.

While women's sexual desires seem healthy to young people, just a short time ago they were feared as signaling mental defects. In her 1976 best-seller *Passages*, baby boomer Gail Sheehy recalled how she and her friends decided only in middle age to challenge the ingrained myth of their adolescence that "normal" women had no sexual feelings:

> Even when it ran contrary to our own experience, women of my generation accepted the mythological profile of the 18-year-old boy who is a prisoner of his hormones and the young girl who is reproductively ready but won't sexually arrive for ten or fifteen more years. Indeed, many of us *willed* ourselves back into sexual dormancy. (448)

Today, even some of the most traditional advisers on courtship recognize women's sexual desires as real, even including Ellen Fein and Sherrie Schneider, the authors of the 1995 blockbuster *The Rules*, a handbook of old-fashioned female courtship wiles. They acknowledge women's sexual desires when they recommend that women hold off so as not to appear to be too eager: "But what if you like sex a lot too, and denying yourself is just as hard as denying him?" (81). Throughout the book, they discuss only men's sexuality as being biologically determined, although they repeatedly stop short of describing women's passive roles (which they heartily prescribe) as reflecting nature. They maintain that when a woman limits sex, she is not listening to her real nature but is *putting on an act*. An example is their recommendation that women not initiate sex, "even if [they] want it badly. Let him be the man, the aggressor in the bedroom. Biologically, the man must pursue the woman" (127).

Of course, the double standard still exists. Sometimes the evidence is obvious, such as the media's castigation of Monica Lewinsky in 1998 for being so overtly sexual, repeatedly calling her a "tramp" and "slut" (Tannenbaum 1999, 97–99). Most manifestations of the double standard are more subtle, however. Instead of fearing being publicly condemned, as past generations of women were, those I interviewed reported that the "bad girl" feels judgment in other ways. Ann, 23, noticed a varying perception of women's one-night stands when she was an undergraduate at Bridgewater State University in Massachusetts. "The next morning, when you went back to your own dormitory or whatever, for the guy it would be called 'the walk of fame' or 'the strut of fame.' But for the women, it's the 'walk of shame.'" Lisa, 25, an actress in New York City, observed that the men she meets now accept the standard that women can be sexual—as long as they don't enjoy it too much. She said she was surprised by how bothered her old boyfriend was by her lack of inhibitions in bed. "He was very, very repressed in his sexuality, so much [so] that he didn't even like me to have all my clothes off when we would have sex. He would want me to keep my shirt on. He would keep his shirt on. And I was like, 'Am I sleeping with Archie Bunker or something?'"

In contrast, other women reported almost no double standard when they were in their twenties, a change from their teen years. "It was a big thing when I was 16, about, you know, how many people you slept with and being a virgin and everything," said Stacie S., 27, who lives in River Forest, just west of Chicago, and attended a Catholic high school. "It's just not like a big deal anymore because everybody is so much more relaxed about the whole sex business." I asked her whether her friends judged one another by how quickly they decided to sleep with men, on the first date or on the third. "No," she answered, "because then I would have to separate the men and the women, and say, 'She's supposed to be a lady.' I don't do that. I don't do that with anybody. It's very rare that you'll hear me talk on who is a whore. They have to be really, really bad. But that's just not in my vocabulary." Stacie attributed this absence of a double standard to her black middle-class and working-class group of friends in the city, but two other students I met from an elite, mostly white eastern school, Goucher College, described almost the same attitudes. Angela, 21, a senior from Baltimore, said that for having casual sex, women "earn a medal of honor. . . . It's about the same as men in the sense that you're cool if you sleep with five thousand people."

The person reporting feeling the strongest double standard was Bridget, 16, the youngest person I interviewed and a student at Wheeling High

School outside Chicago. "I had a guy who was like a best friend of mine," she said. "And he would tell me about the things that he did. And I would say what I did. And I heard from other friends of mine that he would talk badly behind my back about how I did. 'Oh yeah, she would probably sleep with anyone.' That kind of remark. He was supposed to be my best friend. But he had just as many, if not more partners, and it's OK for him. I never said anything [about him]. It never even crossed my mind."

The diminishing double standard is illustrated not only by what society thinks of women but also by what women think of themselves. With less shame, young women also have less guilt. In 1991, Nancy Friday reported this as a trait of her twentysomething interview sample for *Women on Top*: "More than any other emotion, guilt determined the story lines of the fantasies in *My Secret Garden* [her earlier book]," she wrote (16). While no woman ever said that she wanted to be raped, a common image in Friday's earlier book was a rape scene, because rape relieved women of the responsibility for these incriminating, seemingly wanton thoughts and allowed them to blame them on an anonymous stranger who "swept them away." But now, as Friday pointed out, women are overcoming the guilt that burdened women's fantasies in the past. She commented in *Women on Top* that "if there is a rape fantasy, today's woman is just as likely to flip the scenario into one in which she overpowers and rapes the man. This sort of thing just didn't happen in *My Secret Garden*" (17).

There are fewer statistics for actual guilt than for sexual double standards. I have found only a few surveys even mentioning guilt, one being a 1995 *Playboy* study of sexual correctness on campus. In response to "Do you ever feel guilty for wanting to have sex without offering an emotional commitment in return?" only 15 percent of the women, compared with 24 percent of the men, said yes (Rowe 1995, 153). The women in my sample expressed some of the complexities of women's new relationships. Certainly many suffer guilt, if not remorse, for what they have done. But at the same time, the majority also saw it as something they felt justified to overcome; instead of feeling that they were personally to blame, they more commonly blamed society for imposing these self-hating feelings on them. As for feeling public shame, they also generally "grew out of" feeling guilty after their teen years and usually did not let their guilt stop them from being sexually active.

Three students I interviewed at the College of St. Catherine in St. Paul illustrate the common experience of feeling and then overcoming different levels of guilt and regret. The first, Laura, 20, reported feeling the most guilt as a result of her strict Catholic upbringing, but she also said that she was actively trying to move past it. "I remember learning when I was really little about it [sex] and then like never again. We didn't talk about it. So when I got into a relationship, there was all this guilt. I was a bad person and stuff. I've become more OK with sexuality, as in like separating myself from the church and more from that aspect of the church. But that played a huge influence in my sexuality, and I don't like it. . . . I really felt horrible about myself, not even having sex, but doing all the other stuff. . . . I had a Catholic boyfriend so it made it even ten times worse. We felt guilty all the time."

Her classmate Taunya, 22, believes that "sex and love go together" but still says: "I've done things with people I haven't been in love with, and been OK with it afterwards because I have to be OK with it afterwards. I'm not going to regret anything I do. I don't ever live with regrets. I did it for a reason. Everything happened for a reason, I believe. . . . I think a lot of those reasons are just big learning experiences for everybody." Reporting the least struggle with guilt was St. Catherine student Aimee, 23, who had experimented more with casual sex. She noted that she had had more guilt over being a single mother and cheating her daughter out of a more traditional upbringing. "I think sex is great when you're in love," she said. "I think sex is great when you're not. I've had one-night stands, and I don't feel guilty about them. I don't think that it was wrong."

Guilt, like shame, is often difficult to measure because it is experienced in subtle ways. It can limit some behavior, as reflected by the fact that women still have fewer partners and are less tolerant of casual sex than men are. The quality of their relationships may suffer, with women feeling too guilty to communicate their needs. Or they may deny their sexual activity and not adequately protect themselves from disease or pregnancy.

"Your Place or Mine?"

As men and women feel more equally entitled to sex before marriage, their tolerance of premarital and casual sex is becoming more similar as well. In the early 1970s, women still felt more restricted while men were pushing to go as far as possible. Since then, as with all sexual attitudes, the greatest change has been with women. While men's permissiveness levels have decreased slightly since the 1970s, women's permissiveness levels have actually climbed. As AIDS and conservative ideologies eroded both men's and women's permissiveness levels in the late 1980s, women were also being influenced by other forces and have consequently become more permissive because of their growing social power and acceptance of feminist values.

Most of the major sex studies reveal this diminishing gap. In Roper's 1970 Virginia Slims survey, 65 percent of women surveyed agreed that premarital sexual intercourse was immoral. In 2000, answering a comparable question, only 20 percent did not feel that cohabiting before marriage was acceptable. Of those surveyed by the University of Chicago's 1994 National Health and Social Life Survey, only 16 percent of the men and 22 percent of the women born between 1963 and 1974 believed that sex before marriage was "always or almost always wrong." Their elders thought differently; of those born between 1943 and 1962, 21 to 26 percent of the men and 31 percent of the women agreed. And of those born between 1933 and 1942, 36 percent of the men and 53 percent of the women shared this response (507).

As discussed earlier, the major finding of UCLA's 1997 report, *The American Freshman: Thirty Year Trends,* was the change in women's values to become more like men's. The report also found a reduction in "the largest gap of all—in support of 'casual sex,'" that is, the notion that "if two people really like each other, it's all right for them to have sex even if they've known each other for only a very short time." The gap in men's and women's responses decreased from 31.1 percent to 21.9 percent since 1974, with men's approval decreasing and women's slightly increasing. In 1996, 31.9 percent of women responded in this way, compared with 53.8 percent of men. In 1974, 29.8 percent of women felt this way, compared with 60.9 percent of men. The 1998 survey showed a slight widening of the gap, to nearly 26 percent.

Though generally narrower, this gap is still considerable, indicating that women still do associate sex with love more than men do. However, more men and women agree when talking more broadly about premarital sex in general, with only a 5 to 6 percent difference between men and women who say that it is "always wrong." About the same number generally answers that it is almost always wrong, wrong only sometimes, or not wrong at all. Also, as chapter 9, on religion, points out, more women than ever before feel that morality is ultimately personal and do not feel condemned by outside authorities. But as the next section explores, what they actually *do* is a different story, with their rates of casual sex higher than their approval of it.

Acting "His Way"

Indeed, perhaps the greatest testament to women's sexual values evolving to become more "male" is their actual sexual behavior. Just as young women are now thinking more like men, they are acting more like them, too (O'Sullivan and Byers 1992, 436; also see Lottes 1993). With the gap narrowed between every group (including gender, race, and class), most Americans now have sex before marriage. When we compare particular sexual behaviors between the generations, we see quite clearly that the old-fashioned bond between sex and marriage has been severed for all. (Note that I'm mainly discussing heterosexual women's sexual experiences here.)

Of course, in the past, men's and women's sex lives before marriage were strikingly different. Forbidden for females, premarital sex was considered proper male terrain for exploration as long as it was with a limited number of "bad girls" or paid partners. Just 12 percent of women born before 1912 reported having premarital intercourse, compared with 61 percent of men, according to the University of Chicago's regularly conducted General Social Survey. But by the 1980s, women had almost as much premarital sexual experience as men did (Smith 1994b, 2). Other surveys reveal this progression throughout the twentieth century. According to the 1995 National Survey on Family Growth, about 69 percent of the baby boomer women it surveyed who married between 1965 and 1974 had their first intercourse before marriage, compared with about 89 percent of women first married in the 1990s. An even more striking difference, only 2 percent of those first married between 1965 and 1974 had their first intercourse five years or more before marriage, compared with 56 percent of those first married in the 1990s (table 25, 36).

Other large-scale studies report that these women are the most sexually active outside marriage ever. Studies through the 1990s consistently recorded about 86 percent of college women as sexually active (Elliott and Brantley 1997, 134), surpassing college men's rates, which ranged from 66 to 74 percent (see Baldwin, Whitely, and Baldwin 1992; MacDonald et al. 1990). One of the largest surveys of its kind, the annual Ortho Pharmaceutical Corporation Birth Control Study, found that the proportion of unmarried women who had had intercourse increased from 76 percent in 1987 to an all-time high of 86 percent in 1992. Among never married women aged 15 to 44 in 1992, 81 percent had had intercourse, a sizable increase from the 68 percent reported in the 1987 Ortho survey (Forrest and Fordyce 1993, 177).

The youngest women most vividly embody these changes. Women's sex lives resemble men's from the very beginning, with both starting intercourse at the same age and reporting the same number of partners in their teen years. Interviewed at the beginning of this chapter, both Shelly and her friend Janine first had intercourse at a typical age, 16, just short of the exact average age, 17.5 years, for those born in the late 1960s and after. This has been a gradual change from the age of the baby boomer women, who started at about 18, and their mothers, who began at 19 (Laumann et al. 1994, 324–25). Closely following teenage male patterns, adolescent girls also have more partners than the boomers did at their age. One of the most striking statistics of this "sexual evolution," the youngest women surveyed, born between 1963 and 1972, were twice as likely as women born just ten years earlier to have had multiple sex partners by age 18. These young women were almost six times as likely to report this as were the oldest generation, women born between 1943 and 1952 (Laumann et al. 1994, table 9.1, 328).

When describing their first experience, many of the young women that I interviewed sounded like men, by not including love in the narrative. Tasha, 20, a Brooklyn social worker, is an example. "I was very much into control," she said. "I basically selected somebody and told my parents that I was going to sleep over at a friend's house. And I crossed three state lines and visited him in school, and did what I had had to do—and came home the next day. 'OK, that's done.'"

It is important to note that the *quality* of men's and women's experiences still differs. Girls are more motivated by love and relationships. At least half of women surveyed by the NHSLS, as well as those I interviewed, stated that they were in love with their first partner, whereas only a minority of men polled felt that way (Laumann et al. 1994, 329). Among those I interviewed, the closer the relationship was, the more positive the experience turned out to be. "I was in a relationship and I was totally ready," said Jennifer, a senior at Boston University, about her high school experience. "It was the next step in our relationship. I was so in love. It was the nicest thing that ever happened, and I learned so much. I got to experiment with sex and figure out what it was all about. That made it, sex, a positive thing."

Another basic but alarming difference is that girls' first experience is often not wanted or even voluntary. In the NHSLS, a staggering number, 24.5 percent, of the women surveyed said that their first experience was "not wanted, but not forced," and about 4 percent said they were forced (Laumann et al. 1994, 329). The earlier the girls had intercourse, the more likely it was to have been forced. The 1995 National Survey of Family Growth reported this forced experience for 22.1 percent of girls whose first intercourse was before age 15 but only for 3.3 percent for women who started at age 20 or older (32).

After they finally become adults, young women also resemble men in their relatively large number of sexual partners. During their long period of singlehood, before and sometimes after marriage, young women have a higher proportion of partners than did other generations at this age. Most surveys report the average for college students from two to seven, with the men usually having more (also see Baldwin, Whitely and Baldwin 1992; MacDonald et al. 1990). Reporting typical profiles were those surveyed in the 1997 *Details* Sex on Campus report. The average number of lifetime partners was 7.2 for men and 5.7 for women (Elliott and Brantley 1997, 17). *Glamour* reader surveys found even higher numbers, with the respondents to a 1998 feature reporting a median number of ten partners (Mansbach 1998, 242), and in a 1999 survey, 20 percent reported at least twenty sex partners. This last survey also found that a quarter of the respondents had slept with more than one person *in the same night* (Boone 1999, 212).

Casual Sex: A Rite and a Right

Another question about the high number of partners is whether they were casual or committed. Most of young men's and women's sexual experiences did take place in the context of a monogamous relationship, even though the definition of "monogamous relationship" varied as wildly from person to person as did their perceptions of God and the universe. "It's hard for me to believe that if a woman has had six sex partners by the age of 23 that she has been in six relationships," Professor Ilsa Lottes maintained in an interview. To be sure, following the patterns of the boomer women, the younger generation acts more "male" by taking casual sex for granted as defining one's sexual experience before marriage. Although women disapprove of casual sex more than men do, for more emotional and moral reasons, they still see it as a rite of passage and a right, even in the age of AIDS. In fact, when discussing their personal conflicts with sex, the women I interviewed most often talked about religion and spiritual and emotional needs.

Statistics reveal that young women assume they are entitled to the casual sex and experimentation promised by the sexual revolution, that they are living the once-shocking vision outlined in Helen Gurley Brown's 1960s best-seller, *Sex and the Single Girl.* When discussing their liaisons, women commonly indicate that love had nothing to do with it. Reflecting the numbers found in other studies, of those questioned in the *Details* college survey, 42 percent of the women and 51 percent of the men reported having a "one-night stand." In a later academic study finding almost the same percentages of such activity, the women and men who reported having "casual sexual encounters" gave similar reasons, mainly personal: both sexes emphasized motivations like sexual exploration/experimentation (24 percent of women, 16 percent of men), to satisfy their own feelings of sexual desire (30 percent of women, 40 percent of men), and spontaneous urge (22 percent of women, 25 percent of men). "The bottom line is both sexes have casual sex for similar reasons. There are a few differences between the sexes, but the similarities outweigh the differences," explained Dr. Pamela C. Regan, coauthor of the study, in our 1999 interview.

Also revealing more permissiveness for women, their definition of "casual sex" has become more flexible. In our interview, Ilsa Lottes added that what young people consider a "monogamous relationship" has changed to become less serious and of shorter duration. That is, they can have sex on the first or second date and not consider that casual sex, even if they do not expect to see the person again. "It's possible for someone to have two sex partners a year and not be considered promiscuous," she observed. A long-time observer of young people and sex, James Petersen, the recently retired *Playboy* adviser, told me that what people perceive as "cautious behavior" doesn't amount to much overall change. "Everyone now knows what causes AIDS and it hasn't changed their behavior one iota, except to maybe put off sex from the second date to the third date."

When the people I interviewed described casual sex, they were mostly referring to a one-night stand, often leaving out a wide gamut of experiences not involving commitment or monogamy, which certainly would have been considered casual thirty years ago. Examples of these shifts in perception and acceptance are two friends, Kris, 22, and Dionne, 23, single women in Anaheim, California. Although both denied having casual sex, both are in nonmonogamous sexual relationships. Dionne, a student at Fullerton Junior College, said she "doesn't consider casual sex an option for myself." However, she sleeps with a man that she knows has "a sexual relationship with someone else." When I asked Kris about casual sex, she said, "I think it's around. I don't practice casual sex, but I think there's nothing wrong with it." However, when I asked her whether she had always had sex in a monogamous relationship, she answered, "I'd honestly have to say no." In fact, she admitted that she was currently sleeping with at least two men to whom she had no commitment, but that was below the number she considered as "casual sex." "I'm not in a relationship with just one person, but then again, I haven't slept around with fifteen people either."

Like the other women I interviewed, Dionne and Kris said they both saw monogamy as ideal but felt justified in not committing to their current arrangements. Dionne noted that it saved her emotional turmoil, which she suffered recently after a breakup with a long-term boyfriend. Kris explained that she wasn't interested in a long-term relationship because it would naturally lead to questions of marriage, for which she was nowhere ready. "How could I be honest in a long-term relationship right now?" she asked.

Like men, a strong and visible minority of women see their college years as a natural time to "sow wild oats" and experiment. Jennifer, 21, a senior at Boston University, described a "bar scene" at her school that was so common that it had become "old hat" for the older students. "You go there and have a drink, and you keep drinking, get drunk, meet guys. Everybody is just getting sick of going home with people and doing that whole bar scene. And when you say 'the bar scene,' everyone knows what you're talking about: the whole pick-up situation."

Young women are also more likely to support and understand flings when the partners are "responsible" and use "protection" and when the man secures the woman's consent. They are least forgiving of teen sex; this was true even for those who started having sex during those years. Considering these numerous stipulations, many view the role of casual sex as similar to that of fast food. Like men, young women have grown up with it and take it for granted. Outside conditions and moods are a factor. For instance, sometimes it is the only available and convenient commodity available to satisfy that distracting desire. But casual sex appeals more to primal physical needs than to more refined and uplifting spiritual sensibilities. And while it can sustain and soothe in the moment, it fails to nourish deeply over the long haul.

AIDS—which overshadowed the 1990s news stories about sex and young people—is still influencing women's experiences. Though not reducing casual sex overall for women, it has curbed some of the most risky behavior of the most promiscuous. Recent studies of the most sexually active women reflect the most changes. One of the most dramatic changes was found by a survey conducted in 1995 of single urban bar patrons, with a high proportion of respondents seeking casual partners. They were questioned in thirteen bars, eight generally defined as for "singles." Eighty percent stated making a change in some way regarding AIDS, the most common being using condoms (about 50 percent of women and 60 percent of men). Forty percent of both the women and the men reported having casual sex less often, but only 30 percent of the women and about 15 percent of the men said they had stopped having casual sex altogether.

This and other studies revealed that changes in behavior so as to prevent AIDS seems to be increasing with awareness. The same researcher found significantly lower rates of condom use from similar 1991 and 1989 surveys. The most recent and comprehensive government data show that a record number of women are using condoms when they first have sex, their numbers tripling from the 1970s to the 1990s (National Survey of Family Growth 1997, table 40, 50). That observation was supported by my respondents. Those I interviewed later during my research for this book said that condom use was standard among women their age: "People I know don't think using condoms is paranoid, just common sense," said Jean Twenge, a student at the University of Michigan, whom I sought out for her published research on Generation-X women. This change has been the main effect of AIDS that she has observed. "Most people just took it [AIDS] as a reason to use condoms, not to be chaste," she said.

The older women in my sample group, in their thirties in the late 1990s, reported a delayed reaction to AIDS. They came of age sexually during the most permissive period in American history, the early to late 1980s, and started using condoms and taking other precautions only in the early 1990s, when messages about the risks to straight people finally sank in. Wendy, who was an undergraduate at Boston University in the mid- to late 1980s, said that she had started using condoms after college only because "of all the propaganda" and also because she had become more mature in general. "I think that the way AIDS is seen, it's not a gay disease. Everyone fears AIDS. I get AIDS tests. All my straight friends get AIDS tests," she said, adding that casual sex still exists. "It's safe casual sex. . . . I think that AIDS has really changed the whole way we look at sex, and I've seen that change even since I first went to college and now. For example, I think that kids are kind of brought up with a whole different mentality toward sex because of this AIDS scare. . . . I think that we're somewhere in between the free love from the sixties and the younger generation. We were able to be kind of liberated, and then we got hip to the whole AIDS scare, and now we have to be careful. Very careful about who we choose as partners."

AIDS seems to have had more of an overall conservative pull on men's overall casual sex. The NHSLS study revealed a slight decline for men and a slight increase for women in their numbers of sexual partners in the late 1980s, when the awareness of AIDS peaked. The men born between 1963 and 1972 had a lower rate, citing two or more partners before age 20 (61.7 percent) than those born between 1953 and 1962 (66.1 percent), and 3 percent more of the more experienced younger women (51.2 percent) than the boomer women (48.1 percent) (Laumann et al. 1994, table 5.5, 198).

Men's sleeping around is more limited by AIDS because they engage in higher-risk behavior and have more casual sex and higher numbers of partners. Studies show that the people most concerned with AIDS and most apt to change their behavior are those in the highest-risk groups, such as men, blacks, and those young in age and living in large cities, using drugs, having many sex partners, and having anal intercourse (Laumann et al. 1994, table 11.29A, 432–34).

Compared with the women in the general population, the men have undergone the greatest consciousness shift because of AIDS. For the first time in more than a half-century since the advent of penicillin, men are suffering the darkest dangers of sex. While heterosexual men are not in the highest-risk group, they now have a serious life-altering danger to at least ponder. All men are now more likely to fear the personal risks of sex—fear that is no stranger to women, even women of the 1960s and 1970s sexual revolution. Men now must join women in worrying about protection, communication, and self-preservation. Today, even if AIDS didn't exist, women would still feel a strong need to treat sex seriously and take precautions, as they still bear the risks of pregnancy or fertility-threatening sexually transmitted diseases (STDs), which often show fewer symptoms in women and thus are less likely to be treated.

AIDS prevention also represents a notable shift in men's thinking, requiring them to take on the burden of condoms, the only form of nonpermanent male birth control. Whereas condoms often alter and blunt men's experience with sex, they are likely to enhance women's sexual pleasure by relieving them of the responsibility of birth control and even prolonging sexual intercourse. The 1995 urban single bar patron study showed that although few people like sex better with condoms, significantly more women (26 percent) than men (6 percent) preferred it (Juran 1995, 57).

Perhaps one of the greatest contrasts between postboomer and boomer women is the effect of AIDS on their consciousness levels. Even though they are still having casual sex, young adults are less casual about it. The greater use of condoms and the closer screening of partners are the main differences from the heyday of the sexual revolution, when the consequences and the power of sex weren't as great a part of the experience. These considerably large and growing numbers of women insisting on using condoms and even supplying them themselves reflects a wider, more radical trend. By actively protecting themselves, young women are consciously recognizing that they indeed are being sexual, instead of just being passively "swept away."

3. Changing Sexual Scripts: A Close-Up

You showed the president your thong underwear. Where did you get the nerve? I mean—who does that?
  —Barbara Walters to Monica Lewinsky, television interview, March 3, 1999

Because they now think more like men and share more of their power, women are also more likely to act like men in bed, that is, to take control and actively seek pleasure. Although this movement has been slow and has only just begun, women are more willing to take responsibility for sex, initiate it, and take an active part in directing and choosing specific sexual activities, such as a wider variety of acts, including oral and anal sex and experiments with other women. Another change is that men are now more likely to accept women's aggressiveness in bed, realizing that women usually need more than just intercourse to have an orgasm and thus are more willing to help satisfy them.

Many of the old inhibitions remain, however. Women are only beginning to define their sexuality and desire, to learn and acknowledge their distinct sexual response, as evidenced by the relatively low numbers having regular orgasms and getting the "basic training" of masturbation. In addition, unlike men, women are apt to act more assertively only under certain "safe" conditions, such as when "love" is attached to sex. Whereas men feel entitled to seek pleasure regardless of the situation—whether or not it's a one-night stand—women are more inclined to "let themselves go" in a monogamous relationship. Likewise, women are more likely to challenge traditional patterns (such as making the first move, making more demands in bed) in steady dating relationships or in marriage, as opposed to casual encounters. Part of this reserve may be the result of the still strong double standard.

Initiation

One of the main areas of study regarding women's sexual progress has been initiation, in both dates and sexual encounters. Although men still take the lead most often in these areas (and still find that scenario most appropriate), women have become more open and not limited to subtle, time-honored flirtation such as dressing in a certain way or holding their cigarette at just the right angle.

Many scholars view women's initiation as significant because it tends to set the pattern for any future dates or relationship. When a woman steps out of her traditional passive role, she is making a lasting statement, obvious or implied. Researchers have also found that when women make the first move, they are challenging the principal definition of women's sexuality in the past. That is, women are no longer interested in being "swept away," an old-fashioned passive coping mechanism that women used to deal with their forbidden sexual feelings. If they told themselves, their partner, and society at large that they had been "swept away," they were portraying themselves as an innocent and untainted player in the sex game. But this tactic was a double-edged sword; although it "excused" them from having sex without love, at the same time, it denied them responsibility for securing sexual gratification. According to Carol Cassell's *Swept Away,*

> [Swept Away] is a tactic, employed unconsciously by women to get what they want—a man, sexual pleasure—without having to pay the price of being labeled wanton or promiscuous. Swept Away is, consequently, a counterfeit emotion, a fraud, a disguise of our true erotic feelings which we've been socialized to describe as romance. (1984, 25)

This fading "swept away" standard is reflected in the popular culture, especially women's magazines. All the respondents to a survey in the June/July 1999 *Jane* magazine answered yes to the question "Is it better to make the first move when it comes to people you're interested in?" (34). A *Mademoiselle* reader asked an advice column, "Are men less aggressive these days? It seems like every man I date, I've pursued" (Dixon 1995, 68). Almost all the women responding to a *Glamour* survey's question about initiating sex stated that they do so one to three times a week "and that their boyfriends and husbands love it" (March 1996, 76). Though sometimes wary, most men's magazines have also recognized women's initiation as a fact of life. In an article in *Details* entitled

"Straight, No Chaser," Blake Nelson rhapsodized about feeling less pressure with women as the aggressor: "Let's face it, being the pursuer is a drag" (1993, 74). The central revelation of a *Spin* magazine article about sex at Vassar College is the rampant sexual aggressiveness of the women, who outnumber the men there (Konigsberg 1998).

The prominence of such behavior also helps put into perspective the best-selling traditional courtship guide, *The Rules*, which is firmly opposed to female initiation of any kind. Instead of representing mainstream ideologies, this guide represents a subculture, a reaction against the uncertainty and disorder caused by eroding gender roles. Accordingly, the book is a guide to traditional roles, which offer a definite, predictable script. As evidence of its challenge to (rather than a reflection of) the prevailing norms, the book assumes that its modern female readers already have initiated dates and tried to be more aggressive. In response to Rule 2, "Don't Talk to a Man First (and Don't Ask Him to Dance)," the authors anticipate their readers' skepticism about traditional passivity: "Never? Not even 'let's have coffee' or 'Do you come here often?'. . . We know what you're thinking. We know how extreme such a rule must sound, not to mention snobbish, silly, and painful; but taken in the context of The Rules, it makes perfect sense" (26). Questioning the traditional female courtship strategies advocated by *The Rules*, many of the women I interviewed stressed the importance of women devising their own strategies. Many discussed the importance of women's being able to ask men out. I asked Kris and Dionne, friends in Anaheim, California, about differences regarding sexual issues between their generation and the last. Dionne, 23, a community college student aspiring to become a lawyer, observed: "Back then, everything was black and white . . . but there [now] are standards of gray that we seem to accept more."

"We have grown up with our own age group in a society where it's OK for the girls to ask the guys out," explained Kris, 22, an office manager. "It's OK for the girls to do the driving. It's OK to do the paying. When I hear my mom and dad talk, it was the boy who had to come and meet mom and dad before they went out. The boy opened the door. The boy paid for dinner. The boy drove." Dionne added: "I think there's still courtship, but I think it's just like you're both courting each other instead of one total dominant role." She mocked women of the past: "'Oh court me, court me because I can't show my feelings without you showing yours.' You know, now I can pretty much say this is how I feel and I don't like it. And if you do like it, where do we go from here?" They both said they prefer this style of courtship, although it leads to more overt conflicts or power struggles than the more traditional type did. "There's always going to be a conflict when you have someone speaking out," said Kris. "But I don't find it to be a problem."

Sex researchers have also noticed that men's being asked out by women is now a standard part of men's romantic history, unlike the 1980s and before. In her study of college students, University of Maryland professor Ilsa Lottes found that the majority (74 percent) of females she surveyed had asked a male for a date, and a majority (88 percent) of males had been asked out for a date. Fifty-four percent of females reported asking out a man more than once, and 75 percent of males reported being asked out more than once (Lottes 1993).

After women work up the courage to ask men out, the results are mixed. Some studies show that women are rejected more than men are (McNamara and Grossman), but citing several other studies, feminist psychologist Naomi McCormick reported that "more men than ever before, especially young and feminist men, are pleased when women take the dating initiative. Typically, men respond positively to female-initiated dates. And, women who are persistent often get their way" (1994, 19). She also quoted a study (Clark and Hatfield 1989) finding that when young adults approached attractive strangers and invited them to go on a date, visit their apartments, or go to bed with them, the women rejected men, but surprise, surprise, the men greeted women's sexual offers with enthusiasm (19).

As is the case with other presumably male sexual actions, the single trait that best determined a woman's likelihood to initiate is her feminist mindset. That is, those women most often initiating dates were more likely to be what researchers considered feminist or were interested in challenging traditional gender roles. In 1983, S. K. Korman found that feminists initiated an average of 5.3 dates, compared with a mean of 2.2 dates for nonfeminists. Furthermore, 69 percent with feminist attitudes reported sharing the costs of dates at least some of the time, compared with 41 percent of the others (Lottes 1993, 662).

Research has shown that women are also becoming bolder in their initiations. Naomi McCormick (1994) quotes a study by a communications researcher, Thomas E. Murray, who recorded his observations of women in singles bars approaching men with raunchy lines. Stacie S., 26, the social worker living in suburban Chicago first mentioned in chapter 1, gave me some other examples. "I've been at a club when my friend's number is in a man's pocket when he came with his girlfriend. I mean, I knew his girlfriend. They came together. They were hugging and kissing. And she was like, 'I want that man. How am I going to get him?' And she was winking at him and everything. . . . It ended up being that I literally, I walked behind him and tucked her number in his back pocket. Now, he must have been with it. He wasn't like, 'What are you doing?' you know. And he did call her, and they did get together."

In a related shift, once the date is under way and the check arrives, women are less likely than ever before to politely look away. In Lottes's study, only 12 percent of men and 8 percent of women had never shared dating expenses, findings that indicate a great jump from Korman's 1979 sample, which found that 31 percent of feminist women and 60 percent of nonfeminist women had never shared dating expenses. Women taking control outside the bedroom translates to greater control inside. As Lottes concluded, "Women, accustomed to a more equal sharing of economic resources, may demand a similar degree of reciprocity in the sexual arena, giving them more authority and confidence to express their sexual needs as well as responding to those of their partners" (1993, 662–63).

Women's initiating sex has also become a more common practice among young women, especially those in satisfying long-term relationships, though often this is more an ideal than an actual practice. Amy and Brad, a married professional couple in Boston, cite this practice as a natural part of their partnership. Just as they strive for equality in other areas, such as housework, they also strive for equality in bed. Amy, 27, said that initiating sex and challenging other submissive roles of the traditional sexual script were difficult for her to learn. "I had a boyfriend who really could not be sexually satisfied if I was on top," she said. "That's mental. That's strictly mental. That was wounding to me. He talked about how I wasn't feminine enough for him. And now I have all that leftover stuff. . . . And Brad, he's not . . . hung up on what I would say is the man's role. He doesn't have to be on top in bed. He likes it when I initiate. These are the kinds of things that I guess are unusual." Her husband said he appreciates her making the first move because "I don't want to have that burden all the time." "Plus," Amy added, "that way I think he feels more desired than if I'm passive, and he has to really wonder if I'm enjoying myself."

A study of college virgins from 1990 to 1995 indicates that the younger students were more likely to make the first move. Among those surveyed about their reasons for being virgins, more college women in 1995 than in 1990 answered, "My current (or last) partner is (was) not willing." "Recent cohorts of women may be more comfortable with the role of sexual initiator and thus more likely to have experienced a partner's refusal to have intercourse," the authors concluded (Sprecher and Regan 1996, 12). In the younger groups of students, a partner who resisted was more likely to be a male. A Canadian study by Lucia F. O'Sullivan and E. Sandra Byers, published in 1993, found that at least once in the previous year, most young heterosexual singles recollected that the woman sought greater sexual intimacy than the man did. "This finding supports the view that the ideal gender role in sexual situations has shifted such that women are expected to be sexually active" (280).

The biggest change in female initiation has been in attitude, regardless of behavior. In a study published in 1992, O'Sullivan and Byers found that women *considered* initiating as often as men did, even though they followed through with it less often. Another value shift is reflected in women's *ideal* to be more aggressive or assertive in a relationship. In a study published in 1996, the college women surveyed described the ideal women's gender role in sexual situations as more "masculine" than they actually acted. Conversely, the men said that the *ideal* male sexual role was more "feminine" and expressive than they actually were (Lawrance, Taylor, and Byers 1996). In Lottes's sample, 76 percent of males and 78 percent of females reported that men and women should be equal initiators of sexual relationships, although only 38 percent of the women reported ever initiating a sexual relationship.

Women's sexual initiations take place most often in committed relationships to which traditional scripts apply less and women's sexual daring is more acceptable; after all, they are connecting sex to love (O'Sullivan and Byers 1992, 1993). According to the 1993 Canadian study, men and women in steady relationships were much more likely to report "disagreement situations" in which the woman wanted more sex than the man did. (Only 3.7 percent of these incidents were reported for first dates, 37 percent for a casual date, and 59.3 percent for a steady date.)

Revising the Sexual Script

Once one of the parties initiates sex, the typical heterosexual couple is much less likely to use the male-defined sexual script of the past. Instead, women are more active in deciding what happens. In the 1994 University of Chicago National Health and Social Life Survey, Edward O. Laumann and his coauthors describe the traditional scenario as being pitifully brief and directed by men with businesslike efficiency, "involving a minimum of precoital stimulation and a rapid move to vaginal intercourse." The most widely read sex manual of the 1950s, *Ideal Marriage: Its Physiology and Technique*, by Th. H. Van de Velde, describes this process in more detail. (Published originally in the United States in 1930, *Ideal Marriage* went through thirty-two reprints between 1941 and 1957.) Van de Velde, a doctor, directed his advice to married men, explaining that they "are naturally educators and initiators of their wives in sexual matters." Her only job was to respond and smile politely. After minimal stimulation, the goal was clearly intercourse and (ignoring many women's biological capabilities) the "nearly simultaneous culmination of sensation—or orgasm—of both partners" (Ehrenreich, Hess, and Jacobs 1986, 78–79).

Though still mainly male directed, this sexual progression has gradually changed since the 1920s. Very slowly, "the sexual script for opposite-gender sex has become increasingly elaborate to include more kissing, more caressing of the body, more manual genital contact, and, more recently, oral sex," write Laumann and his coauthors in *The Social Organization of Sexuality* (1994, 106–7). They state that these practices increased most dramatically in the 1960s and 1970s when sex became a new recreational sport for the urban singles culture. Responding to this new sexual revolution and feminist consciousness raising, advice books (such as Alex Comfort's *Joy of Sex*) began challenging the old medical texts that prescribed one, narrow, "normal," and "adjusted" method.

Even though much of the old sexual script is still intact—intercourse as the ultimate goal defining sex itself—it now often includes detours and consideration of the woman's orgasm. Instead of going from first to third base in a linear fashion, young women are more inclined to design their own meandering and experimental patterns. Women started to make strides in this direction after feminists in the 1970s raised awareness of the male-centeredness of the sex act and turned their attention to the long-neglected clitoris. As a response to their consciousness raising, advice books began focusing on women's sexual gratification independent of the penis. These books include *The Hite Report*, a critical study of women's sexual experiences and frustrations, and Loni Barbach's *For Yourself*, on women's masturbation.

A more recent influence on redefining sex from a woman's perspective is a more general awareness and acceptance of lesbian practices. That is, heterosexual women and men are able to observe a group that is perfectly sexually satisfied with sexual acts not necessarily involving male equipment. An example of this consciousness shift can be seen in the 1997 film *Chasing Amy*. The main character, Alyssa, questions her boyfriend Holden's traditional definition of sex. After taking note of her lesbian past, he notes that she must still be "a virgin." She asks him to define sex. He answers, "when the hymen is broken." She says that happened to her as a child after falling. He retorts that it means penetration. She makes a motion about fisting, making a thrusting motion with her hand. Earlier, in a club, she shocks him with an elaborate discussion about "eating out a woman." What he considers just "foreplay," a prelude to intercourse, she considers full-fledged bona fide sex.

Throughout the 1980s and 1990s, this focus on the clitoris and women's varying responses and desires became more commonplace. As with all sexual changes for women, the more "progressive" practices have gradually been accepted by younger and younger generations. Reflecting this shift is the popular 1995 book *Mindblowing Sex in the Real World*, by sex adviser Sari Locker. She stresses this now prevalent individualistic ethic of variety, with everyone's sexual script differing in levels of adventure. In a chapter called "The Wide World of Sex," she discusses practices as diverse as abstinence, sadomasochism, foot preferences, tantric sex, and masturbation with sex toys. "You can engage in any of these sexual activities or none," she writes. "You do not have to pick one practice over another. You can dabble and even combine some component from any of these practices. You can fantasize about anything, and you can share the fantasy, act it out, or keep it to yourself" (202).

"Outercourse"

With women exerting more control, one of the most common sexual changes among experienced adults is more concentration on nonintercourse forms of sex. Formerly termed "foreplay" for adults or "heavy petting" for teens, these activities are now considered sex in their own right, whether they precede or substitute for intercourse. The Monica Lewinsky scandal is a good illustration of this shift in perception. According to the media, Americans considered what she did with the president, which allegedly did not include intercourse, as bona fide sex, a "sexual affair."

Statistics fail to reveal the actual choreography of sex, how much time people devote to which activity, although studies have found that more people are engaging in less traditional practices, such as oral sex. This nonintercourse activity, using hands or mouths for stimulation, has many different names. In her March 1999 interview with Barbara Walters, Lewinsky termed it "fooling around." In a 1996 *Mademoiselle* article, Valerie Frankel uses the descriptive term "outercourse" and reports that a new emphasis on the woman's pleasure has revived a series of acts that were once described as "petting" for teenagers or foreplay for adults.

Today's "petting" is a broader and more creative array of practices. The main change is more oral sex for both partners, which the landmark 1953 Kinsey study, *Sexual Behavior in the Human Female* rarely documented. Another twist in modern petting is that men don't necessarily initiate it, with women resisting at every juncture. Frankel's definition of outercourse also sidesteps the linear path from base to base to base. Rather, these activities can take place in any sequence, which she describes as "the circle" model:

> Imagine yourself as a dot in the center. Extending out of the dot are arrows going in all directions to points on the circle. The points are whatever you feel like doing, from light kissing to massaging to blow jobs to talking dirty. They're infinite and can be pursued in any sequence you want. (Frankel 1996, 153)

Those who engage in outercourse now may be in a different age group than they were in the past. In their 1953 study, Alfred C. Kinsey and his coauthors described those engaged in "premarital petting" as teenagers trying to satisfy themselves until their wedding day. While such behavior wasn't limited to teenage years, it was mainly described as engaged in by un married persons. Today, however, petting is regarded more often as legitimate for adults who already may have had intercourse. "Women of the '90s are not squeamish little virgins," says Frankel. "We've had intercourse—lots of it—and think that Outercourse kicks its ass" (1996, 152).

Whether or not petting without intercourse is more popular today is difficult to determine. Our principal source of sexual information, the 1994 National Health and Social Life Survey, is actually much less detailed than the Kinsey study, which even features multiple columns detailing the various techniques men use to stimulate women's breasts. Modern studies of sexual practices cover only those that are most risky, meaning mainly vaginal and anal intercourse, and multiple partners. They don't talk much about plain old making out, which encompasses so much of humanity's sexual experience. The only acts of outercourse cited by the University of Chicago's NHSLS as more common today are oral and anal sex.

The increasing public discussion of "fooling around" as actually being sex is, in fact, evidence of its prevalence. Frankel describes the popularity of outercourse as the result of women's becoming more aware of their desires and biology and acknowledging the risks and power of intercourse. In my sample, Tasha, 20, a social worker in Brooklyn, outlined her goals for her relationship with her live-in boyfriend: "Yes, we as women have now demanded our twenty-one minutes of foreplay, as Masters and Johnson have approved, but that's not the issue. The issue is that I had a conversation with Mark once how I want someone to make love to my elbows and my knees and my toes and the back of my thighs, and my neck and the back of my head. We don't have to have intercourse per se. Or intercourse doesn't have to happen for hours. I understand that people don't always have that amount of time, but still I think it's a point that we have to start striving towards."

Other women I interviewed still limited their outercourse to the old parameters, as something to do when you're not yet having intercourse. Leslie and Mark, who live in Santa Barbara, California, both from religious Christian backgrounds, decided to wait until they got married to have intercourse, four and a half years after they first went out together. For the second two years, she slept over almost every night. "We kind of had this stupid rule that, you know, if we were messing around that one of us had our underwear on. It was just a rule that we stuck by and we never changed that," said Leslie, 24, a ground support supervisor for an airline.

While they seem novel, many "foreplay" activities, except oral and anal sex for women, couldn't be more old-fashioned. Indeed, the statistics from the 1953 Kinsey study and the fact that "premarital petting" merits an entire chapter prove that this behavior was standard. It was a clearly defined sexual stage, most commonly first experienced by women in their last two years of high school. The Kinsey report describes the most common acts as kissing, deep kissing, manual and oral "stimulation of the female breast," "apposition of genitalia" (grinding the privates together without penetration), and, less commonly, "manual stimulation of the male and female genitalia." About 23 percent of teens 16 to 20 and a third of women in their twenties and thirties at that time had petted to orgasm. The report also explores the texts of ancient cultures describing the variety of these petting acts, as well as the elaborate customs of past generations of Americans, including the already forgotten slang terms of "bundling, spooning, mugging, larking, and sparking" (231).

Much of this dominating and often creative behavior ended in the 1970s, when young people began to feel entitled and, partly thanks to the Pill, able, to proceed right to intercourse. But by the early 1990s, Frankel explains, "we woke up and smelled the Nonoxynol-9. . . . Twenty-five years was, apparently, enough time for singles to realize that there had to be a better way" (1996, 152). One obstacle to exploring petting, however, is that it remains mysterious. In the media, we see people either kissing or going straight to intercourse, with no visible interaction between. Ironically, a supposedly repressed "coed" in a ponytail and poodle skirt in the 1950s, better versed in petting, may have known more about what turned her on than does a woman today in a tight-fitting micromini who "hooks up" every weekend with a different guy.

The Big "O": Great Expectations

The force directing outercourse is the pursuit of the female orgasm. Even though many old female frustrations remain, mutual orgasms are now considered a basic part of what it means to have sex. For young heterosexuals, women's orgasms are no longer mainly considered a lucky bonus or an afterthought, which marks a shift away from sexual guilt and toward women's pursuing their own desires, as men always have.

"I think men know that if they get off, but didn't satisfy the women, it's not such an ego thing for them anymore, just to get a woman in bed. Now the ego boost for them is to know that they satisfied her," said Wendy, 26, who works in the entertainment industry in New York. Her friend, Eric, 25, present in the room, made the observation that men are feeling more pressure than ever from women. "I think before women just went along with it, and now women are saying on talk shows and in books, 'We're over it. We want to come, too.' So there's the pressure."

Wendy agreed that she and her friends are learning to make more demands as they get older. "My friend Susan brought up a good point on the phone. She said, 'Nowadays I won't give a blow job to a guy to please him. I'll give one to him if he's pleasing me.' And this is like my reaction, my thank you, kind of." But she and her friends arrived at this realization only when they reached their mid-twenties after being sexually active for several years. Wendy said that she didn't have her first orgasm until she was 24, long after her first sexual experience at 16. Even the most sexually experienced women I interviewed were slow to make this connection. Mary, 27, who became a prostitute as a teen after running away from home, didn't have an orgasm until she was 22 or 23, at the beginning of a seven-year relationship. "I didn't know anything about it," she said (for her transition to abstinence, see chapter 4).

Studies comparing young men and women reveal some common experiences in pursuing orgasms and pleasure. According to the *Details* survey, 94 percent of the men and 87 percent of the women reported ever having an orgasm. A 1999 *Glamour* survey on orgasms obtained similar figures. A small percentage of both—only 7 percent of the women and 1 percent of the men—said that they typically had no orgasms "per sexual encounter." Fifty-three percent of both the men and the women said that they had had one, and 35 percent of the men and 26 percent of the women said that they had had more than two (Levin 1998, survey of 288 men and women). In Ilsa Lottes's 1993 study, a majority of sexually experienced young women stated that they usually had at least one orgasm with their partner, and almost a third said that they usually had more than one orgasm.

According to other data, heterosexual women have a long way to go to rival men in regard to orgasms. The University of Chicago's National Health and Social Life Survey found that an average of 28.6 percent of women "always have an orgasm" during intercourse but that men had a vastly greater rate of 75 percent. In this study, age is not relevant. The group of women with the lowest response rate were those aged 18 to 24; only 21.5 percent reported always having an orgasm. (The NHSLS didn't ask about orgasms in other categories besides "always has an orgasm," not considering a more realistic "most of the time" option.)

The *Details* survey also discovered an orgasm gap. When asked how often they achieved orgasm, 56 percent of the men answered "always," compared with 13 percent of the women, but they both answered "most of the time" at similar rates, 35 percent of the men and 40 percent of the women. Current studies also found much more widespread sexual dysfunction among women, especially young women, than among their male counterparts. A University of Chicago study, published in the *Journal of the American Medical Association* in 1999, stated that 27 percent of women aged 18 to 29 said that sex wasn't pleasurable, compared with 17 percent of women in their forties and fifties (Laumann, Paik, and Rosen 1999).

Even the most sexually active women during the height of the so-called sexual revolution fared no better. In the *Cosmo Report*, published in 1981, only 20 percent of the readers surveyed said they always had an orgasm during partner sex of any variety, including intercourse, manual clitoral manipulation, or oral sex. Half *usually* did; a fifth *sometimes* did; and a tenth *seldom* or never did, based on a survey of 106,000 readers assumed to be among the most experienced and interested in sex in the population (Wolfe 1981, 84). Clearly, even these "liberated" women had a long way to go.

When comparing current data with those from earlier surveys, we find that the present rate is not as high as might be expected considering the relative abundance of popular information about orgasms. In fact, in the 1953 Kinsey report, a surprising third of married women reported having an orgasm most (90 to 100 percent) of the time. The Kinsey study also recorded a high rate of those who *never* have an orgasm, including 25 percent of women in their first year of marriage, and another third of the married females responded "only a small part of the time" (Kinsey 1953, 375, 408).

The reasons that women are less apt than men to have an orgasm are varied. Sex therapists talk about women's becoming more secure about their sexuality as they age, with women reaching their maximum orgasmic capacity in their late twenties and early thirties, which then remains constant through menopause. Many women I interviewed mentioned the lack of information in their formative years about how women achieve orgasm. When I asked them what specifically they didn't know, information about the clitoris was the most common answer. They often found out about its prominent role accidentally and later in their sexual lives, usually through friends and women's magazines. Crystal, 25, a law student in Washington, D.C., said that she was encouraged after hearing a nurse talking about masturbation in seventh grade, about "how you shouldn't feel bad if you touch yourself." She later got some tips from *Cosmo*. Her friend Jeanne, also 25, said that she read about it in the book, *How to Make Love to a Man* by Alexandra Penney.

Many women spoke critically of younger men's continuing indifference. Lisa, 25, and Tasha, 20, two African-American friends in Brooklyn from working- and middle-class backgrounds, said that only a few of their partners had made such an effort. "The idea that all the stuff you do in foreplay is in actuality all a woman needs to come and be totally satisfied—'There, that's fine. Go home now'—they really just can't quite grasp that. I don't have anything against actual intercourse penetration sex, but the manner in which it is normally gone about, they don't have a fucking clue," Tasha noted. Like other men I interviewed, Michael, 32, a graphic designer from suburban middle-class Chicago, explained that this concern is a function of both age and the type of relationship. Now married, he admitted that he was more selfish when he was younger.

Still, there are some signs of change. In a recent *Glamour* orgasm survey, a clear majority of men said that women's orgasms during sex were a priority, with 45 percent answering that their partner's orgasm was "extremely important" and 43 percent, that it was "very important" (Levin 1998, 174). Explaining such evidence, Susan Crain Bakos, the author of *What Men Really Want* and a frequent contributor to major men's and women's magazines, told me in an interview that young men are better informed and giving more than ever. "I think that men have come a long, long way. Most men know about the clitoris. They may not know exactly how to find it in every woman because it's not easy to find in some women." Rather than men's selfishness, she blamed women's communication as a more likely problem: "I think men get a really bad rap in sex. I don't think that men are selfish in bed. I think they really want to please their partners. Every time I interview men, they tell me how important it is for their partners to have an orgasm, because they don't think they're any good if they can't please their partners."

Oral Sex

One major route to women's orgasms recently received an unprecedented amount of public attention. The younger generation of women stands out most prominently as adopting a decidedly woman-centered practice: receiving oral sex, which is now standard both as an act of outercourse and before or after intercourse. "If there has been any basic change in the script for sex between women and men, it is the increase in the incidence and frequency of fellatio and cunnilingus," report the authors of the 1994 NHSLS (Laumann et al. 1994, 102).

Women receiving oral sex is an act most directly reflecting women's growing power in both their sexual relationships and society. The practice depends on both women's and men's recognition and respect of this power. Oral sex on women is an inversion of the old sexual script and now involves a man "servicing" a woman, and the most powerful women are the most likely to demand it. A major variable for receiving, as well as giving, oral sex, as with other recreational sexual activities not involving reproduction, is education. About half of women with less than a high school education have received oral sex, compared with 83.1 percent of women who have finished college (table 13.6, 98).

So much has changed. In the 1940s and 1950s, Alfred Kinsey and his colleagues reported oral sex as prevalent only among the more elite and experienced groups in his married samples. Among the younger females in his 1953 study (those born between 1920 and 1929) who were virgins, only 3 percent "had allowed the male to touch their genitalia orally." Among those born before 1900, the rate was only 1 to 2 percent. The numbers were higher for the more sexually experienced, reaching 20 percent of those with some "coital experience" fewer than twenty-five times) and to about 46 percent for those with "extensive coital experience" (more than that). These figures were comparable for those who had experienced fellatio (257).

But today, according to the 1994 NHSLS report, a clear majority, 74.7 percent of women aged 18 to 24 have received oral sex, compared with 73.7 percent of women 30 to 34, revealing that younger generations are engaging in it early on. Surprisingly, considering that men's experiences in this area are more widely discussed and visible in popular culture, men's and women's rates of fellatio and cunnilingus are equal, with only 8 percent fewer of the female respondents having experienced both (Laumann et al. 1994, 102). Women and men aged 18 to 39 incorporated it most regularly into their sex lives, with 22.3 to 24.2 percent of these women reporting having done it during their last sexual experience. The shift was most pronounced between them and women in their forties and older; for women aged 40 to 44, the rate of having engaged in it during their last sexual encounter fell by almost half, to 12.6 percent.

The increased number of women receiving oral sex has been particularly dramatic in the past few decades, rising steadily since the 1970s. In contrast, men's rate of receiving oral sex peaked and leveled in the 1960s. Reflecting this recent shift are the younger males' attitudes, as they are more likely to describe giving oral sex as "very appealing" (Laumann et al. 1994, 157). Those participating in this act now are more likely to come from all walks of life, not just from the better-educated and middle-class groups. Part of the shift is a result of the sexual revolution, with its singles culture emphasizing the recreational aspects of sex. Author Susan Crain Bakos attributes this change in practice to magazines and erotic videos, which now show women's orgasms. "I would say that any young man that reads the magazines and rents an occasional video is going to figure out how to perform oral sex, which probably his father didn't know because he didn't have these opportunities," she stated in an interview.

Another reason for the popularity of oral sex is its effectiveness in bringing about an orgasm. In a study of sexually knowledgeable and experienced women who use vibrators, the most common type of stimulation that "usually or always triggers orgasm" was oral sex, was cited by 61 percent of the sample, compared with clitoral-manual at 56 percent, and clitoral-vibrator at 54 percent. Following all these "outercourse" techniques was old-fashioned vaginal intercourse, at 44 percent (Davis et al. 1996, table 3, 316).

Oral sex has also become prevalent before intercourse, either to arouse the woman or to bring her to orgasm. Bakos told me that this is now standard practice: "In each love-making session, men like to start with oral sex. A lot of them tell me they do. The men in their twenties have grown up understanding that women need more than intercourse."

One difference in the practice of oral sex from the past is its casualness. Oral sex used to be considered something that happened at a stage after a couple was already having intercourse, as an expression of intimacy in the most committed and trusting relationships. Today, both men and women are more likely to engage in oral sex outside marriage. Only 12 percent of married women reported that their partner usually performs oral sex on them, compared with about more than three times that in a short-term partnership (29.9 percent) and about twice that in a long-term or live-in partnership (about 19.6 to 19.8 percent) (Laumann et al. 1994, table 3.8A, 130). In addition, oral sex has recently become a standard teen alternative to intercourse. A 1994 national poll by Roper Starch found that 26 percent of the high school students surveyed had had oral sex, and among those who already had had intercourse, two-thirds also had had oral sex (Lewin 1997). Newspaper articles report that even young teens take oral sex very casually, as a way to avoid the risks of intercourse (Lewin 1997; Stepp 1999).

Also attesting to its increased popularity is the presence of oral sex in men's and women's sex books and glossy magazines. In *Women on Top*, Nancy Friday wrote that this was an area "where women have finally come of age. Having discovered it, they can't get enough" (1991, 352). Even the readers of the more sedate *Ladies Home Journal* cheer this practice: in a February 1993 sex survey of American wives, 25 percent chose oral sex as what they liked best about sex (130).

In the early to mid-1990s, oral sex even reached mainstream music as a politically charged demand of truly liberated women. The three young women of the group TLC had a top-ten hit with "Ain't 2 Proud 2 Beg," which endorses "kissing both sets of lips." Mary J. Blige's "Real Love" video features a couple making out in an elevator until the woman grips the guy's head and pushes him to his knees. Janet Jackson repeats the same move in her videos for "If" and "Again." The women of Jade make this motion pushing down imaginary heads in their "Don't Walk Away" video. Finally, female rappers SWV muse on this theme in their top-ten hit "Downtown," pleading "Baby don't stop / Let me be your lollipop" (Sheffield 1994, 64).

"Alterna-Sex"

Whereas oral sex is by far the most common "adventurous" practice, others are also becoming popular. According to the surveys, women are willing participants in these practices, with men and women taking part in equal numbers. When asked to describe themselves sexually, the most common response in the *Details* magazine's Sex on Campus survey was "adventurous," cited by about a third of both men and women (Elliott and Brantley 1997, 16).[8] At about the same rate as men, 63 percent of women said they talked dirty; about a quarter had engaged in spanking or bondage; 16 percent had had sex with a much older partner; 13 percent had taken photographs; 14 percent had role-played; and 10 percent experienced a threesome, online sex, or a "golden shower."

Another increasingly common experiment for women, even for those who identified themselves as heterosexual, is sex with other women. The NHSLS study revealed that women in their thirties (5.4 percent) were more than twice as likely than women in their fifties (1.9 percent) to have had a same-gender sex partner. A large number of these women saw themselves as "straight"; only 1.8 percent of the women in their thirties and 0.4 percent of the women in their fifties called themselves lesbians (Laumann et al. 1994, table 8.2, 305). Education was a major variable. Whereas only 5.3 percent of high school graduates reported ever being attracted to another woman, 12.8 percent of college graduates reported these desires.

Other, more recent surveys have found much more experimentation. Reflecting perhaps the greatest sexual generation gap of all, a staggering 18 percent of females aged 18 to 29 reported sexual activity with another female in a Yankelovich Partners Survey released in October 2000. A more recent *Glamour* sex advice column quotes a source from the Institute for the Advanced Study of Human Sexuality pegging about 18 to 20 percent of women as having "been sexually intimate with someone of the same sex" and about 3 to 4 percent of women as actually gay (Czape 1999, 82). The article also explains that a woman is a lesbian only if she is "sexually interested in only women—period." This definition makes heterosexual women feel freer to explore without having their sexual identities analyzed, changing their social status, and risking discrimination.

When women talk about being "adventurous" or "new," they also may be referring to anal sex, previously a largely gay male practice. Just as lesbians have increased women's awareness of how to have orgasms without the aid of intercourse, gay men also have transformed heterosexual sex. Again, like all "recreational" types of sex, this is more common among the better-educated people. Mirroring the *Details* Sex on Campus statistics, the NHSLS reported that 28.6 percent of women with a master's degree had had anal sex, compared with 16.6 percent of high school graduates, whereas 29.2 percent of men with a master's degree and 23.1 percent with a high school education had had anal sex. Women in their twenties were slightly more likely than other groups (at 10 to 12 percent) to have engaged in it in the past year (Laumann et al. 1994, table 3.6, 99). Anal sex represents women's next sexual frontier for practice and public discussion. As society becomes more sexually sophisticated, it will become a commonplace sexual topic, just as the Monica Lewinsky affair revealed the popularity of oral sex.

Beyond Pillow Talk

A less risky sexual practice is one that can take place while fully clothed. Indeed, communication about sex—before, after, or during—is a new and widely accepted and practiced way of deriving pleasure. Once again, Monica Lewinsky revealed this practice in her enthusiastic public discussions about her phone sex with President Clinton, which is based completely on talking. In their spring 1999 interview, Barbara Walters's ignorance of this practice reveals the generation gap in connecting the verbal with the carnal.

In the 1990s, communication in all aspects of relationships became more valued. When I asked women what the most important part of a relationship was, this was their usual answer. They see communication as an essential tool for fairness and equality. When two people follow a predetermined sexual script, such as that ordained by the medical textbooks of the 1950s, they don't need to talk to each other, and silent scripts do not allow as much room for individual preferences and experimentation. Communication has grown with the rising popularity of the condom in the second decade of AIDS, as its use must be actively negotiated by two people. The widespread movement against acquaintance rape on campuses also encouraged communication to avoid misunderstandings and ensure consent. Joseph Weinberg, based in Madison, Wisconsin, who has conducted antirape workshops for thousands of men on campuses, explains that open communication challenges preconceived notions of sex as silent and mysterious and notions of men as aggressive and adversarial (see

Kamen 1991, 328–33). Weinberg makes these men think about how much more arousing it might be to hear a yes from a woman than not asking her anything and assuming consent. He stresses the positive aspects of hearing from women: "'Yes, why did it take you so long to ask?' and 'Where do you like to be touched?' 'How are you feeling?' 'Does this feel good?' 'How about that?'" A fear Weinberg commonly confronts is "Wouldn't it break the spontaneity?" His answer: "It might, for the moment. But what's spontaneous about getting her drunk, pushing her over, and doing her? I don't believe that's particularly spontaneous."

Jennifer, a senior at Boston University, also cited the modern procommunication influence of therapy, which has spilled over into her sex life. "[My family] went to family therapy, not necessarily because there was something wrong. But we just sort of started doing it, and it turned out to be a good thing. And that's basically what it is. I try to bring that out in my relationships. Sometimes it's hard and it doesn't always happen that way, but I always try to make sure there's a lot of communication." I asked her whether this ruined the mystery, a common old-fashioned fear of communicating during or about sex. "Oh, no. I think that talking can be just as sexually [exciting]. Talking about what you're going to do, or what you're doing, or what feels good. I think that actually has to do with women feeling comfortable about themselves to say, 'I like this.' Or, 'Will you do this to me?' And that takes a lot of guts for a woman to do."

Many other women also confirmed that they felt more comfortable communicating in a long-term monogamous relationship than in a casual one. "In a more casual relationship, I think you have to watch yourself," said Francine, 26, a graduate student at the University of California at Santa Barbara. "You don't want to be so demanding because you don't want to put the guy off or you don't want to like scare him away. And so you want to be more pleasing to him."

The advisers on MTV's *Loveline* commonly tell callers that if they aren't ready to talk to their partner about sex, they're not ready to have it. Popular sex adviser Dan Savage writes in the introduction to his 1998 book *Savage Love*: "After all, nothing makes a person better at sex than good communication. All sex therapists, advice columnists and marriage counselors—serious, mainstream, pop culture, religious—are all in agreement on this point" (8). The February 1996 issue of *Glamour* asked women about "how you tell a man what you want in bed" and found that some women preferred straightforward discussions at a predesignated time (56). A *New Woman* article advises women how to approach men who might be sensitive to criticism: "How will he know what you want if you don't tell him?" (Felder 1994, 111).

Nonetheless, women still have a long way to go to openly acknowledge their sexual desires. "When you're with a guy, they don't care if you're getting off or not. And I felt guilty for even asking, you know, or talking to them. I wouldn't ask," said Amy, 26, a law student in Washington, D.C. Her friend Crystal agreed: "I wouldn't have it [orgasm] through college. I would never ask." Writer Laura Miller, an editor of the web magazine *Salon* and a former staff member of the Good Vibrations vibrator store, said that she noticed this lack of communication as common, even among women bold enough to enter her business. "I've had women coming in wanting to buy dildoes so that they could simulate intercourse and teach themselves how to have an orgasm without clitoral stimulation, because their current partner won't do that and their last partner did. And rather than just ask their current partner to do what their last partner did, what worked for them, they try to figure out how they can respond to what a new partner is doing. That's a common thing."

Observing this phenomenon, Julia Hutton, the author of *Good Sex* (partly a study of how people talk about sex), told me that the women she interviewed frequently cited resistance from male partners when they communicated to them during sex. The younger males, especially, tended to interpret any suggestions the woman made as criticism of their performance. She pointed out that communication counters the cultural stereotype that a man should naturally know what turns a woman on, that "a man is in control, a man has superior knowledge, a man is invulnerable." Indeed, we see few examples in pop culture of people actually talking in bed. The usual movie image is two bodies grinding to orgasm in perfect nonverbal harmony. The man, an Oscar-level star or Cinemax softcore leading man, never receives even basic instruction. Even though all women are different, he just knows what to do.

Masturbation

Another bold move that women make in their quest for gratification often takes place in private: masturbation. Though less stigmatized today, the practice is still largely a neglected tool for women. In this aspect, men have the advantage, with earlier and higher rates of self-exploration and, hence, considerably more self-knowledge, control, and satisfaction in bed. By masturbating, women learn the particular ways they can be brought to orgasm, which differs greatly in every woman. What they do in private also influences how they respond to a partner. As Kinsey documented in the 1950s, women who masturbate are much more likely to have orgasms with intercourse. Like a man, such a woman has demystified sex, separating it from love, and is prepared for what to expect. As Friday writes in *Women on Top* (1991), it is also a prerequisite to oral sex, requiring the acceptance of and learning about one's private parts.

Despite much cheerleading by feminists from the 1970s to today, from Betty Dodson to the publishers of the magazine *Bust*, a surprisingly large number of young women don't masturbate. The *Details* Sex on Campus study reported that only 55 percent of women had masturbated to orgasm, compared with 86 percent of men. Ilsa Lottes's study found that only 14 percent masturbated weekly or daily, whereas 40 percent of the men surveyed did. According to the NHSLS, the numbers are lowest for the youngest and the oldest women and highest for those in middle age; 64.4 percent of women 18 to 24 had not masturbated in the past year. This compared with 58.3 percent of women 25 to 29, and 50 to 52 percent of women in their thirties and forties. The number of abstainers rose sharply among women over 50, with at least 71.8 percent not doing it in the past year. But the tide may be turning. The most recent survey I consulted (and admittedly the least scientific and with the smallest sample), in the March 2000 *Glamour*, reports that 94 percent of readers it surveyed masturbate regularly (a survey of one hundred women aged 18 to 35; see Holmes 2000).

For both women and men, education was a major variable in the increase in masturbation's acceptance and practice. In the NHSLS, only 25 percent of women who had not completed high school had masturbated in the past year, a figure that rose steadily at each educational level to a high of 60 percent of those with a graduate degree. The best educated are also the most likely to always or usually experience orgasm during masturbation, ranging from 45.6 of those with less than a high school education to 87 percent with a graduate degree (Laumann et al. 1994, table 3.1, 82).

Masturbation is still a topic controversial enough to cause a national political uproar, as illustrated in the case of Jocelyn Elders, the U.S. surgeon general who was forced to resign in 1994 after she recommended discussion of masturbation. And for women, it is especially secret, so much so that women aren't warned against it as much as men have been. Even the Old Testament cautions against the sin of Onan, spilling one's seed on barren ground. Maybe the greatest proof of its secrecy is the lack of any vulgar street names for women doing it, in contrast to men who "jerk off," "spank the monkey," and the like.

According to popular culture researchers, however, some of these attitudes are becoming more accepting. Shere Hite discovered this change in two studies, from the 1970s and the 1990s. In her 1994 *Hite Report on the Family*, 61 percent of the girls she surveyed had a positive attitude toward masturbation, compared with 29 percent in her 1976 *Hite Report*. Nancy Friday made similar observations of the younger generation, who had been raised with at least some awareness of the subject. Friday found a major difference in acceptance in her two generations of interview samples of women in their twenties, from 1973 and 1991. Friday's work is well known for describing women's sexual fantasies in great detail, serving as both reports about and facilitators of masturbation. According to her, most of her postboomer early 1990s sample didn't share the negative feelings about masturbation that prevailed in the earlier boomer group:

> They have an ease with the subject of masturbation that is a pleasure to hear, a vocabulary so rich in description of when and how they masturbate that I am dazzled; their sexual fantasies soar into a realm of adventure that makes most of the reveries in *My Secret Garden* read like tentative stuff. . . . How can women today know how hard it was for those first women to speak, having no familiar words, no ease with masturbation or in expressing something no other women had yet given them permission to do. (1991, 32)

References to women's masturbation in the popular culture are still rare but more common than twenty or thirty years ago. One person that I interviewed mentioned first reading about it as a child in Judy Blume's *Deenie*, in a memorable washcloth scene. Cyndi Lauper celebrates it in "She-Bop" and the Divnyls, less subtly, in "I Touch Myself." Tori Amos, a preacher's daughter, praises it as an act of rebellion in "Icicle" from the 1994 album *Under the Pink*: "Getting off, getting off, while they're downstairs singing prayers." My interview sample reflected the influence of such media exposure and "women's locker-room talk" among friends. About fourteen women from my core sample spontaneously mentioned masturbation in our interviews. It usually came up while talking about orgasms, as a method of learning to have one. Two sets of women, including the Florida high school teachers and the College of St. Catherine students profiled in chapter 10, said that it was a topic that their friends regularly discussed. Two other women mentioned it as an important lesson they learned from *Our Bodies, Ourselves.*

These women, the most definite superrats, spoke confidently about the practice as their right. Connie, 27, an Asian writer in California, said that she discovered it on her own in grade school and has never felt guilty about it. She said that it kept her sexually fulfilled before marriage (both she and her husband were virgins when they married) and still gives her even better orgasms than she experiences with intercourse. "What's wrong with masturbating?" she asked. "I'm not hurting anyone. I don't have the religion to stop me from it. I'm preventing myself from having a disease, and there's no real loss of reputation, since everyone does it anyway. . . . I am absolutely not ashamed of it." She traced other women's fear of masturbation to their fear of sexual pleasure. "I am actually surprised sometimes that when I tell people, some of them are ashamed of it. Some of them are kind of frustrated because they've never had an orgasm before. And I said, 'I can't believe you have never had an orgasm.'. . . And some of them feel like sex is wrong, that even having sexual pleasure is wrong." Most of the other women had to learn to overcome their guilt about the practice. One woman explained how *Our Bodies, Ourselves* relieved her anxieties. "That's the first book I ever read that made me feel sexually free. I could do this, and I'm not going to go to hell. And I don't have to have the covers over me and the lights off, and my parents have to be asleep. That was the first book that made me feel other people do this, and I'm not the only one. Because I thought I was the only one," said Tasha, 20.

Four lesbian and bisexual friends in Denton, Texas, were also particularly open about discussing masturbation. When we broached the topic of religion, two described fighting long battles to overcome their guilt about masturbation. Lisa, 26, a graduate of Brigham Young University who was raised in a devoutly Mormon family, said that the issue of masturbation was the major wedge between her and the church. "I masturbated from a very early age, and had a lot of guilt in masturbating and growing up Mormon and learning how wrong it was to masturbate. So that gave me a lot of problems. And Mormonism stresses sexual purity, being morally clean, sexually morally clean to such a degree that I was unable to stay sexually and morally clean under the Mormon principles. So it really did separate me from my religion and kept me from feeling close and faithful within the religion because it had such strong rules and requirements. So I really feel like I cannot be Mormon. I cannot practice my religion."

Annette, 30, from a small Louisiana town, said that her Catholic religion "played a big, big, big deal" in keeping her from masturbating until her late twenties. She had heard that "women weren't supposed to" and so abstained. When she heard a friend talking about it, she became curious but still considered her "such a pervert." "I was convinced that something bad was going to happen if I did. When I took a bath or anything, there was no way the skin on this was going to touch something else. No way in hell. It just wasn't going to happen."

But they said that they shed their guilt after reaping the rewards. "Once I finally did experiment with it, I learned more about myself," said Annette. "I learned how to . . ."

Her partner, Crystal, interrupted, "Make love?"

"Yes," she said. "Really make love with someone. And I do it without shame."

Lisa added: "I have a good friend who is a terrific lover. She is a terrific lesbian lover. She practices on herself all the time—what feels good, techniques."

Like a few others I interviewed, Lisa volunteered that she often masturbates just to relax. Tasha, the most open about the topic, also described this effect, demonstrating that women masturbate for the same reasons as men do, as the studies show. "I mean I've masturbated in front of friends," she said. "I've just been like, 'Look, I'm really stressed out today. I need to relax. And it's like I can smoke or I can do this. And I'm going to do this because smoking gives me cancer." Clearly, in the past thirty years women have learned a great deal about distinguishing sex from love. Starting to have sex earlier and to have more partners are the most significant indicators. Changing what they actually do in bed has been more gradual, as it involves making demands of men and knowing one's own desires and needs.

II

Doing It "Her Way"

4. Virginity Reimagined: No Sex and the Single Girl

Why should I feel ashamed for taking care of myself; for bucking a trend: for doing my best to ensure my physical, emotional, and spiritual integrity in a world of numbness and violence?
>—Loolwa Khazzoom, sex educator, in the 'zine *Moxie*, summer 1999

You realize that you've seen his orgasm face, but you don't know what he likes for breakfast.
>—Louisa, 30, quoted in "Casual Sex: Why Confident Women Are Saying No," *Glamour*, September 1997

In the past decade, we have witnessed a mass exodus out of the closet of the most suspected and stigmatized groups: lesbians and bisexuals, the cohabiting, and single mothers.

And then there are the virgins. Like these other individualists, no longer on the defensive and apologizing for their choices, virgins are expressing a new pride and are starting to stand up for themselves and be counted. Like the women who say yes, those who say no are operating from a basic ethic of the sexual evolution: the right to control their own sexuality.

Susan, 23, reflects this emerging philosophy of having sex on one's own terms and with a higher level of consciousness. A volunteer in the Lutheran Volunteer Corps in Washington, D.C., working with the urban poor, Susan's religious views are basic to her sense of self. They were the driving force behind her past sexual restraint, not by inducing shame, but by emphasizing the spiritual component of sex, which she can't easily separate from the physical. As a result, Susan said that she waited to have sex for the first time until just recently with her fiancé, whom she had met two months earlier. "I recognized that I have certain talents and certain gifts, and I owe it to myself to take care of those gifts," she explained. "I'm not going to just throw it around, throw my body around. And I see that sexuality is part of that. The sexual revolution—I guess we grew up in that—I think a lot of it has cheapened something that isn't cheap."

Like the others I interviewed who spoke about virginity, Susan is not prudish or judgmental of others. In fact, she greatly values sexual openness, and during our interview in a café, she was more comfortable than I was. I thought we would talk privately, but when we began our conversation, people were seated nearby on both sides of us. Noticing my own growing self-consciousness, I told her we could move somewhere else. But she kept talking openly, and openness about sex is an important part of her relationship with her fiancé. "It's not like sex is this big pinnacle you can't really talk about or it's kind of weird to talk about it. It's all a part of the full relationship. To talk about how you feel in a situation, positions or otherwise, isn't as big of a deal."

Susan also supports societal openness about sex. Growing up in the 1980s when sex became more open, she said she wasn't bothered by its omnipresence in the media. She especially admires Madonna, also from her hometown Detroit area and a prominent figure during her teenage years, for making people aware of sexual issues such as AIDS. But what she favors in the media is critical thinking about sex and the responsibility that it should bring, not just sensationalism. She says that this is a perspective that the teenaged mothers she works with could use. "It's got to be an overall societal thing where it's talked about more openly, and it's not a dirty thing. Something you have to be mindful of, though. Something you realize you have a responsibility for. You have to be aware of the risk you're taking. Some people are able to have sex and just really enjoy it, and they are able to separate their spirituality from it. And I believe to a degree that it's everyone's prerogative; if that's what they want to do, it's fine. But I think it should be a conscious choice and not just something you fall into."

Especially in the late 1990s, a chorus of similar voices emerged from the media, positive about their choice to abstain: "I'm 25 years old and I'm a virgin. At least by popular standards. I've never had sexual intercourse," wrote rock critic Tara McCarthy in her 1997 memoir *Been There, Haven't Done That*.

I am not a right-wing religious fanatic nor am I a prude. I'm not a wallflower nor have I ever had any trouble finding guys who would sleep with me. I've actually shared beds with quite a few. . . . Truth is, I've had very satisfying, very intimate physical and emotional relationships with men in my life. I honestly do not feel like I'm missing out on anything except the elation I've seen women feel when a late period finally arrives. (3, 4)

Probably the most visible young female proponent of chastity is the recent Williams College graduate Wendy Shalit, author of the 1999 book *A Return to Modesty,* who realized the absurdity of her embarrassment about her virginity after reading Kathryn Harrison's 1997 memoir *The Kiss.*

After reading her revelation that she had had sex with her father, I realized how upside down things have become. Here she was sleeping with her father, for God's sake, with few qualms whatsoever, and here I was, ashamed of my sexual inexperience, devoting all my energy to keeping up appearances and worrying that someone would find out what I hadn't done. It's high time sexual modesty came out of the closet. (Shalit 1999, 191)

The sexual evolution has enabled women to take control of their sexuality in a variety of ways. Just as they are now more confident about engaging in more and earlier premarital sex and putting their own pleasure at the center of their experiences, they are also more confident about saying no. As a result, even though the number of virgins has not noticeably increased and women are acting more like men than ever in the sexual realm, *attitudes* toward abstinence have dramatically changed in a short period of time. In contrast to the past, this greater acceptance of saying no isn't based on traditional feminine norms of virginity; it has a new twist. Instead of abstaining out of fear, of reducing one's "market value" for marriage and becoming "damaged goods" and ruining one's reputation, young women today view remaining a virgin as a *positive* choice, rooted in their own individual preferences. Furthermore, since they no longer depend as much on men as their sole route in life to financial support and social status, they no longer feel the same anxiety about "saving themselves" for a husband.

Young women today have also shed some of the stigmas of virgins created during the sexual revolution of the 1970s when the norm of women having to say no reversed to a mandatory yes. The virgin was downgraded as hopelessly retro: "uptight," "frustrated," "prudish," "defective," "repressed," "hung up," "rejected," "frigid," "antisex," or "Victorian." Today, more positive meanings are associated with "virgin" or "saying no," including "self-esteem," "integrity," "self-knowledge," "control," "independence," "mindful," and even, as Tara McCarthy wrote (1997), "sexually fulfilled" and "sexually knowledgeable." Today, no single sexual role is the norm, as was the case with the virgin in the 1950s or the promiscuous woman in the 1970s. Like women who choose to sleep around, women who decide not to are also accepted as making their own decisions.

This was not a movement I fully anticipated. Considering that admitting one's virginity was taboo when I was in college in the late 1980s, I was surprised how openly the women I interviewed discussed their status and how confident they were about their decisions. More young adults are taking offense at the assumption that they are sexually active. The incoming freshmen at Stanford University for the 1992/93 school year complained in written evaluations that their orientation presentation, "Sex in the '90s," failed to mention abstinence as a choice (later orientations do now include celibacy.) (Glaser 1994, 121). An academic study of college students from 1990 to 1995 confirmed this trend, finding that women's experiences with virginity were more positive than negative and that later groups had more pride than did earlier ones. The authors, Susan Sprecher and Pamela C. Regan, attribute this confidence to "a greater number of publicly visible, virginal role models to emulate" (1996, 12).

Surveys show that many women are still holding back (even when these same surveys track considerable numbers of women moving quickly to sex and with many partners). The situation today is the opposite of that in the 1950s: now the number of virgins is larger than one would expect, just as the number of nonvirgins was then. When *Glamour* magazine asked readers, "When is the right time to have sex?" 46 percent said they would consider it in the first four dates. But the other 54 percent would not: 11 percent said they would wait until marriage; 11 percent said they would wait until they had dated for six months; and 30 percent said they would wait until they had dated for three months (Harris 1997, 314).

These same figures apply when measuring the number of virgins. We are used to looking at only how many women have sex early, that is, those who are *not* virgins. Nightly newscasters and government researchers regularly wring their hands in exasperation over the legions of amoral and lust-crazed teenage girls getting knocked up. But they fail to consider the many young women who take their time. Even though about 83 percent of women have had sex by the time they reach age 19, this also means that roughly one in five has *not* had sex (Laumann et al. 1994, 326). Today, a slightly higher number of women remain virgins than did those in older generations at their age, who married much earlier and were more obligated to be sexually active with their husbands by a certain age. The National Survey of Family

Growth estimates that the percentage of virgin women aged 20 to 24 to be 11 to 12 percent, those aged 25 to 29 to be 4.3 percent, and those aged 30 to 34 to be 2.8 percent (41).

The Media

In the entertainment world, hip virgins, fictional and real, came out in full force in the 1990s. Whereas Helen Gurley Brown created shock waves in 1962 with her book celebrating premarital sex, *Sex and the Single Girl*, others today attract attention by arguing for the right to say no. Rock singer Julianna Hatfield declared to *Rolling Stone* in the early 1990s that she was still a virgin. During the same period, the long-running TV series *LA Law* ended with the virgin lawyer Jane Halliday remaining true to her religious beliefs. At the age of 27, both sitcom star Crystal Bernard, of *Wings*, and Lisa Peluso, of the soap opera *Loving*, declared their unpenetrated status. Representing the characteristically enthusiastic media coverage of virgins, a *Chicago Tribune* headline about Bernard in its "KidNews" section proclaimed: "Sex? Cool Your Jets!: 'Wings' star practices what she preaches (Yep, she's a virgin)" (Herrmann 1993).

In 1999, when Wendy Shalit's prochastity book was published, the media produced a wave of features about a new crop of virgin heroines. "Hollywood—a town where the most virginal thing is the olive oil at the Ivy—has lately become obsessed with sexual innocence, of all things," wrote *Entertainment Weekly* (Jacobs and Shaw 1999, 10). This article cited the chaste character played by Drew Barrymore, a journalist returning to high school for an assignment in the film *Never Been Kissed*, and Kevin Williamson's ill-fated ABC drama, *Wasteland*, featuring a 26-year-old virgin. The statistics demonstrate, however, that these mostly positive characters signal more of a change in social attitudes than an increase in the number of virgins. For example, almost every article about virgins in pop culture in the 1990s discussed Tori Spelling's character Donna, who managed to stay chaste for seven years on *Beverly Hills 90210*. But at the same time, in every episode, all the other characters were busy jumping from bed to bed. The same is true of the college drama *Felicity*. The virgins aren't plentiful, just more vocal and less apologetic about their status than they would have been in the 1980s. In its first season in early 1999, Felicity ponders her virginity and decides not to be ashamed of it, a move that would seem to reveal a new chastity. However, as she notices, she is the only one.

A New Standard: Thyself

Like the women I interviewed and these media virgins, young American women are guided by the principle of following their own voice. In our individualistic American culture, that standard of being true to oneself is the driving force behind young women's sexual decisions, and more are deciding not to have sex until they are personally ready, no matter how long that takes. Whereas their mothers tended to define morality according to the teachings of their religion or other outside institutions, today's young women see it as an intensely personal matter. Their generally higher educational level also is liberalizing, making them more critical of organized religion, traditionally women's most sexually restricting force.

The young women I interviewed constantly expressed their belief in the ethic of following their own counsel. In response to my many questions, from whether casual sex was wrong to whether a mother should work outside the home, they used various forms of the phrase "It depends on the person." I asked Beth, 24, a graduate student at Texas Women's University, to tell me her ideas about sex in relationships. "It's so up to the individual," she responded, adding that it depended on the types of men she met, whether they viewed her with respect or were just getting conquest material to share with friends. In the same group interview session, I asked Letha, a junior in nursing at Texas Women's University, about premarital sex. "I think it depends on the person. I haven't said I'm going to wait until I'm married. If I find someone before, I probably will." Using that measure, Andrea, 28, put off sex for three years with her boyfriend and future husband, a contractor in Plymouth, New Hampshire. Andrea, a secretary, met him at the University of New Hampshire, which she attended briefly. They had a long-distance relationship, which they didn't consummate until just before they married, when she was 24. "I felt I wasn't ready. To me, having a relationship with a person, I wanted to know the person as a whole. Not just in a physical way. . . . I wanted to know how he felt, how he thought. I basically wanted to know him inside and out before committing to a physical relationship."

The idea of having sex only when it matches one's personal beliefs is reflected in teens' and women's magazines. In the 1990s *Seventeen*, "Sex & Body" columnist Deborah Kent often stressed using the self as a measure, such as in the feature "Virgin Territory" (December 1993). In response, a reader wrote, "Bless Ms. Kent for saying my sexuality belongs to me" (16). Sex advisers in the January 1998 *Glamour* gave the same advice to a woman asking how she would know that she was ready for sex. They answered, "Keep in mind that postponing sex until it's right for you—regardless of what anyone thinks—means that you know your own mind" (56). In *Essence*, Tara Roberts, 24, explained why she wouldn't settle for less than full respect. "I did not want to be involved with anyone who could not reinforce the positive, life-affirming image I had constructed of myself." She quoted a definition of a virgin as "one in-herself; not belonging to a man" from the 1987 book *The Great Cosmic Mother*, by Monica Sjoo and Barbara Mor (118).

The therapists also subscribe to the popular emphasis on the self. A frequent guest on *The Oprah Winfrey Show,* Iyanla Vanzant is the best-selling author of a spiritually centered book for teenagers, *Don't Give It Away,* the "it" being "yourself," she stated on Oprah's show in 1999. In a similar vein, Karen Bouris's 1993 book *The First Time: Women Speak out about "Losing Their Virginity"* concludes with a similar message, and in an afterword, sexologist Louanne Cole advises young women to consider their own needs: "A key ingredient for an enjoyable 'first time' is mutual, not unilateral, interest in creating pleasure for and with one another. Regrettably, too many young (and older) people engage in sex for secondary reasons, and young women are most likely to do so" (199).

Sex and Meaning

Saying no is also a way of seeing sex as having *power and meaning*, not necessarily for everyone in every situation, but for that particular person at that time. In contrast, if one views sex as always signifying nothing, as completely neutral and without consequence (as dictated by sexual revolution ideologies), one will not hesitate about always saying yes.

While many feminists fought the sexual revolution because they thought it enslaved women to men, others from a separate camp might be skeptical of this new movement, associating any such provirginity symbolism with more traditional times when women's sexuality was repressed. During the sexual revolution, which stripped sex of its centuries of "bad girl" baggage, many were relieved to see sex in more neutral terms. These feminists pointed out that the concept of "virginity" seemed to work only against women, to control and repress them. In 1978, Adelaida R. Del Castillo wrote that whether mental or physical, virginity is "more an obsession created by and for the use of men than actual feminine state of being" (144). Rosalind Miles later reiterated this view, commenting in *A Woman's History of the World* (1988) about women's practice of giving her virginity as a gift to her husband on her wedding night. This practice, she wrote, ensured a patriarch's "divine right to a vacuum-sealed, factory fresh vagina with built-in hymenal gift wrapping and purity guarantee" (74).

But again, more women regard virginity not as being preserved for a husband's later consumption but as a way of having sex on their own terms. The social influences behind this notion are numerous. Certainly those most vocally favoring virginity are the fundamentalist Christians, who have sparked much public discussion about the value of saying no, such as in their political advocacy of abstinence-only education programs, which have mushroomed in recent years. At the opposite end of the political spectrum, feminist activists underscore the importance of consent and assertiveness in campaigns against unwanted sex, such as acquaintance rape.

In the wake of AIDS, even the most politically progressive campaigns for safer sex alert people to the risks of casual sex and have legitimized the right to say no. Many women I interviewed cited the physical risk as a reason for rejecting casual sex, although it didn't usually stop them if they really wanted it. In a Gallup Poll follow-up question to those who opposed sex outside marriage, 25 percent mentioned the risk of pregnancy, and 14 percent cited the risk of disease (Smith 1994a, 92–93). The top reason given in a 1996 study of virgins was wanting to wait for a relationship, and the next three reasons were, in order of importance, pregnancy, AIDS, and STDs (sexually transmitted diseases) (Sprecher and Regan 1996).

Women's greater reserve than men's also seems to be the result of practical thinking. The fact is that women still suffer disproportionately from the many consequences of sex, from a crisis pregnancy to more physical vulnerability to contracting HIV. In an act of intercourse, a woman's chance of contracting AIDS is at least several times greater than that of men. Shelly, 24, interviewed in the beginning of chapter 2 about women's acting like men, listed that risk as her only reason not to have casual sex. But like others I interviewed, AIDS didn't stop her from experimenting, and she questioned the risks she took only years later. "I think I was very lucky not getting sexually transmitted diseases and not getting AIDS. I think I was lucky, and I think about it all the time." In response to these risks, society is more tolerant of other sexual acts that don't include intercourse. Virgins today can still be sexually active. Tara McCarthy (1997) observed that not having intercourse forced her to experiment more than other women did with "the other stuff" and to get in tune with her sexual response. "A boyfriend once said to me that he thought if his parents knew what we did in bed together, they'd probably prefer [it] if we were just having sex" (88, 89).

To honor this greater significance they attach to sex, young women are more likely than men to wait until they have the support of a committed relationship. Indeed, women are still more likely to attach love to sex. Despite the genders' views having come closer than ever before, about 26 percent fewer women approve of casual sex. In a 1996 academic survey of male and female college virgins, the respondents' most common reason was that "I have not been in a relationship long enough or been in love enough" (Sprecher and Regan 1996, 6). (More women than men explained their virginity in this way.) While men's and women's age of first sex has never been closer, their motivations differ. As a reason for having their first intercourse, many more teenage girls, 47.5 percent, gave "affection for partner," which was chosen by only a quarter of the males. But these responses were reversed when citing curiosity/readiness for sex as a motivation (Laumann et al. 1994, table 9.3, 329).

Because attaching the reason to have sex to an emotional commitment is regarded as female, society has devalued it as "weak." But as young women gain more power and security in society, they are recognizing their need for emotional commitment as a natural human preference and not necessarily the result of a double standard. For both women and men alike, a close and loving relationship ideally offers security, vulnerability, and intimacy, conditions that are basic and necessary for making the deepest human connections. They might also find it less strange to "get naked" and lose their inhibitions with someone they genuinely care for. In fact, both men and women rate their emotional and physical satisfaction as highest in committed relationships, according to the University of Chicago's National Health and Social Life Survey. A comparable number of men and women rated themselves as "extremely physically satisfied" (51.1 percent of men and 40 percent of women) and "extremely emotionally satisfied" (48.1 percent of men and 41.5 percent of women) with their marriage. This rate declined for live-in relationships and long-term partnerships, and the lowest ratings were for "short-term partners," with only 15.9 percent of men and 16.1 percent of women seeing themselves as "extremely physically satisfied" in these situations. Only 10.6 percent of men and 12.6 percent of women regarded themselves as "extremely emotionally satisfied" with "short-term partners" (Laumann et al. 1994, 130).

The importance of commitment seems to signify that women's and men's satisfaction depends on more than just their orgasm. In fact, they reported

being more likely to "always have an orgasm" during sex in a casual encounter (Laumann et al. 1994, 130), perhaps because of the singularly sexual focus of this situation. In a long-term relationship, emotional bonds have
a greater impact on producing satisfaction. Edward O. Laumann and his
coauthors explained that short-term relationships entail more anxiety about
the future and are less likely to have "established methods of emotional communication and support" (1994, 132).

Rethinking the Sexual Revolution

These considerations are part of a broader reanalysis of the sexual revolution.
As young women see casual sex demystified, they are more likely to consider
the risks and sacrifices. Unlike the baby boomers at their age, today's young
women are not consumed with battling an overreaching double standard, so
they can now move on to other issues. Sarah, 24, a student at Wheelock College in Massachusetts, discussed this issue: "At least we [as a generation]
have had sex. At least that part of it is kind of over. Now we're on to the
moral and ethical issues that surround it. What are the ethics of sexuality?
And where do we fit into our own sexuality? That's a huge question for
women—we have been the subject of sexuality, the object of sexuality for so
long, and now [we are becoming] the actor in that drama."

The young women I questioned about the sexual revolution agreed that
it was a male invention, geared to men's satisfaction and control. They
criticized the era's prevailing male definitions of "sexual freedom as
promiscuity" as ignoring the possible meaning and power of sex. (This
was the case, even though most shared many of the male values of permissiveness outlined in previous chapters; almost all had had premarital sex;
many were cohabiting; and several were divorced or had had children out
of wedlock.) Even those with the most promiscuous pasts gave the sexual
revolution of the 1970s (and 1980s) a very mixed review, inclined toward
the negative. They viewed the revolution as cheapening sex, making it
more compulsory for women, and overlooking the consequences and responsibilities. Indeed, the very thing that made the sexual revolution liberating for many women, stripping sex of all meaning, is what could make
it oppressive and misleading today.

Holly, 27, who owns a small business in Austin, Texas, explained why she
feels she has more sexual freedom in a monogamous relationship, a new twist
to traditional male ideals of sexual liberation. "There was a time when I was

promiscuous. But now I feel completely free sexually. I'm very comfortable with it, and I guess it's because I have that partner and we're sharing it together and we're relearning our sexuality. . . . The message [of the sexual revolution] was free sex was with everybody, and now I get . . . better sex. I see more freedom staying with one person who I feel I can explore all the possibilities with than from going from bed to bed to bed. . . . I think the sexual revolution was a big joke. I really do."

"I think we have lost the concept of divine sexuality," responded Cheryl, 31, a lawyer, commenting on the need to look at the quality of sex before quantity. "We separate love from heart, from thought, from God—and that's not organically what we as human beings are. Those things are not separate. And the sixties may have gotten us past behavioral prohibitions, but it didn't get us to divine sex."

Some women expressed similar regret for their promiscuous college years. "People are really carefree now, and I don't like it," said Megan, 22, the graduate of the College of the Holy Cross described in chapter 1. "Like the sexual revolution females feeling that they can kind of go out and do whatever. And I don't think that's right. It's almost as if they don't have any respect. . . . They feel, 'I'm free. I can do whatever.'" She described people at her school treating sex "like a game." After a week of studying, men and women went out on the weekends with the goal of picking someone up as a way to vent their stress. "And if they came home alone, they would be all disappointed the rest of the week. They would have this greater need the following weekend. It was really strange." Megan herself, who represents some of the conflicts between permissive male and restraining female values, got caught up in the action. She slept with her fiancé the first night they met, in a bar. "We were both pretty drunk that night, and things just got carried away. . . . We both regret having done it because it just didn't mean anything later on. Now [sex is] as simple as kissing."

Ann, 23, a graduate student in Plymouth, New Hampshire, made similar observations about sex's being devalued by those prowling the bars for conquests. She doesn't condemn people for having casual sex or judge it as wrong, but she does criticize them for having it irresponsibly without condoms to protect against AIDS. "I feel [the sexual revolution] was definitely [bad for] our generation. . . . The way it affected us was with a very laid-back attitude toward sex, and now our generation is dealing with some serious health issues when it comes to sex. And I think we would still like to have that laid-back freedom about it, but we can't." As a result, she said, people are still "using that seventies' mentality" of not caring about risks now, when the stakes have changed. I interviewed Ann in the early 1990s when condoms were used less automatically. "We're in the 1990s, and it's time to realize it's a life-or-death issue for us now. It's kind of like playing Russian roulette, whereas in the 1970s, the worst you could get was an STD."

A few of the women I interviewed complained that because sex is so casual now, it has become more compulsory, especially for teens. When I brought up the sexual revolution to the group of three high school teachers in Miami, they all maintained that it had made teens feel pressured to have sex too young. Two of them had had sex at ages 15 and 16 and regret not having been mature enough for the experience, blaming society for giving them no alternatives.

Also complaining about increased sexual pressures, Maureen, 24, an engineer in Boston, said that she found it too difficult to uphold her preferred "traditional values" and abstain from sex until marriage. Nowadays, she thinks that men are "too aggressive" with sex and that women have lost their "morals." One result is that she had sex with her present boyfriend, who expected it "in a dating situation." She admitted she was curious about having sex with him but, in another era, would have waited. "I think I probably would have been better just waiting. But at the time, it was a toss-up between losing him, just keeping him as a friend, or giving into it." (However, she did refer to herself as "a hypocrite" because she is continuing to sleep with him after they broke up.)

Becky, 23, a graduate student at New York University, agreed that the sexual revolution was really for men and had ruined family life. She said Hugh Hefner's *Playboy* of the 1950s defined its tone: "I think the whole sexual revolution was based solely around men's desire at the time to have a lot of sex with a lot of different people, which I guess is understandable. But I think that basically it's mythologized into somehow women wanted it too."

The oldest person in my core group, Linda, 36, a college student in 1993 at Texas Women's University, also criticized the 1970s notion that sex was compulsory. She came of age at the end of the sexual revolution, when she was a student at an East Coast college. "What I know about myself is that I thought sex was something I had to do. Something that I was expected to do. Whereas I don't think that young women feel this way. It's like, 'Now I don't have to have sex with you just because you want me to, just because you took me to dinner.'"

These frustrations with the sexual revolution are not limited to young women. Even in the 1970s, women voiced such concerns. While appreciating the sexual revolution for bringing more openness and information, the women surveyed in the 1976 *Hite Report* overwhelmingly condemned it as a male invention. "The crux of the matter—the effect of declaring sex healthy and necessary, and women 'free' to do it—was to take away women's right *not* to have sex. Women lost their right to say 'no,'" Shere Hite explained. She quoted disgruntled women, such as the following: "To me, the sexual revolution is just a simple reversal of the pressure I grew up with to be chaste—now there is one path for all to follow, and it makes just as little sense. Both enforced sex and enforced abstinence are bad" (457).

The 1981 *Cosmo Report,* a survey of 106,000 *Cosmopolitan* readers, found the same bitterness. According to its author Linda Wolfe, a majority "are disappointed or disillusioned with the sexual revolution. . . . Many believed that, like the heirs to political revolutions, they had been betrayed. They had participated in the overthrow of one tyranny only to see another installed in its place" (Wolfe 246, 247). Even women's magazines, which largely swallowed the sexual revolution ideologies of women's imitating men, have recently shown signs of reflection. Recognizing women's emotional needs, Lynn Harris explained in the September 1997 *Glamour* why the women she interviewed

> have stopped bed hopping and slowed the sexual momentum of their developing relationships: The new standards they have set for themselves are not medical precautions. The safety they practice is emotional, the consequences they weigh internal. When the women and men I spoke to eschew or delay sex, it's not because they're scared or bitter; it's because they're, well, busy. It's because they've begun to care about someone deeply, and they want to savor anticipation and make sex special. It's because they're in charge and comfortable. It's because they're happy. (315)

Harris also observed that often the thrill of casual sex just wasn't worth the hassle. Many women recognize their real feelings of emptiness and loneliness only after such an encounter, which may offer just a taste of the actual intimacy and human connection they are craving. But even those who had mixed feelings about the sexual revolution acknowledged that it had helped relieve women of the double standard and freed them to explore sex more openly and with fewer restrictions. Francine, 26, an Asian American graduate in chemistry from the University of California at Santa Barbara, recognized that "women can express what they want as opposed to always being the submissive one. I mean, the way my mom puts it is, my mom is pretty funny. She talks about sex like it's the man's right and the woman's duty, and the woman has no pleasure derived from it whatsoever. And I know that that's a big difference [from today]."

"Sexual Pluralism"

Since the sexual revolution, some of this shift to value a diversity of choices has been generational, often more prevalent in "politically correct" populations. And nowhere is this "sexual pluralism" more evident than on college campuses, where moods are often created without interference from the greater messiness, pressures, and restrictions of the outside world.

In a poll for the *InView* college magazine, 80 percent of the eight hundred students surveyed said they did not believe it was embarrassing to be a virgin. But 91 percent believe it's OK for women to be sexually aggressive. "A new sexual morality for young people, which is neither hedonistic nor traditional, is slowly emerging on college campuses," wrote reporter Raina Sacks in a 1990 article summing up *InView* magazine's survey of college students' sexual attitudes. Long-time observers of college life note this new variety and atmosphere of tolerance, even for conservatives (who, ironically, tend to be less tolerant themselves). Northwestern University professor Nicola Beisel, who teaches a popular class on the sociology of sex, described on National Public Radio how the climate had changed since the sexual revolution:

My vision of what's happening on campus is that here's a number of different subgroups of students, and they are in some ways contesting over what the norms of sexual behavior are going to be. When I think back to being an undergraduate, there was, I think some sort of consensus that we were supposed to be sexually active. There was also a very small Christian movement on campus. They were next to nonexistent. We thought the Young Republicans were something of a joke. There was also sort of a heterosexual hegemony on campus. So, men who came out of the closet at my school were beaten up. I mean, so in coming with a vision of one thing that's happening on campus, I don't think there is one thing. When I ask my students about this, I get lots of different stories about what the meaning of being sexual is. (*All Things Considered*, January 18, 1995)

Fighting Stereotypes

The women that I interviewed offered different positive reasons for saying no to sex. This group included not only virgins but also women with considerable experience who had chosen to abstain from sex for a while, exemplifying the emerging social view that women who are celibate aren't necessarily opposed to sex. Instead, they discussed this choice as rooted in their self-esteem, not in negative feelings about sex. Lisa, 25, an aspiring actress from Brooklyn, said she valued her "time out" from sex as much as her earlier decision to become sexually active: "I'm giving myself a break in just trying to deal with some things within myself and sort some things out. And so I feel confident. My best friend is a guy, and he knows that I haven't been having sex and he made some comment to me the other day like he knew that I was going crazy and it probably has been so long and I was like, 'No, I'm not going crazy, and to tell you the truth, I feel good the way I am now.' I never thought of it in the context of me being pro-woman or whatever. But yes, I guess to an extent because of where I am and my convictions about women and just where I am as a woman and where I am as a black woman that I feel totally confident and totally comfortable with the decision that I've made for myself. And at the time when I was sexually active, I felt no shame about that either."

Texas graduate student Beth volunteered that she also was taking a break from the demands of a relationship. For the past three years, she had had other concerns: "School was it," she said. "I just wanted that degree." That break allowed her to spend time on herself, in contrast to when she was with a time-consuming boyfriend, who depended on her emotionally and otherwise. "I pick up just after myself," she said. "I spend money on the things that I want. I like being in a relationship, but I want someone who can take care of themselves. I don't want to play mom anymore. I don't want to have to do that." With women forming their own identities, this preference to be alone rather than in a bad relationship is gaining acceptance. "It's not worth it if it's not good," Beth noted. Her classmate Letha agreed: "I would never date a guy just to have a guy."

The positive effect of personal integrity as a sexual motivator was a finding of Susan Sprecher and Pamela Regan's 1996 study of college virgins. "Women to a greater degree than men were proud and happy, and men to a greater degree than women were embarrassed and guilty" (9). These beliefs, the source of women's pride in remaining a virgin, ranged from not being personally ready to following religious principles. In contrast, men's negative feelings were associated with another set of reasons, labeled "inadequacy/insecurity," which involved feeling shy or being rejected. For both the sexes in the study, the most common reason for not having sex was not being in a relationship long enough or not being in love enough. The next reason was the fear of pregnancy and AIDS (more often listed by women than men). Following more closely for women was "I have not met a person I wanted to have intercourse with," and then "I do not feel ready to have premarital intercourse." These results contradict many of the stereotypes of virgins. First, the explanation that "I lack a desire for sex" was the least-cited reason by both women and men. Second, religion was rated only seventh. Third, women commonly chose abstention in combination with several other reasons, such as wanting to be in love. Fourth, most virgins aren't waiting until marriage. Having a relationship was the leading reason, and the belief that "I believe that intercourse before marriage is wrong" rated eighth, after feelings of not feeling personally ready to have sex (rated sixth).

Reflecting women's overall positive motivations, in 1992 *Glamour* magazine announced a new kind of virgin, "Virgins with Attitude," based on almost two thousand letters from exasperated virgins who demanded that their decision be recognized as valid. The author of the article, Amy Pagnozzi, acknowledged the many "retro-virgins" who used "chastity as a commodity" and the "blessed virgins" who based their decision on religion, but she also found many motivated by control. "Virgins with Attitude would rather choose than be chosen, even if this means exercising great discipline in suppressing their own physical needs. The world may see them as antisex; they see themselves as pro-choice" (296).

None of my interviewees listed the lack of sexual desire as a reason for their virginity. The most frequently chosen reason (named by six) of the twelve women surveyed who were virgins or had waited to have sex until after age 19 was waiting for a relationship. Four named this as their principal concern; another combined this answer with a fear of pregnancy and her spiritual/religious views; and still another cited religion combined with not being ready. A total of three women chose marriage and religion, with two listing both. Yet like Susan, the Lutheran Job Corps worker, and author Tara McCarthy, they generally discussed delaying intercourse as something they wanted to do for themselves, not for a man or religion. One of the two women who waited to have sex until they married said that she was mainly guarding against being exploited (AIDS was a secondary concern). "I would read Dear Abby columns and all these magazines about sex, and I would see the way these women were being exploited, and even as a child, I was so determined that this would never happen to me," said Connie, 27, an Asian American public relations writer in California, who first had sex at age 23 with her husband. "It wasn't so much that I wouldn't have sex out of moral reasons. It was because I didn't want to be hurt, and I didn't want anyone to ever take advantage of me, ever." Besides, she said, she was satisfied with male companionship, and she also "never had a shortage of orgasms, because I can achieve that myself. So I found a way to circumvent the sex thing by finding out how to fulfill myself at a very early age."

Most of the women who mentioned religion as a motivation said that they "grew out of it" after adolescence. Terry, 25, a graduate student at Plymouth State University in New Hampshire, said that in high school, her ideas about keeping her virginity stemmed from religion, although she didn't have a "really strong religious upbringing." When she reached college, her motivations changed when she "saw some women really sacrifice who they were for guys. I thought, 'I'm not going to do this unless it means something to me because I'm worth more than that.'. . . It wasn't so much an issue of, 'I have to be married.' It became more of an issue of 'I think more of myself to compromise myself in that way.'"

Earlier, she had told me about her guarding against being someone's conquest. Like many other virgins, she sees her sexuality as worthy of more respect and is acutely aware of many of the negative ways in which men treat women. "My personal philosophy is that sex has to be meaningful." For two years, she witnessed, in exaggerated form, the degrading mentality of sex as a game when she was an assistant "house mother" at a fraternity at a state university in Ohio. "Thursday night was a big night to go out, and Friday you would hear about all the women that they had over at the house. You would hear things like 'Don't you ever bring that fat pig back here.' 'Did you stick her?' And if they saw someone walking by the windows that they thought was 'blah,' they would yell things out." She also talked about being bothered by the men's common admission that they lied to women and said they loved them in order to get them to have sex. "I think it's emotionally abusive to do that to people. . . . Sometimes I really didn't know if they knew they were damaging a human, a real person with emotions and feelings. And I think that kind of attitude, part of a conquest is that you're usually trying to win something, not someone." Now she has no regrets. "So many of my friends have said, 'I regret this' or 'I wish I hadn't started so young.' And I was like 'I love being able to say I can look back and I have no regrets about how I have handled myself. . . . I can honestly say I haven't compromised who I was for a man."

Another reason frequently given by the older virgins was that they took longer to personally feel ready for sex and/or to form a relationship to support their first encounter. Writing in November 4, 1998, in the web magazine *Salon*, New York University graduate student and virgin Mindy Hung expounded on her sacrifice of a personal life to her long-term goals: "Getting sex takes dedication, courage, interest and effort. It's not as if losing one's virginity is a common and unavoidable household accident. Penises do not fall from high shelves."

The virgins I interviewed expressed tolerance for others' decisions. Mary, 24, a Boston engineer, had sex for the first time in the past year, with her first boyfriend. She said that she had wanted to wait until marriage because of traditional beliefs (not tied to religion) but that curiosity, escalating hormones, and pressure from him were too strong to resist. A solid relationship with a man she met through a personals ad provided the support she finally needed to go through with it. "I used to think that you shouldn't have sex before you get married. But my opinions have changed. I guess it's up to the person. I have friends who still believe in that, and I have friends who never believed in that." Lan, 23, a law student in Washington, D.C., admitted that she "probably will have sex before marriage." While she used marriage as a criterion in high school when she was more religious, she now looks forward to a relationship as giving her the needed emotional support. Like Mary, part of the delay is due to shyness and a result of her highly sheltered traditional Vietnamese and strict Catholic upbringing. "In a large group setting, I'm a very shy person," she said. "Not much of a social butterfly. Part of that is I didn't have the experience doing that in high school. I feel like it's very hard for me to make small talk with people."

Spirituality and Religion: For Christ's Sake

Four women who were waiting or had waited until their twenties to have sex also mentioned religion and spirituality as an influence. Susan, quoted at the beginning of this chapter, considered spirituality to be more important than religion. "My sexual being is distinctly mine, and whomever I want to share that with better be really special." Three others who mentioned religion as a reason for maintaining their virginity were fundamentalist Christians. Of all the women I interviewed, they exhibited the most pride in and the least embarrassment about their decision. Three out of four said I could use their names, a higher proportion than for the entire sample. They also noted that they got the most support from friends. Laura, 20, a sophomore at Texas Women's University, told me in front of a group of three nonvirgins: "I have always made the personal choice that I am waiting until I get married. My friends feel that way too, even the ones that date a lot."

One of the most dramatic Christian outpourings of support is the teen program True Love Waits, founded in April 1993 by youth minister Richard Ross of the Tulip Grove Baptist Church in Nashville. The program asks teenage girls to sign pledge cards that they will "be sexually abstinent from this day until the day I enter a biblical marriage relationship." The group gained national recognition in July 1994 when 25,000 teens attended a rally in Washington, D.C., bringing with them 200,000 signed cards, which they spread out on the Mall. Just like the male Promise Keepers, they regularly hold rallies in large stadiums, often attracting thousands of teen supporters.

I witnessed this movement on a smaller scale at Auburn University in Alabama in the spring of 1997. In a lecture hall, the Campus Crusade for Christ was holding its regular Thursday night meeting of more than four hundred students. Campus director Bill Voldt told me that attendance had doubled in the past year. As at Auburn, this campus Christian organization was growing at high schools and colleges nationwide, in membership and number of chapters. It was second only to the largest, the Intervarsity Christian Fellowship of the USA, with more than seven hundred chapters. After some introductory announcements, the student leader, Mark, said that he wanted to talk to the women alone and asked the men to leave for a separate meeting. When the men left, Mark, 27, an incredibly articulate and quietly charismatic man, dressed casually in a blue and white striped shirt, talked to the women about the importance of modesty, preaching biblical precepts of women's chastity and modesty in a Western culture of revealing and personally expressive dress. He described in sometimes excruciating detail how women should and shouldn't dress in regard to tightness, lack of coverage, and transparency. He painstakingly specified what to avoid, such as "leaving your headlights on" (when nipples show through a bra). "All of a sudden, the man has a reference point," he said, invoking some nervous laughter from the audience. "He knows more about what's going on there." The danger? Mark carefully explained how such careless exhibition could drive a "good Christian man off his path" toward prohibited autoerotic stimulation. To explain a man's reaction, he asked them to imagine themselves in a health club and accidentally seeing a man's shorts fly open. "The degree to which that was nasty to you guys is the same degree that this is appealing to [us] guys." The women, many of them dressed in skimpy halters and miniskirts in the humid southern night, nodded appreciatively, often stopping to look up in their own dog-eared copies passages of the Bible he cited. They often laughed nervously when he used slang and became especially specific (such as with the headlights comment). "He just cracks me up," whispered a woman to her friend.

I talked to several women afterward, who said they were grateful to be told how their dress affected men. When first approached, an outgoing attractive blonde woman, Wendy Whatley, 21, from Valdosta, Georgia (whom I didn't include in my core sample), told me that she was "really excited about tonight." I asked her why. "I'm a Christian and a virgin and a believer in the principles of the Bible and want to hear more about the guys' perspective on godly attitudes for mating." We went quickly from the subject of modesty to virginity. I was startled how open Whatley was with me, a stranger with a tape recorder (and one who had just given a lecture on feminism that night on campus). Her primary motivation was "Christian principles and beliefs," which she does not perceive as a limit: "It's not a restriction at all because Christ came to free us from the bondage of sin and I don't want to sound clichéd, but I feel like his plan is definitely what's best, and if I stay under the things that he's established, my best interest has already been taken into consideration. He's looking out for me and the laws that the Lord has established for a godly woman." Whatley admitted this view was not mainstream at Auburn but represented "a huge sector of students. . . . I feel like I run in more conservative circles than most. Most of my friends feel the same way. Like they'd be humiliated to come in and tell me that they had slept with a boyfriend."

I commented that this decision to remain a virgin in today's culture requires a lot of faith. "Yeah. It's never anything I've ever struggled about. Like I've never thought twice about not waiting until I get married. It's almost inherent for me." Whatley also said she "would never be embarrassed" admitting she is a virgin. I observed that she was being "a nonconformist to the culture," and she agreed. "Just like in recognizing that just because a guy wants to do something, like I don't have to let him. Even in just taking my hand. Some people are like, 'That's not a big deal.' And it's a big deal to me. And if you're going to kiss me, it's a really big deal. And I don't have to let you do that. So it should be a commitment that you're willing to back up with your actions and words," she said, pausing. "Is this weird?" I later asked her more about her doubts. She said that in one close relationship with a man, she did gain sympathy for those who don't wait. "I did date a guy in high school, and that was the first time that I realized why anyone would want to have sex before they get married. . . . I mean, you date somebody and love somebody and that's a totally natural response. . . . And yet at the same time, when you're not dating anyone, looking back, I can see how detrimental that would have been had I allowed myself to respond to natural desires or whatever, and how much I did preserve my heart and how much it was in my best interest to hold out and not succumb to that or whatever." But what about women's desires? Whatley clearly saw Scripture as taking precedence: "If you're going to base Scripture as your authority as a Christian, it's just kind of understood. If it restricts you in any way, well, then it should."

Expressing similar confidence and faith in the Bible's teachings on virginity was another fundamentalist Christian woman, Mary, 27, who had had sex at an early age as a teenage runaway and prostitute. Mary (whom I didn't count in my tally of twentysomething virgins), is now happy to next have sex when she gets married. This mother of one represents a population of so-called secondary virgins who have had sex but are now waiting until they are married to have it again. Her recent conversion changed her life in every way. Now living in a homeless shelter in Anaheim, California, she has received material help from church members in getting back on track. They have provided her with temporary shelter and even a loan to get her car fixed.

The church has also given her needed spiritual guidance and support. "Nothing worked in my life when I tried to do it by myself and by my own choices. . . . Now I do what Scripture says," she said. This includes following its teachings against premarital sex: "I just believe that you should be married because it's not classy when you're not married. It's not special. You're just getting each other off and that's it, that's what I think. It's just like you make me feel good, and I'll make you feel good, and then that's it. And then it's over with. 'Come back next week and we'll do it again.' It's not special." I asked her whether she ever did "get anything out of" sex in the past, such as with her former boyfriend of seven years. "Not really, no. I don't remember a time when it felt good. It may have felt good physically at times, but inside there was still, it just wasn't right. . . . There's all kinds of things you can do to feel good physically. But there's more than your physical body there. You have a soul."

Fundamentalists as Individualists?

It is difficult to determine whether these fundamentalist Christian women are following the same individualist wave of the other virgins cited here or whether they are directly challenging it. On the one hand, they are making Scripture, and not themselves and their desires, the final authority. But at the same time, they are nonconformists and individualists in actually choosing this way of life, against the majority of society. Instead of being forced to follow the Bible, as they would have done in the past, they are actively deciding for themselves. Finally, in the past when a single, powerful religion was able to dominate the community, women were usually forced to follow it without question.

Fundamentalists are also more likely in this age to speak in therapeutic terms of the self and integrity, rather than of sin (though terms like "low self-esteem" may be euphemisms for more condemning language and opinion of the sexually active). In addition, in another modern twist, this personal choice especially applies to fundamentalists living in settings they do not dominate, such as public universities and urban singles centers. Texas undergraduate Laura, for example, said that on her own, at a public school, she had chosen a stricter religious path than her mother had at her age, as her mother had admitted that she had had sex with her father before they got married. The community of friends that supports her way of life is one she freely chose, not one she was born into and could not escape. The irony is that making one's religion a guidepost for sex is an individual decision to follow a nonindividualistic philosophy.

Lingering Stigmas

The Christian fundamentalists also stood out from the rest of the sample in their proud and public declarations of their virginity, whereas the fact that none of the other virgins let me use their full names was an indication of their relative discomfort. Most of the nonfundamentalist women said that they felt much more isolated, especially because they had much more experienced friends. Terry, 25, at Plymouth State University, said that her friends often assume that she has had sex when they routinely go over the details of their romantic lives. At these times, she said, "I just become very quiet. . . . I remember even in college, being 20 years old, and a guy said, 'You aren't a virgin, are you? Well, what's wrong with you?' That was at 20; God knows that at 25, he would be stunned." As she grows older, with fewer other virgins around her for support, the isolation gets worse. "In fact, one of my friends—she's 26—she just lost her virginity last summer. . . . And she had a hard time telling me because she thought I would be disappointed in her or something like that. I was like, 'God, I'm not that pious. It has nothing to do with that.' But in a way I was a little let down because I'm like, 'Oh. I stand alone.' I'm the only one left among my friends that I know of."

Even though the fundamentalist virgins enjoy the most support from friends, virgins as a whole still confront stigma and stereotypes. While more of them are coming out in public, the journey for acceptance and under-standing has just begun. A dialogue is still needed to respect every woman's choice to say no, whether for "politically correct" reasons of challenging un-wanted sex and harassment or because of traditional respect for biblical pre-cepts. In a letter to *Ms.*, one reader, Hanah Parish, expressed this challenge best. She was reacting to an article from an earlier issue condemning a fun-damentalist True Love Waits prochastity rally:

What is important is that girls decide to have sex when it is right for them, not when society says it should happen. So if one girl is ready at 16 and an-other girl wants to wait until marriage, they both are making the right de-cision, if it is an informed and personal one. If we women are going to start taking control of our own lives, we have to accept that some of us will live our lives differently from others. (July/August *Ms.* 1997, 5)

III

Redefining the Family and Relationships Her Way

5. Modern Marriage: From Meal Ticket to Best Friend

A vibrant marriage has to be more than just problem-free. When a marriage is strong and healthy, it is a powerful vehicle for personal growth.
—"Steps to a More Spiritual Marriage," *Ladies' Home Journal*, March 1998

When I asked women what the most important part of a marriage was, no one brought up the leading answer in the past: to be financially supported by a man. Instead, the reasons I heard most often (in order of frequency) were "communication," "friendship," "equality," "honesty," "partnership," "compromise," and "openness."

"I kind of feel that for a lot of this generation, it's really not a question: 'Is he a good provider?' I always assumed I'd be working at some point; my mother worked," said Leah, 26, a graduate student at the University of Texas. "But I was looking for someone who was just going to treat me as an equal in a lot of ways: in the kitchen, with housecleaning, with everything. A partnership. That's our marriage." Today, women's roles in marriage are more equal, and as a result of their greater power in marriage, women today are happier with it. In a 1995 CBS News poll, women were more likely than men (63 to 49 percent) to say that their marriages were better than their parents'. When both genders compared themselves with their parents, 56 percent said their marriages were better, 36 percent were the same, and only 3 percent were worse (Bowman 1999).

Today, even for the most traditional couples, marriage, like the American family, has changed. Just as young women have more choices about their sexual behavior and principles, they also have more freedom to tailor their family according to their own personal preferences. In addition, even though marriage and family are still major life goals of most American women, they are not mandatory as they once were. Because women are now less dependent on men as a meal ticket, they can choose not to marry at all, whether they live with a man, have children, or are gay or straight.

"American Family Values"

The conditions for this move toward a more democratic family have been developing since the turn of the twentieth century. One hundred years ago, the divorce rate began to increase but so slowly that few people took notice. During World War II, an unprecedented number of women entered the workforce. Then after the war, although many women left their jobs to raise families, many kept their jobs, never viewing themselves and their abilities in the same way again. These changes and others became most visible in the 1960s and 1970s, when even more women started pouring into the workforce, getting more education, and initiating divorces. Since the early 1990s, however, this very dramatic change has slowed, and the American family has actually been stabilizing. Statistics indicating the "breakdown" of the American family, based on such factors as divorce and out-of-wedlock children, have plateaued. After skyrocketing in the 1970s and 1980s, rates of divorce, abortion, cohabitation, premarital sex, and single motherhood now are steady, with the figures matching those of other industrialized nations. From 1970 to 1990, the number of married couples with children under 18 shrank from 40 percent of all households to about 25 percent, where it has remained until 2000 (*Household and Family Characteristics* 1998).

In regard to female ideals of commitment, the young women I surveyed were stricter than their counterparts in the late 1970s and most of the 1980s. Indeed, family priorities for women actually resembled the more conservative 1960s levels. And even though more women are attending college than ever before, college women's most ambitious "power career" aspirations have declined to 1970s levels, lower than those of the 1980s but still higher than those of the 1960s and earlier. The result is that women want to "have it all," both marriage and work, but they also expect to sacrifice some of their career or fit it in to family needs (*American Freshman* 1997).

Writing in the *New York Times*, graduate student Elizabeth McGuire talked about young professional women wanting balance, refusing the boomer extremes of having to keep up a "frenetic pace" or quitting their jobs to raise a family. Accordingly, they make career decisions that are more amenable to raising and enjoying children, such as entering more flexible fields and starting their own businesses. In this way, they differ from the career-oriented boomers and even the older Generation Xers, who viewed children as an afterthought, not considering until after establishing their careers the commitment that children require. "Many people may think we are nearing the end of the workplace revolution," McGuire wrote. "In reality, we are only just beginning" (McGuire 1998, A9).

At the same time as they support "family values," young American women have a broader definition of "family." They acknowledge that most women want to work or must work out of necessity and that a family may be different from the white straight suburban nuclear model. For example, when I asked Becky, a New York University graduate student who had been raised by her divorced mother, to define a "family," she stressed that the important thing in the end is that two parents are present. "Does it have to be male/female?" she asked herself. "I have to be perfectly honest and say in the child's interest, it's certainly better if they have a male and female parent. I certainly would have appreciated that. But I'll tell you. I've seen plenty of documentaries about lesbian couples and gay couples, and I think they are fine parents, and are much better than foster care or just shuffling through the different boys' homes or girls' homes." While Becky values the traditional two-parent family, she still resents much of the self-righteous rhetoric about it from conservative politicians. She described her mixed feelings about former Vice President Dan Quayle's insistence that a breakdown in family structure had caused many of society's problems. "He's right to a certain extent. But what's wrong with that is his term 'family values' is loaded in the same way that 'New World Order' is," she explained, using another sound bite from the past Bush administration. "When he's talking about 'family values,' he's talking about a Christian-oriented white family. And that's true. There's no denying that they're talking about Christianity. That bothers me. Because I think that creates its own set of problems."

Throughout history, politicians' narrow definition of the family has lagged behind that of most citizens. The failure to recognize working women proved to be a fatal mistake in the 1992 Republican presidential campaign. At the national convention, in their vague platform of "family values," conservative leaders such as Marilyn Quayle and committee chairman Rich Bond emphasized the worth of only the traditional family of a nonworking mother. In the process, they alienated the majority of American women who do not—or cannot afford to—fit that profile. In response, the Clinton campaign four years later prominently featured the issues of working families.

Even Leslie and Mark, both 24 and religious Baptists, the most traditional couple I interviewed, admitted some modern concessions. Married at 21, they both believe in defined gender roles in marriage. When they have children, Leslie plans to leave her job as a ground-support supervisor at an airline and raise them. She has already lowered her original career expectations by quitting college and moving to Santa Barbara to join Mark, where he is enrolled in a graduate program in engineering. "I'm not like an old-fashioned fifties woman or anything," said Leslie. "But I believe in women's work and men's work. Taking out the garbage is definitely men's work." However, they both emphasized that they respect others' choices and don't "ride a high horse" because of their decision. Leslie views herself not as a conservative but as an individualist by not following one "politically correct" model of womanhood. She pointed out that in the 1970s and 1980s, women had more to prove than they did today. "Instead of showing your independence by being part of the revolution, you show your independence by being your own self," she said. At the same time, however, Mark's and Leslie's marriage is also more flexible than that of their parents. Mark plans to spend much more time with his children than his father did, who was singularly focused on his career, and also he does some of the housework.

Marriage Traditions Old and New

In this transformed American family, young women still remain devoted to the concept of marriage. Perhaps the greatest testament to its enduring appeal is the booming bridal industry, accounting for $32 billion in retail sales in 1996. Nearly 3 million weddings took place in the United States in 1997, half a million more than in 1995. And people are spending more. The average cost of a wedding in Chicago, for example, climbed from $10,000 in the mid-1980s to about $20,000 today (Kerrill 1997).

While attending a typical American bridal fair in Chicago as a spy for this book, I kept thinking about how, on one hand, so little had changed on the surface. Judging by the overwhelming enthusiasm and open pocketbooks of those in attendance, I saw firsthand that marriage is still romanticized and prized enough to make grown women swoon. The centerpiece of the fair was a fashion show. The crowd, mostly conservatively attired women in their early twenties, some husbands-to-be, and mothers, overflowed into the aisles and sections behind the rows of chairs. With every movement and expression of the models on the runway, the audience clapped and moaned and sighed and often howled, displaying the unswerving attention and devotion usually reserved for fundamentalist revivals.

One of the event's organizers told me that the surest sales are for the big purchases: the dress, the photographer, and the reception. She commented that no matter what their budget, women are not likely to skimp on those three items. Speaking of the bridal industry, she noted, "We pride ourselves on saying that we're a recession-free business." She added that the women will do what it takes to save for these items, commonly delaying the wedding and living at home with parents to save money (as were several young women there whom I interviewed).

Still, while so many women continue to pay homage (along with large sums of money) to wedding and family tradition, much has changed under the surface. The once fringe idea of marriage as a partnership has become utterly mainstream. A large part of the reason that marriage has changed is that women have changed. With more power and higher expectations, young women enter marriage on an entirely different footing than did the generation before the baby boomers. A majority of women (55 percent) now earn at least half their household's income (1995 Whirlpool Foundation study, "Women: The New Providers," *Glamour*, October 1995, 124). The proportion of women working to support their families doubled in the past twenty years, from 19 percent in 1980 to 46 percent in 2000 (Virginia Slims Poll 2000). Now that they have less need of men to support them financially (and know that they can't necessarily count on them, anyway, for life), women are making other, more intimate demands of their husbands for partnership. Although finances are still important and a major source of marital strife, they aren't the only one. According to the 2000 Virginia Slims/Roper Starch Opinion Poll, in response to the question "What makes a good marriage?" women and men rated "respect for each other" at the top of the list (selected by 85 percent of women and 83 percent of men). Following that, selected by seven in ten women and men, were being in love, the spouse's sexual fidelity, communication about feelings, and keeping romance alive— all rated above "financial security" by a slim majority, 59 percent each of men and women.

The ideals of the women's movement, on society's fringes in the 1970s, have become those of the nation. This current young generation as a whole seems to have more progressive attitudes toward women's place in society and marriage. Using the 1972 Attitudes toward Women Scale, University of Michigan researcher Jean Twenge (1997a) compared seventy-one subjects from 1970 to 1995 and found a steady trend toward more liberal/feminist attitudes. Women changed most in the late 1970s and early 1980s, but men lagged a generation behind. (It was not until 1986 to 1990 that they equaled the attitudes toward greater gender equality that women had in the 1970s.) Twenge's findings reflect the results of the past thirty years of surveys of college freshmen by the UCLA Higher Education Research Institute. Over the years, student attitudes have become much more liberal and accepting of married women's roles outside the home, even though other attitudes (such as toward marijuana and the death penalty) became more conservative during the 1980s (*American Freshman* 1997). In an interview, Professor Ilsa Lottes of the University of Maryland remarked that more egalitarian values were the key force separating young women from the boomers of her generation, that in the 1970s, these values were new and not as widely and fully absorbed. "It [the women's movement] was just coming into being," she said. "I wasn't raised to think I could do anything. I'm 53. I was raised to be a teacher so that it wouldn't interfere in my more important roles as a wife and mother. Now I would be called sexist for saying the same thing to my women students."

Just as more Americans approve of women's having a career, professional career women also have a more positive view of marriage. Building on boomer patterns, they feel free to marry later, when it won't interfere with their career, and to have fewer children later in life. Younger men are willing to share housework and child rearing. A woman's marriage vow no longer signifies a total retreat from the outside world into the traditionally womanly sphere of the home and family. She no longer is assumed to be forming her entire identity as a Mrs. Somebody, an accessory to a man, sacrificing all her own ambitions. And thanks to the pioneering efforts of the boomer career women, the workplace, at least for the more affluent, is more family friendly and accepting of women.

Beyond Race and Religion

As new ideals for marriage emerge, some of the old ones disappear. Consistent with young women's individualist philosophies, they are less likely to base relationships on religion or race, more traditional concerns. (This is true even though marriage partners still tend to have similar backgrounds.) In the 2000 Virginia Slims Opinion Poll, more than 90 percent of the women said that marriage between people of different religions is acceptable, and 85 percent agreed that interracial marriage was acceptable. Accordingly, the number of such marriages has skyrocketed. Between 1960 and 1990, the number of interracial marriages increased by 800 percent. Roughly one in twenty-five married couples today are of different races. In 1990, according to a study by the American Enterprise Institute, nearly 2 million children lived in homes in which the primary adults were of different races; this number doubled in 1980 and rose more than four times the number in 1970 (Holmes 1996).

The figures for intermarriage vary by race. Although they still account for only 1 percent of all marriages, the pace of marriage between whites and blacks is rapidly accelerating. According to the U.S. Bureau of the Census, in 1993, of all new marriages by blacks, 12.1 percent were to white partners, up from 2.6 percent in 1970 (most of these were black men marrying white women). This is dramatic considering that just forty years ago, these marriages were illegal in many states. The intermarriage rate is much higher for Hispanics, Asians, and Native Americans, of which at least 30 percent marry outside their race. In fact, with higher intermarriage rates than their male counterparts, Asian American women are just as likely to marry a white man as they are another Asian. A majority of both Native American men and Native American women (53.9 percent) marry whites (Lind 1998).

Young adults also more often marry persons of different religions, with about three-quarters marrying and about one-half dating or cohabiting within their religion (Michael et al. 1994, 46). Only one-third of mainline Protestants marry persons of their own religious identification, compared with 61 percent of evangelical Protestants and 68 percent of Catholics (Laumann et al. 1994, 244). The intermarriage rate for Jews has more than quintupled, from 9 percent for Jews married before 1965 to at least 52 percent for those married after 1965 (Steinfels 1991).

In addition to finding a different partner than they would have in the past, young women also have other expectations about the relationship itself. The women I interviewed indicated that communication was essential, just as it was for their sexual relationships. In contrast, in the past when women were expected to fill predetermined passive and subservient roles, they had no need for such communication with their partner. Although fundamentalists were more insistent than most on maintaining traditional gender roles and male domination of marriage, they also promoted communication between the partners to help support their commitments.

Also observing these changes was Mary Ann Hanlon, 54, who was perhaps the most experienced social observer of modern marriage whom I interviewed. For the past twenty years, she and her husband have held pre-canna classes (premarriage counseling sessions) for working- and middle-class Catholic couples in their Queens, New York, home. Even though the format differs from parish to parish, a course on marriage is a standard requirement for couples taking vows in the Catholic Church. Hanlon's six-week course has always emphasized the importance of communication. She has noticed that couples now more fully accept and absorb these lessons because they have better and "more realistic" communication skills. "They actually talked to each other about the things that were going to have an impact on their lives. The nitty-gritty of how they were going to share the chores, or who is going to handle the money."

In my interviews, women of all classes and educational backgrounds emphasized the importance of communication. Lana, 29, a student at Alladin Beauty College in Denton, Texas, emphasized communication when discussing her faith in marriage and family. "I think you have to work hard at it," said Lana. "Very hard. We work hard at it. I mean, communication, that's the biggest work." A student at Plymouth State University, Ann, 23, also listed "communication as key to a good relationship," explaining that "it shows the person you care enough about them to talk to them about, 'What's going on?' Or work something out when you're having a disagreement." Such themes animated my conversation with three mothers on public aid in the University Settlement on the Lower East Side of New York. I first asked them about challenges that are part of their lives but that their parents did not face. The women, two African Americans and one Latina, elaborated on their greater expectations for communication and partnership. Vernadette, 33, who is married and has an 11-year-old daughter, observed, "The challenge for me is communicating and negotiating with family. That would be breaking the pattern that I've gotten from my mother and father. . . . In my family, feelings were not expressed. They were denied. . . . And dealing with my daughter, I don't want her to continue in the same cycle. If you have a problem, communicate it. Don't talk like it doesn't exist." Vanessa, 25, who never married, said that a great challenge was communicating with men, along with men's lack of responsibility and commitment. (The father of her child abandoned them and refuses to pay child support.) Like Vernadette, she expected a marriage to be an equal partnership. "It's supposed to be fifty/fifty. There should be an equal thing, not just with sex, but in taking care of the kids, you know, fulfilling each others' needs, being there for each other."

Similarly, the women hoped that the husband and wife would be "best friends," rather than exclusively a "wife" or a "husband." Maintaining this type of relationship is more natural to a generation of women and men that is more likely to cultivate friendships with the opposite gender. As they grew up, today's young men and women shared more of the same values and educational experiences, and in college in the 1990s, they were more likely to live in coed residence halls, where they formed friendships and learned to demystify the opposite sex. Bellinda, 22, said this made a difference when she was a freshman at the University of Texas at Austin. "I went to an all-girls Catholic school, so I didn't have really good interpersonal communication, anything like that. I wasn't used to being around men, so it really helped a lot that I was living with a bunch of guys. I had to learn how to be friends with men and how to be more than friends with men, and how to keep those relationships different." After her dormitory experience, she moved into an apartment with two females and one male friend. After our interview, she planned to move in with her boyfriend at Purdue University, who shares a three-bedroom apartment with his brother and a female friend of theirs.

Several other women I interviewed had male best friends and male roommates, and almost all of them pointed out the difference between themselves and their parents' generation. Karen, 26, who is an accounting clerk at a hospital in southern California and whose best friend is a gay male, said that she had witnessed this difference with older coworkers. When she goes to lunch with a man in her office, the women in their forties and fifties seem confused. "He lives with his girlfriend. I live with my boyfriend. We talk a lot. We eat lunch together and stuff, and they think there's something going on. Because how could you guys just be friends? . . . When they were 22 or 23, most of them were married. I don't think they came from a time where men and women were friends as much. It was like you dated them, that was fine. But you didn't just socialize. When you needed advice, you wouldn't call some guy that you talked to or whatever, some guy that you were friends with. There was always like a sexual conflict or something underlying or some kind of tension."

Sexual fulfillment has also taken on new importance. Now that the wife is not required to "serve" her husband sexually with "wifely duties," her needs have become more prominent. A 1994 EDK/*Redbook* survey of married couples revealed that "married couples value their thriving sex lives, which they nurture with romance, intimacy, sexual variety. Today's married sex is red-hot and experimental, women are every bit as interested as men," stated the report, "Married Sex Sizzles." According to this survey, almost half (47 percent) the married couples rated the sexual aspect of their marriage as "very good," and another 35 percent said that it was "good." To keep the spark alive, the most popular way cited by both men and women (73 percent and 78 percent) was experimenting with different positions. A third were adventurous enough to do things not associated with traditionally tame marital sex, such as acting out fantasies, watching erotic movies, and using massage oil or vibrators. Those rating their sex lives as hottest also reported happier marriages. Eighty percent who gave their marriage a high "sizzle rating" also said their marriages were happy (versus only 42 percent of low sizzlers).

A *Mirabella* magazine article, "Hot Monogamy," about this greater emphasis on sexual pleasure in marriage observed that

> we have entered a radically new era of sexuality. . . . Monogamy is definitely the ideal among young people today. Sticking together. Having kids. Concentrating on family life. You could say things were just like they were back in the Fifties—except for two enormous differences. The fact that women work. And the fact that these young monogamous couples are insisting on good, hot sex. (Wolfe 1995, 127)

Dr. Helen Singer Kaplan, a couples sex therapist quoted in the article, attributes this insistence on good sex to the greater importance of commitment and a fear of risks, such as AIDS. Young people take a dimmer view of adultery and so are more likely to turn to their established partner for experimentation and novelty. Also, now that the double standard has diminished, a man has less of a whore/madonna complex about his wife, seeing her as a sexual being as well as a mother/"good girl." In the past, a man seeking a hotter sex life would be more likely to have an affair with a different kind of woman, a "bad girl." This adultery is evident in films of the 1960s and 1970s, including *Shampoo*, which treated adultery as a joke.

Although people are still having extramarital affairs, statistics show that American adults are becoming less tolerant of cheating. Also, the younger generation of men is having fewer affairs, no longer seeing them as a standard alternative to a tame and lust-less marriage. The National Health and Social Life Survey found that older generations of men were more likely to have had additional partners during their marriages. Of the men born between 1933 and 1942, 23 percent said they had had another partner besides their wife. But of the men born between 1963 and 1974, the number reported was only 10 percent (Laumann et al. 1994, 208). Men in their forties and older were twice as likely to have paid for sex in their lives (20 percent) than were men in their twenties (10 percent) (Smith 1994b, 75). (However, the NHSLS charted women's rates of infidelity as remaining more stable through the years, at 7 to 9 percent.)

Demands on Men and Fathers

As women demand more of marriage, they are also demanding more of men. As a result, the roles of husband and father have been transformed. Women now expect men to share the housework and child rearing, and according to the polls, the men think this is reasonable. In the 2000 Virginia Slims Opinion Poll, more than 80 percent of men and women favored men's sharing household responsibilities. (Their record of actually helping out was less commendable, however.)

In the 1980s and 1990s, fathers assumed and enjoyed new involvement at home. A recent study of employed adults by the Families and Work Institute showed a smaller gap between working men's and women's contribution to housework. In 1977, men spent about 30 percent as much time as women did on household work, compared with 75 percent as much in 1997. (The gap in 1997 was 45 minutes.) The same study also found that children received more attention from working parents, mainly because of the change in men (Lewin 1998b). Fathers participate in child care from the very beginning, with 90 percent of married fathers present in the delivery room when their children are born, according to Robert L. Griswold, author of *Fatherhood in America* (see Gibbs 1993). In the 1980s, bookstores introduced titles like *Expectant Father*, *Father a Successful Daughter*, and *Father's Almanac*. The magazine *Modern Dad* was started in 1997 by a 28-year-old former financial manager who noticed that when his friends became fathers, they wanted to be "very connected to their kids" but didn't know how (*Chicago Tribune*, 26 January 1997, sec. 13, p. 6). In polls, men claim more interest in their children than in their career. In a 1990 survey by the *Los Angeles Times*, 39 percent of fathers said they would "quit their jobs" to spend more time with their kids. Another survey found that 74 percent of men said they would rather have a daddy-track job than a fast-track job (Gibbs 1993, 56).

Only recently has the government noted the growing role of fathers in caring for children. A 1994 U.S. Census Bureau report described them as the central force holding down the need for day care. The study found that the proportion of families paying for child care fell from 40 percent in 1988 to 35 percent in 1991, a trend attributed mainly to the increase in care by fathers. In 1988, 15 percent of preschoolers with working mothers were cared for by their fathers, a figure that rose to 20 percent over the next three years (Vobejda and Cohn 1994).

Like the other aspects of marriage discussed, this dual parenting role is growing for Americans from all walks of life. Beauty school student Lana, of Denton, Texas, is grateful that her mechanic husband helps take care of their two sons. They cannot afford day care, so they each take shifts when the other is working. "I think men are getting more level. They're coming around," she said. "They're trying anyway. I mean, my husband has been babysitting all day today. He's good at that." Much of this change has been voluntary, with fathers regarding involvement with their family as rewarding and not as a sacrifice. Representing this emerging view is Gary, 30, a college administrator in Chicago. Like several others I interviewed, his real father had abandoned the family, and Gary has no memory at all of him. His parents divorced when he was an infant, and he now considers his stepfather his real father. (In fact, he didn't know that his stepfather wasn't his real father until recently when he was going through his mother's papers.)

Gary planned his entire career around being able to make more time for his wife Kerry and year-old daughter, Alyanne. After working his way through law school, he chose his current, more flexible job instead of joining a law firm. When Kerry went back to work, as a high school math teacher, he enthusiastically took a month off for child care, under the new Family Leave Act, which took effect in 1993 and has been used by millions of fathers since. "If I had gone into a law firm," he said, "it was quite clear there would be no taking this leave. To do so would mean sacrifice—you will not be promoted. You will forever be stereotyped and cast in a certain way. Yet at my work, it was so natural. There was absolutely no hesitation, no backlash. It was admired."

Gary noticed some other gaps in society's acceptance of a more involved father. Mainly, he had some clashes with his more traditional stepfather, a mechanic in a small Pennsylvania town. "When we were getting married, my father sat down to tell me how important it was that I take charge and not let Kerry make certain decisions. Because if I let her make any decisions, then she'd probably make all the decisions. . . . And trying to explain to him what my concepts of equal relationship are—the word had no meaning for him." As a result, his father insinuates constantly that Gary is being pushed around by his wife. When he tells his parents something "that they don't want to hear, they'll say, 'Did Kerry make you say that?'" Kerry's parents, who are from Jamaica, also are skeptical. "When I [Gary] go to her house, if I try to help do the dishes, her mom, her pop will joke, 'Oh we have to put a dress on you' because I'm doing 'women's work.'"

Even though men of all classes might wish for this more enlightened role, only a few, like Gary, are able to make it happen. White-collar employers are far more likely than most even to consider making the workplace more family friendly. Despite the fact that the majority of women work, the workplace has been slow to offer child care, family leave, and equal wages for women. In the 2000 Virginia Slims Poll, 63 percent of women surveyed said that employers should give women more flexibility. In addition, men still earn more money than their wives do and most often demand that women be the ones to make the career sacrifices. Many women are grateful, however, just to have fathers involved in their families at all, for about a quarter of households are run by a single parent, almost always the mother.

Negotiating Roles: Four Couples

Because of these higher expectations and demands, marriage today is more complex than ever, constantly requiring hard work, flexibility, and discussion to maintain. Illustrating these modern challenges are four professional and well-educated couples, aged 25 to 27, whom I interviewed in Austin, Texas. They all had met while undergraduates at the University of Texas and had been married for three to four years. Compared with their parents, they all have taken a much more active and individualistic approach to their marriages. Even the details of their lives, such as the women's choices for their last names, reveal their consciousness in personally tailoring their roles. Two of the women, Heather and Leah, took their husband's last name. One, Pat, kept her unmarried name, and Dylan chose a hyphenated middle ground. Repeatedly during our long conversation, these women and their husbands compared themselves with their parents. One major difference was the traits they sought in a partner, as their marriages were primarily intellectual and emotional relationships rather than financial arrangements.

Reflecting this shift, these four couples, who were raised in some kind of Christian faith, didn't make denomination a variable as their parents had. "With my mom, religion was a big issue," said Heather, a sales representative in Wadsworth, Texas. "We are Presbyterian way back, like into the 1600s. My dad was going to the House of Christ Church. That was something they had to deal with." The other couples laughed at that comment. "That [religion] wasn't a big deal to me," she continued. "I think that what I wanted more than anything else was someone I could really talk to that I respected," adding that she was first attracted to her husband Rodney after he helped her edit a paper for class.

Pat, who grew up in Houston in a Mexican American family, said that the difference in race and class backgrounds didn't keep her from marrying her WASP husband, Mason. Her family is working class and his is upper middle class (his father is a vice president of a state university). Whereas Pat's main goal was to find "a responsible person," her less well educated and more traditional mother had other priorities for her own husband and then, after divorcing him, for her boyfriends. "The first one was married. The second was a blackjack guy. The third one was a bail bondsman. And the only thing they had in common was the fact that they were Hispanic. And that's really what she's looking for," said Pat.

Despite the rewards, these couples spent more time talking about the conflicts caused by their demands for equality in marriage. Indeed, even as these couples rejected their parents' models of marriage for their lack of authenticity and communication, they also yearned for their sense of stability and certainty.

Rodney, a technical writer who has floated through a variety of careers since college graduation, stated that his parents "saw a clearer path" for their lives, as well as for how they conducted their marriage. "My parents are both from Iowa. At a certain age, you got married. I mean I think that was it. They just happened to be dating at that time. I would like to think that there was a lot of deeper thought to it, but it just turns out that they got married. It was the same way he [Dad] picked his major. It was the same way they did a lot of things. . . . There wasn't a lot of deep planning when I was growing up. But everyone here has had numerous deep conversations hours in length about what we are doing here."

Because they don't take their roles for granted, these couples must work harder to define them for themselves, and often this lack of structure causes misunderstandings. "An example is that my parents have very strong ideas about how they do things, about who does what," said Rodney. "You can name any task in the household, and it's Mom or Dad. There's no problem; you don't even have to think about it. My mom does the books. She handles all the money, paying the bills, and so on. Dad works. The problem is that neither of us [Rodney and his wife] knows how to take care of the books. So I'd work and come home and thought that the books hopefully would be balanced, and I couldn't understand why [they weren't]. So it took us a while to work these things out."

But as a result of their flexibility, Rodney and Heather also have the rewards of doing the chores to which they are more personally suited, instead of following a predetermined role. He explained: "I hated mowing the lawn; I grew up mowing the lawn. I don't want to mow the lawn. And she was like, 'Mow the lawn; it's tall.' I'm like 'I'm not mowing the lawn.' She went out and mowed it and didn't think it was that bad. So I cook, and she mows the lawn. But it took us three years to realize when we did that, it worked out a lot better." "I was happy. The lawn was nice," Heather commented.

The women also reported some confusion between expecting a more equal marriage and also following their traditional mothers. They said they were intimidated by their mothers-in-law who had immaculate standards of cleanliness, which they were not able or willing to replicate because of other commitments. They also felt themselves resisting their husbands who wanted to share control of the domestic sphere. "We didn't really do this, but I would tell people we had a prenuptial agreement that we would have no cute soaps in our house," said John, a graduate student in mathematics who is married to Leah. "I always hated it when people had those cute soaps and it was just like a symbol, like I didn't want to have it that she controlled everything in the house and you couldn't touch it or do with it how you wanted."

But perhaps a more serious conflict is the compromise of careers. The mothers of all eight of these young adults did not work full time when they were growing up, and they did not expect to have a real career. In contrast, these four wives have college degrees, and two are planning on earning doctorates. In the old days, the husband, the one person with career ambitions, directed the family's relocation according to his educational opportunities and job promotions. But with two ambitious partners in the picture, the result can be constant uprooting. All four couples have moved at least twice in the past several years. "Never throw away your boxes," said Mason, who then moved twice in the next three years after our interview to different engineering jobs in California. For two of these couples, having to compromise on their careers didn't pose a great problem. Pat said that her editing career was more flexible and less important to her than her husband's as a computer engineer was to him. And Rodney is still undecided about what he wants to do but is planning to enroll in an MBA program. But the other two couples, both with two highly career-oriented partners, experienced more conflict. Leah's husband interrupted his education to drop out of the University of Michigan to move with her back to Austin, where she entered a more affordable architecture program. And Shawn felt uprooted moving to Berkeley for his wife's (Dylan's) education. Now back in Austin, Dylan and Shawn are tensely debating the future. He has settled into a career-track job as a technical writer and feels more established and grounded than ever. But Dylan's field, Persian studies, is so specialized that she knows she must move to pursue a doctorate. "We have to have something that is good for both of us," said Dylan. "I mean I'm obviously going to get a Ph.D. in Persian. I don't want to say, 'You know,' imitating an old-fashioned feminine Scarlett O'Hara at barbecue giggle, 'Forget that idea.'"

They also all differ from their parents in putting off having children. With more emphasis on their own relationships, education, and current financial crunches, all have decided to wait. "We feel like we are still learning about each other," Dylan explained. "You feel you want to get at least the major neuroses in your life discovered before you have a family," said Heather. I asked whether they were more practical than their parents. "We have birth control," offered John. "My mom got pregnant when she was 16," said Pat. "She had to get married." "I always thought growing up I would have children by this time," said Heather. "I was growing up and my grandma was like, 'You get married at 20 and have kids at 22.' And I think here I am at 26. I actually found a job that I kind of like, and barring terrible things, it might be something I would want to do for a while." She added that she wants to wait until she and her husband could afford to have her stay home with their children. Like the other couples, she was adamant about avoiding day care while her children were little.

Dylan commented that her generation of women is no more realistic and no less romantic than their predecessors, who expected a man to rescue and define them. "We're engaging in [fantasy] just as much. A woman now wants a career, and her happily ever after is not going to be, you know, 'a house in the suburbs and two kids and a station wagon, da da da.' It's going to be: 'I'm going to find a man who wants me to find a career with him, who is going to treat me exactly the way I want to be treated. I'm going to have kids, and we'll have a two-income family. We're going to go to Europe every year. And we're going to do this, and everything is going to be fine.'"

God and Feminism

Perhaps the greatest challenge to this more egalitarian model of marriage is its threat to some men, as it denies them the centuries of power and domination that they enjoyed in the past. For that reason, the evolving democracy of the American family is by no means universally popular, and the concept of equality is facing a backlash. According to surveys, the group most fiercely opposing the democratic family is the evangelical Christians. Significant minorities of white evangelicals (37 percent) doubt the wisdom of sending women into the workplace, according to a Pew Research Center survey. In June 1998, representatives of the Southern Baptists, representing 16 million members, approved a doctrine that a wife should "submit herself graciously" to her husband. In contrast, three-quarters of all Americans say that society has benefited from women's presence in the workplace (*Diminishing Divide* 1996).

The largest visible uprising against women's power sharing in the family is the Promise Keepers, a national fundamentalist Christian group of men. Founded in 1990, the group has attracted thousands of men to rallies, often held at football stadiums. On one hand, the message seems refreshing and sensible for men to assume more responsibility as husbands and fathers. But the group's leaders have expanded that goal to mean that they should take over the family and not share power with their wife.

Bill Voldt, 37, campus director of the Campus Crusade for Christ at Alabama's Auburn University, explained the group's mission to me. He works while his wife home-schools their five children. They accept the biblical model of a male leader, though he is enlightened enough to help her with her housework. "To me, you can't have two people be in charge," he said. "If everyone is in charge of a football team, to me it wouldn't be common sense. . . . My wife in our marriage, she looks to me to be the leader of the family. But I change more diapers and do more dishes and cook more meals."

The desire of some men to control their family explains some of the fervor of the "family values" debate. Much of the Religious Right's argument for "family values" is often a not-so-thinly veiled attack on feminists and the reality of women taking more power in the family. Indeed, they recognize the sexual evolution's radical shift toward women's taking control, which threatens to overturn hundreds of years of male rule. The Religious Right has pointed out some of the negative effects on the family, such as the weakened commitment to the family and marriage. Although young people appreciate commitment and devotion to the family in principle, they are unable to realize these ideals entirely because of their higher personal demands, which closely mirror the baby boomers' priorities.

I noticed in my interviews a large gap between theory and practice. Even though many women were firm, even passionate, about the importance of marriage and staying home full time with children, in the end they refused to make the sacrifices their grandmothers did, for either emotional or financial reasons. As a result, they are more likely to divorce and work outside the home. Yet women's personal changes and the women's movement itself account for only some of the changes in families. Commitment has also been weakened by global economic pressures. In *Habits of the Heart*, an attack on extreme American individualism, the authors point out that an economic crisis caused by not having enough money to support a family is often unfairly blamed on a lack of "family values": "Being unemployed and thus unable to get married or not having enough income to support an existing family due to downsizing, can certainly be understood as a family crisis. But why is the crisis expressed as a failure of family values?" (Bellah et al. 1996, xii).

6. Choices for Remaining Single: "She's Gonna Make It After All"

I want to teach my daughters that you have to please yourself first. It's the most important lesson you can give them.

—country singer Faith Hill, explaining what she learned from her divorce, to Parade magazine, January 20, 2000

When discussing their lives when they were in their twenties and thirties, the women who I interviewed spent a lot of time telling me how different they were from their parents and grandparents at their age. Usually that difference was marriage: "My grandmother says to me, 'I can't believe you're not married yet,'" said Dionne, a student at Fullerton Junior College in California, with ambitions of becoming a lawyer. "Every time my grandfather comes to see me, 'When are you getting married?' I'm only 23. There's school. There's a lot I want to do before I get married and have babies."

When Lynn, 26, raised in an upper-middle-class Chicago suburban home, accidentally became pregnant during her last year of college at Illinois State University, she decided to keep the baby. Although she recognized the tremendous hardships that decision would bring, she was grateful to have had a wider range of choices than her mother did at her age, including the option to raise a child alone. "I'm not going to be like my mother and depend on somebody. . . . She's still dependent on my father. She doesn't have a lot of her own resources. I guess I don't want to end up like her."

Karen's parents were married early, in their late teens. So when she told her father, a fireman, that she was moving in with her boyfriend but not marrying him, "he did not react well at all," said Karen, 26, an accounting clerk at a hospital outside Los Angeles. "He said, 'When this doesn't work out, nobody is going to want to go out with you.' He has that very fifties mentality. It's like, 'Your reputation is going to be shot.'"

Media commentaries about the status of the American family that cite social phenomena such as single motherhood and divorce use common terms such as "crumbling," "decay," and "breakdown." And indeed, these words often do describe the devastating effects of economic pressures and a general devaluation of commitment by society. However, the media often fail to discuss the *positive* advancements for women behind many of these individualistic shifts, mainly for those women who have the power to control their lives. Many changes, such as divorce, have coincided directly with women's obtaining more education and independent means of support. As women acquire more power in society and marriage becomes more egalitarian, their ability and desire to live without any commitment at all has become more prevalent. Whether by choice or circumstance, more women of the post-boomer generation are remaining single without shame and often with enthusiasm, even if they are living with a man or have children. They see living without marriage as a positive choice, or the best choice possible under the current conditions. Although some of these living situations, especially single motherhood and divorce, are often far from a woman's ideal, they are preferable to the old and even more limited alternatives, including being shipped off secretly to an unwed mothers' home or being forced to stay in an abusive or empty marriage.

Permission to Remain Single

Remaining single, even in one's thirties and beyond, has become so common that young women assume that it is a right; they have forgotten about the strong social stigma attached to being single that was prevalent just thirty years ago. By the late 1970s, only a third of Americans disapproved; 15 percent actually thought it was preferable; and the rest felt it was up to the individual (Bellah et al. 1996, 110). Since then, remaining single has become even more acceptable.

Again, as with most of the sexual changes described in this book, the greatest changes have been with women, and women have gone even further than men to legitimize remaining single. For them, the stigma has always been worse, as exemplified by the negative terms of the past describing a single older woman, such as "spinster" or "old maid," which sharply contrast with the equivalent terms for a single older man like "bachelor" and "playboy." The growing number of single women is testimony to this new permission to remain single: 66.7 percent of women aged 20 to 24, 35.7 percent of women aged 25 to 29, 20.1 percent of women aged 30 to 34, and 13.5 percent of women in their late thirties are single (National Survey 1997, table 32, 43). The average age of marriage for women, 25 (26.7 for men) in 1998, has never been higher (*Marital Status* 1998), and in the past fifteen years alone, the number of single women living alone has increased by almost 50 percent.

The number of married adults of all races has fallen but most for blacks, who are least likely to marry. The reasons are complex, based on a combination of economic and cultural forces and often partly attributed to a loss of high-wage industrial jobs for black men. Among black adults in 1994, fewer than half (43) percent were currently married, a considerable decrease from 64 percent in 1970. In comparison, in 1994, 63 percent of white adults were currently married, down from 73 percent in 1970 (*Marital Status* 1996).

Not only do women of all races have less shame about remaining single, but they also are more likely to be satisfied with this arrangement than in the past. According to several studies of single adults, unattached women are happier than their male counterparts. One reason is that after being divorced, men have fewer coping skills and thus are at greater risk for emotional disorders (Fowlkes 1994, 157). In a 1993 poll of singles, half of the single women said they wanted to get married, compared with two-thirds of the single men. When asked whether people who live alone are basically lonely and unhappy, only 23 percent of the women agreed, compared with 41 percent of the men. Physical well-being is also an issue, as most studies show that marriage adds more years to a man's life than to a woman's (Angier 1998, 10). Other studies explain that single women have much more socially and emotionally developed lives than do single men, with closer and wider networks of friendships (Fowlkes 1994, 156).

Some statistics concerning women's contentment can be found in the business pages. As an indication that they are not just waiting for a man, single women have recently become a major home-buying force. From 1985 to 1997, their share of the housing market rose by a third, accounting for 15 percent of the total number of home buyers. In 1996 and 1997, single women outpaced single men in home ownership as an investment goal (Iovine 1999; statistics from Kermit Baker, economist at Harvard University's Joint Center for Housing Studies).

Single men and women also give different reasons for remaining single. Men more often cite a desire for sexual freedom or a fear of commitment, whereas women mainly avoid marriage to avoid being subordinated to men. "Women who remain single identify the advantages of preserving and fully developing their personal and social autonomy by not accommodating to the secondary status of the traditional wife role," wrote researcher Martha R. Fowlkes in a review of academic literature about single Americans. "The freedom valued by these women, though, is not comparable to the relatively antisocial freedom sought by unmarried men" (1994, 159). Single women commonly use their freedom to get ahead, and they typically have a higher social status than do single men. While upwardly mobile, successful, educated professional men are most likely to marry early, their female equivalents are more likely to stay single. One 1991 study showed that single, never-married women had higher incomes and more education and were professionally more advanced than other women. Single men, on the other hand, were in the lowest such categories (McGavin 1996; study by the University of Wisconsin's Institute for Research on Poverty).

Now, as men traditionally have done, women see their single years in their twenties and thirties as a time to build their career, which means more attention to education and less to children and marriage. Reflecting the motivations of many others that I interviewed, the three single friends in Miami (mentioned at the beginning of chapter 2) discussed how their decisions to remain single contrasted with those of their mothers. All three of their mothers married right after high school, and two of them divorced and then earned a college degree. Accordingly, the three friends said that they were more cautious about marrying, wanting first to learn more about themselves. "I would consider myself knowing my first boyfriend better than my parents knew each other before they got married," said Tammy, 24. "It's not really accepted among our friends, especially in college, to go out and just get married," said Shelly, 24, who is also studying for a graduate degree at Florida International University. "It's frowned upon. Like are you stupid? Have you read the statistics lately?" She added that she viewed delaying marriage as "having family values" because that step ensured that when a woman did marry, she would know herself better and so could better avoid a divorce. This view reflects statistics showing that the earlier a woman marries, the more likely she is to divorce her husband.

Owing to the high divorce rate, many women now have less faith in marriage as a solution to all their problems. African American women are least likely to marry. Stacie S., 26, a social worker who lives in Forest Park, Illinois, said that although she would like to get married, she doesn't expect to do so. She lost faith in married men after seeing them try to score at bars and clubs. "But why are you here with your wedding band, or worse, a tan line from your wedding band? And you're like trying to go home with someone. Every time I see you in the club," she said. "Or you could see it in your own family. Everyone has a cousin, brother, uncle that just goes out, really out, and you know what he's doing. And it gives you no hope for getting married." I asked her if there now was less faith in marriage. "No, there's *no faith* in marriage. And then it's so easy to get out of. Even if you do it, you're like, 'Oh well, it didn't work out. We'll just get a divorce.' They make it so easy now. They're talking about how you can go to a machine now and get your divorce degree, like a little ATM machine that'll shoot the document out. You guys sign it, and take it down to the clerk's office, and it's a done deal."

Cohabitation

The sexual evolution for young women has also resulted in unprecedented levels of cohabitation, or what used to be called "living in sin," as well as a new openness about it. We forget the effort that people took, even in the 1970s, to hide the fact that they were living with someone of the opposite sex. A student would have hesitated mentioning this to a professor; an employee would have not let anyone in the office know. Today, the premise of the popular 1970s sitcom *Three's Company*, that a man has to say he is gay in order to make his living arrangement with two female friends socially acceptable, seems more ridiculous than ever.

While premarital sex is certainly not new and middle-class couples before the 1970s certainly did spend the night with each other, they were less likely to live together openly. In this age of coed residence halls, it is hard to picture the scandal that cohabitation caused a short time ago. In 1968, a Barnard College sophomore, Linda LeClair, became a national celebrity for living off campus with her boyfriend, a Columbia University graduate. The *New York Times* had a front-page story of her battle with college authorities, and *Time* had a feature story on "Linda the Light Housekeeper." But today, cohabitation has become a rite of passage, with more than half of marriages preceded by it. Since 1970, the rate of living together outside marriage has increased fivefold, from 1.1 percent to about 6 percent of couples. About 10 percent of women in their twenties are currently cohabiting with a man, and about half of women 25 to 39 years of age have cohabited with a man at some time during their lives. This practice differs little by gender, education, or income, although it is higher in larger cities. African Americans are more likely to have cohabited at some point in their lifetimes, but not at the present. Finally, the rate of cohabitation is markedly higher for people who have been divorced (National Survey 1997, 5).

Like single people's other family arrangements, cohabitation is reflected in the popular culture. Women's magazines regularly contain features on the special problems of cohabiting couples (see Forsyth 1995, 1997; Nelson 1996). In the "Couple Time" section in the January 1995 *Glamour*, a reader from Davenport, Iowa, wrote in with a romantic suggestion: "When you live with someone and you're getting ready to go out, you see each other during every step of the process. . . . For my birthday this year, my boyfriend took me out on a 'real' date: He got ready at a friend's house before picking me up" (94). In a September 1998 "Q&A Sex" column, a *Mademoiselle* reader, unaware of even recent stigmas against premarital sex, asked: "When my live-in and I visit his folks, they put us in separate rooms. Why do they do this? And what should I say?" (128).

Reflecting the prevalence of cohabitation, about ten women I interviewed were currently living with a man or had done so in the past, and they expressed no shame for their decision. Their parents' reactions were more mixed, however, with about half disapproving. But two others said that their mothers, learning from their own mistakes, even encouraged them to do so. "My mother told me to live with a guy before I get married," said Beth, 24, a student at Texas Women's University. "If she had lived with my dad, she wouldn't have gotten married."

Today this arrangement is the natural result of marriage at a later age (and of more premarital sex), less worry by women about a "bad reputation," and the practicality of sharing a home and expenses. Some of the stigma about cohabitation has diminished because of its status as a rite of passage before marriage. Indeed, half of all first cohabitations do result in marriage. In accordance with this statistic, a significant share of the couples that I interviewed had lived together before marrying. Of the four Austin couples profiled in chapter 5, three had lived together before marrying. While some of their parents disapproved, they generally felt absolutely no shame about cohabiting, especially in the college town of Austin. (To placate their parents, however, they all became engaged while living together.) Their reasons were practical. They decided to live together because they were not yet ready to get married. Furthermore, living together was cheaper than maintaining two households, and besides, they all were really living together anyway. "We made all our meals together," said John. "We would bring food over to the other one's house," said his wife, Leah. "We were going back all the time anyway," said John. Like other couples, they did not view marriage as transforming their relationship. "I don't think that when you get married, something magical happens," said John. "We just felt that we wanted to stay together after the university experience was over with."

Pat and her husband, Mason, also said that when they graduated from college, cohabiting was a natural stage before marriage. "I thought we were living together in college, even though we didn't have the same housing. We were at each other's places all the time. I mean you were over at my apartment freshman year more than you were at your dorm," said Mason to his wife. "My sophomore year, when I was living at a dormitory, people would come up to me sometimes: 'Did you always live here?'" Pat added that her divorced parents did not protest this arrangement because they both had lived unmarried with partners themselves.

The third couple, Heather and Rodney, also emphasized convenience. Even though they did not technically live together in one apartment, they took turns living at each other's cooperative houses, usually filled with roommates. "If you had air conditioning and I didn't, and I was hot, then I'd be over there," said Rodney. "Or if her stove was out, she would come here. We were all living in sub-par housing. So it doesn't take a whole lot of reasons or very important reasons to [cohabit]."

Divorce American Style

With single and cohabiting people cautious about marriage, one might assume that young adults would have a lower divorce rate. But the fastest-growing group of single people are the divorced. The number of divorced adults quadrupled from 4.3 million in 1970 to 17.4 million in 1994, an increase from 3 percent to 9 percent of all adults age 18 and older in 1994. Young adults share the boomer rate, with about 40 percent of marriages still ending in divorce.

Strong competing currents are leveling off the divorce rate. On one hand, more young people do appreciate the benefits and morality of commitment (especially because more of them have been raised by single parents). Yet at the same time, they are also fiercely individualistic, with women having higher standards for how they are treated by their spouses and feeling more secure about leaving a marriage that doesn't suit them. With the boomers paving the way with the skyrocketing divorce rates in the 1960s and 1970s, young women now feel much less stigma than did past generations about getting divorced. With less emphasis on a woman's virginity defining her as quality marriage material, the old feared label of being called "used goods" is as outdated as that of "spinster."

As with other sexual changes for women, their greater earning power is also behind this one. Because more women can support themselves outside marriage, the majority of divorces are now initiated by women. "Marriage has always been an economic arrangement," said Gary Becker, who won the 1992 Nobel Prize for his studies on the effect of economic forces on people's behavior. "It's not new that people are unhappy. Women are now in a stronger position to go ahead with the divorce" (Stein 1995, sec. 4, 1). For the poorest women, another force leading to divorce is increased economic pressures from outside. Poor families are twice as likely to split up, according to U.S. Census Bureau statistics. Of the six women I interviewed who were divorced or separated, five were from low-income families.

Whatever the circumstances, many of the divorced women I interviewed, most of whom married young and were poor, would not have expected or been able, before the 1970s, to get a divorce. Even though their feelings about divorce were mixed, they all were relieved to have this option. One example is Kristi, 29, who had divorced her husband a few years earlier because she wasn't satisfied with their personal relationship. She described the differences in women's higher standards for marriage today. "I'm all for giving it 100 percent and trying, but if I don't see any reason to be there, I'm not the type to just stay married because you have to be married," she said. "Maybe women are realizing they can get divorced now. Before, with our parents, and more so even before our parents, their parents, I don't think that divorce was a thought, and the woman was pretty much subservient to the man in general. I'm not saying everyone was like that. But women are realizing that you don't have to be miserable, if it's something that you're miserable about." While she speaks highly of her first husband, she complained that she wasn't in love with him and that he did not understand her. Having been married right out of high school, at 19, she was not ready for the quiet married life that he wanted. Now, happier in her second marriage, she said, "I feel love like you read in books." She explained her priorities: "I have changed a lot since I was 19. You need to find somebody who is going to change with you, that you're not going to change in different directions. I think that's one of the most important things."

But other women talked about getting a divorce because of more serious complaints, thereby countering the attacks of conservative critics who blame divorce purely on selfishness and who refuse to recognize external economic pressures. The five other women I interviewed who were divorced or separated all described much more serious cases of physical and emotional abuse, which made them feel as though they were living under siege. Like Kristie, Maria, 21, said that she mistakenly married too young, at 16, and for the wrong reasons. She also said that she appreciated the importance of commitment. And just as she appreciated her new freedom, she was critical of people who divorced too easily. "I just don't think that people take [marriage] seriously. Marriage is something sacred, and people don't appreciate it. I think people get married too young. They feel like they have to sometimes."

But while Kristi said that she had been deluded by notions of romance to marry early, Maria saw it as a practical last resort to get out of her parents' poverty-stricken home in Dallas. She ran away with an older German man, and then they moved to Germany and then back to Dallas in a two-year period when she was deeply isolated from others. "I was sort of his housewife. I wasn't happy with him. He was violent with me. And so I just left," she added, describing her divorce at age 18. "I have lived by myself since then." After working at a health food store, Maria is now attending beauty school in Denton, Texas. During those times when she had nowhere to live, her friend Laura, another student there, took her in. "It takes nine months to get certified," she said. "Nine months. If you show up every day." She hopes to have cutting hair as a backup career, with the goal of eventually attending North Texas University or Texas Women's University.

Often the reasons for divorce are complex, a combination of financial and emotional factors. Ivy, 25, who works as a telemarketer in Austin, mentioned financial pressures (as well as her modern standards for fair treatment from her husband) as the central reason for her collapsed marriage. She appreciates being able to end her marriage, recognizing that in the past, pressures from her Catholic and Hispanic family background would have kept her trapped in the marriage, no matter what the circumstances. Still, because of tremendous financial hardships, life is not easy for Ivy. Her two young children are with family in Puerto Rico at least until she is able to get back on her feet. She talked about her stresses when we met in her apartment complex, an oasis with lushly landscaped bushes and flowers in a tattered neighborhood. Her main complaint about her apartment was its emptiness, despite her constant attempts to cheer up the place. During the interview, we sat on the rose-colored carpet of the empty living room. On the bare bar separating the room from the kitchen was a vase with three pink carnations.

"I have the fear that by the time I'm 30, in five years, the experience I've had in life is going to catch up to me and I'm going to look like an old prune," she said, smoking her ever-present cigarette. "It hasn't caught up to me yet. A lot of people say they admire me, and it's not easy. Every day I wake up and it's a struggle. You know. Every day I wake up and I force myself. I have to think about what I have to do for my children, what's right for my kids. I mean my children are tomorrow's future. They are the ones who are gong to make a difference. And if I give myself that example, and if I don't try hard enough for my children, then what are they going to become? And it's a very scary feeling, you know, and I think the most beautiful gift in this world is children."

I asked her about the start of her relationship with her soon-to-be ex-husband (the divorce was in the process of being finalized). "I fell in love. I fell in love. One of those naive young things. . . . He was in the military at that moment. . . . And we had it made, you know. Everything was going great. Economically, financially, emotionally, physically, everything. I guessed it was meant to be. At the time we were three months married and that's when we decided really NOT to have any children, you know. But I guess it wasn't meant to be because in three months of marriage, I got pregnant. It was something like, wow, it was shocking. It was a gift." Ivy had another child a few years later when her husband was stationed in Kileen. Then their problems started. He hurt his back in the army and had trouble getting the care he needed for rehabilitation. His sick mother repeatedly needed emergency surgery and blood donations from her son, forcing the family to fly back and forth to Puerto Rico three times in one year.

To help out, Ivy tried to go back to work to earn more money, but her husband's jealousy forced her to quit two jobs. "The last year and a half, it was just like we grew apart. He had his own little world. We couldn't communicate. He had his own thoughts. I had my own thoughts. You know. The pressure. The children," she said. "I wasn't credited as a wife, as a woman, as a mother. You know, and basically, if a woman feels very low extremes, feels like she isn't doing her job right, as a housewife and mother, then me, I felt, I thought I lost everything."

Ivy cited their financial problems as finally breaking them apart. "I would see the pain in my kids, and I couldn't deal with it. I just couldn't deal with it. It got to the point where we would be out in public, and he would just raise his voice at them. And all I would do is hold on to that pain and lower my head and keep going. . . . I was seeing everything that was going wrong and I tried to communicate with him. We would try to go to counseling. It wasn't there. It was something that wasn't there anymore. . . . So I just decided. I decided, 'I'm sorry. This is it. It's over.'"

Then the financial problems became worse. After three months of separation, he stopped paying child support, as well as their overdue bills and loans. "I lost everything, I lost the house, I lost the car, I lost all my furniture, my children's furniture, because of this." She said the worst part was when their mobile home was repossessed. When she called the finance company, they told her they had her things but failed to add that they would trash them after forty-five days. "When I went to pick it up, it was all gone. All my personal pictures. The newborn pictures of my children. It's like four years have been erased in my life, in my children's life. When my children grow up, what do I have to show them? I have no memories. The only memories I've got is in my head, of what I can tell my children. The pictures, personal items, little things that you treasure, they're all gone. Everything is gone. Four years is gone. No memory trace. No nothing. No proof." Ivy's goal now is to be able to fulfill her "dream of computer science" by going back to college. "I feel I will be qualified for grants with my situation and my income. Me, right now I'm getting by with a job that helps. I'm able to have a roof over my head. Right now I got another raise. I've been working there for ten months and got two raises: $6.15 hour. Rent is $359, all utilities paid. And then I have to buy my own food, transportation, cigarettes. My kids are receiving child support in Puerto Rico. I send them money for what they need."

Single with Children

When Ivy gets her children back, she will join the growing ranks of single-parent families. When they plan their lives, most women in college do not realize how great the odds are that they will be raising their children alone. Today, one-third of single, divorced, and widowed women between 18 and 34 have children. In 1998, single parents accounted for about three out of ten, or 27.3 percent, of all parent-child living arrangements, compared with only 13 percent in 1970. A majority of single-parent families, 64 percent, were white. But a higher proportion of black families were headed by single parents: two-thirds of black families, compared with 25 percent of white ones. (In 1970, the corresponding proportions were 36 percent for blacks and 10 percent for whites.) (*Household and Family Characteristics* 1995). A two-parent home is no longer the most common family arrangement. The 1995 movie *Toy Story* did not feel the need to explain that the main character had only a mother and no father. Formerly based on married units, family sitcoms are commonly structured without a husband, from *One Day at a Time* in the 1970s to *Grace under Fire* and *Murphy Brown* in the mid-1990s to *Once and Again* in the late 1990s.

The factors leading to single motherhood have changed. A decade ago, children were twice as likely to have lived with a divorced parent than a never-married one. Today, they are just as likely to live with a parent who has never married. In 1994, about 36 percent of single parents have never married; 37 percent have been divorced; and 23 percent were separated from spouses because of marital discord or another reason. A greater proportion of whites are divorced, and twice as many white single mothers are divorced as are married with their spouse absent or never married. These numbers are reversed for blacks, with about three times as many never married than divorced or married with a spouse absent (*Marital Status* 1996).

The rise in unwed motherhood has been dramatic for all groups. From 1983 to 1993, out-of-wedlock births soared 70 percent and then leveled off. Today, one-third of births are to unmarried mothers, and the rate for white women has doubled since 1980.

Despite social outcries about the promiscuity of teens, since the 1970s, women in their twenties and older accounted for 70 percent of out-of-wedlock births. Through the 1990s, the birthrate for teens fell; it stayed constant for women in their twenties, and it rose slightly for women in their thirties. The number of out-of-wedlock teenage births actually dropped by 50 percent between 1957 and the mid-1980s; the numbers seem larger now only because unwed mothers are no longer hidden from society. In the past, they were much more likely to marry the fathers or be shuttled off to an unwed mothers' home and later give up their children for adoption. Today, these girls go to school obviously pregnant, openly discussing their circumstances. (In reality, the teenage birthrate reached an all-time low in 1997, reflecting the overall record low U.S. birthrate.) At the same time, married women are having fewer children, further inflating the share of babies born to unmarried mothers. Also contradicting the stereotypical belief, the majority of unmarried births are unintended pregnancies, not motivated by the promise of welfare benefits (National Survey of Family Growth 1995 report for Child Trends Inc., a nonpartisan research firm, prepared for the U.S. Department of Health and Human Services).

Unlike divorced and single women, never-married single mothers are more likely to be less educated and be from lower-income groups. The odds of becoming an unmarried mother sharply decline as educational achievement rises. About half of births to high school dropouts occur out of wedlock, whereas among college graduates, the rate is just 6 percent. Forty percent are long-term welfare recipients, compared with 14 percent of divorced women, and 50 percent are poor, compared with 10 percent of the general population.

It is significant, however, that professional and educated women are beginning to see single motherhood as an option. According to the U.S. Census Bureau, the number of single professional women who become mothers has tripled since the 1980s, and the number of those with some education has doubled in that time, reaching 11.3 percent in the mid-1990s (Bachu 1993).

The reasons for unwed motherhood are disputed. Liberals like Harvard professor William Julius Wilson blame it on economic crises that produce fewer eligible men. Marriage is simply out of the grasp of poor women, as fewer partners are available to them who are able to support a family. While falling wages cannot explain these rates entirely, unwed motherhood is indeed more common in areas with few young employed men. Moreover, these factors seem to be the product of a modern, industrialized society and are not unique to the United States. The number of out-of-wedlock American births are comparable to those of other Western nations, with one-third of all births in Britain and France being out of wedlock, and about half of all births in Denmark and Sweden.

Today, some unmarried women intentionally become mothers. Of the women polled by Virginia Slims/Roper in 1990, one-third said that if they were single and nearing the end of their childbearing years, they would consider having a child on their own. Likewise, the term "shot-gun marriage" has become outdated. In the 1960s, marriages immediately followed half of unwed pregnancies, but by 1989 only a third of them led to marriage, according to U.S. Census Bureau reports. One reason for the decline of the "shotgun marriage" is that women have less faith in marriage as an automatic solution to their problems. As observed in chapter 5, more young women define marriage as an emotional relationship rather than a financial arrangement. "I don't want a guy to marry me because I'm going to have a child," said Vanessa, 25, a single black mother in New York City who is raising her 4-year-old daughter on her own. "I want him to marry me because he loves me. He accepts me for what I am." She added that if he does not, "you'll just break up anyway."

Two women whom I interviewed represented the greatest changes in single motherhood in the 1990s. Like divorced women, they have mixed feelings about the effects of their choice on their children but ultimately take the view that they have made the best decision possible under the circumstances. Lynn, 26, introduced in the beginning of the chapter, does not fit the stereotype of the single mother. She lives with her parents in their new custom-built ranch house in an affluent section of a far-south Chicago suburb, a former farming town. Her father, who belongs to a country club, is a retired general manager of a steel company. In the past, at least before the 1980s, Lynn's life after her accidental pregnancy in college would have been much different. She said she would have hidden the pregnancy and given her child up for adoption or have been forced to marry the reluctant father. (Even though she is prochoice, she said that she did not believe in abortion for herself.) But in the 1990s, she had another choice: raising her son herself. While she regretted quitting college, she said she was never as enthusiastic about it as she was about her son, who could not wait. "I guess I felt that this was more important," she said. "Whereas with college, I knew I could go back."

Above all, Lynn knew that she was not alone. Two friends from college, including a roommate, had also decided to raise their babies on their own. "Without [my roommate], I would have had a harder time picturing what was going to happen to me," she said. "But I knew that she made it. And she was supportive. She told me it would be OK. 'You can do it. Your family will support you.'" But Lynn wasn't sure if she could count on her parents' support. On what she describes as "the worst day of my entire life," she told them. They both were shocked and upset, with her father hardly acknowledging the pregnancy until its final weeks. But when the baby was born, he started to feel pride in his first grandchild and was soon showing off pictures of him to his friends. Like Americans in general, he has moved from outrage to a resigned acceptance of unwed mothers.

Today, Lynn's parents' main contribution to her and her son is giving them a rent-free place to live. With her part-time job as a sales clerk at a local mall, Lynn can pay the rest of her expenses, including her phone bills and clothes for her child. After a long battle, the father of her child, who was her boyfriend for almost five years, grudgingly agreed to have child support deducted from his paycheck. He works as the operations manager of a women's clothing store in another mall downtown. Only recently, in the child's second year, has he warmed up to the idea of being a father, paying him additional visits. When the child was born, Lynn explained, "he had just graduated. He was looking for work. So he was at a point where he wanted to be independent and start working. And he didn't want the responsibility at all. He just wanted to do his own thing. He wanted to go out with his friends."

Lynn is ambivalent about the lack of pressure that the baby's father feels to marry her, which would have made her life easier financially. But in the long term, she knows that they probably would have been divorced. "I guess that this is what was meant to be. I don't think that we were meant to be together. We argue a lot."

The only time Lynn has felt any stigma is while talking to older adults at her workplace, ironically, a maternity store. "One man said, 'Is your husband excited about the baby?' And then I said, 'Well, I'm not married.' And then I felt really stupid. I guess I don't want to admit that I'm ashamed, but maybe just a little bit because . . . people from the older generation, I know what they're thinking: 'Oh gosh, she isn't married.'" Another problem is isolation. All her friends from high school live in Chicago, an hour north, and going out with them is a major production requiring a baby-sitter and spending time away. Also, in her affluent suburb, she is surrounded by stay-at-home mothers who don't share her money worries, making her feel even more alone.

Despite her confidence in her decision to keep her son, Lynn finds this life more difficult than she expected. Her energy is spent on caring for her son and worrying about their future, with no time for herself, not to mention dating. Her goal is to take computer classes and get a 9-to-5 job, with a schedule more amenable to day care, and eventually to move into a two-bedroom apartment. Like other independent single women, she looks only to herself for rescue. "I'm not going to sit around waiting for some guy to pick me up off my feet. I can't depend on my parents forever. They're already in their sixties. So, there's going to be a point where I have to take care of this by myself."

Another single mother I interviewed was Aimee, 23, a senior at the College of St. Catherine, in St. Paul, Minnesota. Her fate was also different from what it would have been a generation ago. Aimee knew this because her mother was a single pregnant student at the same school in the 1970s. But like many others at the time, she and her boyfriend were forced to get married by their strongly religious parents. They divorced five years later.

"My grandma, who forced my mom and dad to get married, came to me when I told her I was pregnant and said, 'I made a big mistake with your parents,'" said Aimee. "This is my Irish-Catholic grandmother. And she said, 'I really want to tell you. Do not make that same mistake. If you can do that, we'll all be here to support you and we're glad you didn't get an abortion. And everything will be fine. Don't get married. If you don't love him, don't get married.'" Today, Aimee feels almost no shame as a single mother at a liberal Catholic women's university. For an internship for a student office, she compiled a report on single mothers at the college, who numbered 376 out of a total student body of fewer than 1,500 for the 1995/96 academic year. Aimee noted that only once did a nun admonish her for being a single parent, when she was not able to do an assignment because of her child. Like Lynn, Aimee is prochoice, but she said that after considerable reflection, she decided that having the baby "was the right thing for me to do. I spent almost the whole time of my pregnancy in virtual seclusion praying a lot in my mom's home and my home, my childhood room," she said. Today, Aimee's job as a college apartment manager pays her rent, and a part-time job at the student life office also keeps her afloat. She now plans to go to law school, as her LSATs were high enough to guarantee admission and to support herself and her daughter with loans.

Welfare Mothers

Aimee also receives a government day-care subsidy, Medicaid, and food stamps. Despite the stereotypes, she is a typical welfare mother: she is white, has one child, and sees welfare as only a temporary source of support. But she does feel some qualms about receiving public aid, more than she does about being a single mother. While she realizes that unwed motherhood is more acceptable now, being on welfare is less tolerated and excused. "I know in the early 1970s, these programs were really accepted, and in fact, women were encouraged to take advantage of these programs. And now there's a social stigma attached to being a welfare mom, that you're producing generations of children that are ill suited to live in our society and blah, blah, blah."

Indeed, Aimee felt so shamed for being on welfare that she got off it temporarily to work as a sales clerk at a department store. But then she realized that she was in the same impoverished financial situation with even less time for school and her daughter and that her long-term future was being jeopardized by short-term gains. She is now grateful for her decision to return to public aid, because if she had waited any longer, the new welfare restrictions imposed at the time of our interview, in late 1996, would have prevented her from receiving benefits.

Aimee also admitted that at first, she felt some guilt about raising her daughter without a father. Like many young women, she has mixed feelings about weighing her needs against those of her children. "It was the wrong way to raise a child. It was like bad, like I was hurting her. It wasn't even that

I felt pressure to get married. It was just like I was bad. I was bad and wrong. . . . And what I was doing was really going to be hard for her. And I really struggled with that." She later realized, however, that besides parents, communities are responsible for raising children. She agrees with the premise of Hillary Clinton's 1996 book, *It Takes a Village.* "The Catholic Church should not be promoting a prolife stance and not taking in children and raising children and being there for parents who choose to do that that way," she said. "It's the right-to-life groups that will be there until you decide not to get the abortion, but then you're on your own."

Other mothers on welfare whom I interviewed, minorities from low-income, urban backgrounds, were more apt to discuss government aid as a positive and shame-free choice. As the Religious Right fears, welfare is often preferable to a husband, giving women independence and control that they would not ordinarily enjoy. Narda, 25, originally from Ecuador, said that she greatly prefers government aid to her ex-husband. In fact, living without him is a relief. "I think that I can do a better job with me being in charge of the kids. They can understand the messages that I try to give them more clearly than if there was a second person putting in their own views. There is no way they can get mixed messages." She sees this as a better arrangement than she had growing up in her two-parent household. "I find that the way my mother was, she had to always double-check with my father what he would like for us to do, how he wanted us to be raised. There was always that kind of conflict because he was a hard person to deal with. I don't have that problem. It's just me." At the time of our interview, she was planning to take care of her two small children and then go back to school. "I don't consider it [delaying education] a sacrifice. I mean I'm only 25. My kids are only going to be this age for a short time, and pretty soon they'll be going to school full time. And I'll have time all to myself. I'm just waiting when the right time comes. That's all."

Another single mother I interviewed with her, Vanessa, admitted that government aid was her best choice for raising her 4-year-old daughter. Despite her tireless efforts, she has yet to receive support from her daughter's father, who has moved to another state. As Aimee acknowledged, life for welfare mothers changed in the mid- to late 1990s with "welfare reforms," which basically mean "no welfare." Without welfare, single mothers' options for independence are few. More low-income and poorly educated single mothers will remain in oppressive marriages, give away their children for adoption, have abortions, or seek desperate means of support, such as in the streets.

Abortion as a Right

For all women who become pregnant accidentally, other options, both old and new, are available. Despite some mixed emotions about the subject, this generation of young women has grown up taking for granted their right to have an abortion. As single women increasingly accept birth control as a right, surveys show that young women especially have overwhelmingly become prochoice (despite some qualifications regarding circumstance). But young American women's actions speak more strongly than opinions in support of this right. According to the National Health and Social Life Survey, 23.5 percent of conceptions in women aged 18 to 24 end in abortion (Laumann et al. 1994, 458). After abortion was legalized in 1973, the annual rate rose steadily until 1980 and then dropped to the 1975 level of twenty abortions per one thousand women aged 15 to 44 (Cooper 1998).

Abortion is mainly used by young single women to maintain independence and control over their lives, which is one reason that it is so threatening to conservatives. Eighty-two percent of women seeking abortions are unmarried, either in school or working. And even though blacks and Hispanics have higher abortion rates, the majority of women getting abortions are white and in their teens and early twenties. Fitting this profile of independence is Kris, 22, an office manager in Anaheim, California, cited throughout this book. She said when she recently became pregnant, she knew she was not ready for a child. She had witnessed the hardships of her twin sister, a new single mother whom she helps support, and did not want to follow in her path. She calls her decision to have an abortion her first "proud, responsible step" to take control of her life and not passively accept her fate.

Although the stigma against abortion has changed, it has not necessarily diminished. Before 1973, the shame of having premarital sex was paramount; today, with members of the extremist Christian antiabortion movement brandishing pictures of aborted fetuses, women who have abortions may be accused of being selfish murderers. Writing in *The Nation,* Professor Rosalind Petchesky, author of *Abortion and Woman's Choice,* discussed the difference in perception:

> When I was a teenager in Tulsa, Oklahoma, in the late 1950s and early 1960s, the abortion experience was of course steeped in shame, but it had little to do with harm to the fetus. My generation of young middle-class women knew nothing about the fetus. Like the pregnancy scare and

"unwed motherhood," abortion meant shame only because it connoted sex, you'd "done it" without the sanctity of marriage. (1990, 732)

However, other controls on abortion today are more formidable than stigmas. Even though abortion is legal, it is harder to find a doctor to perform it. In the 1990s, legislators imposed new restrictions on poor and young women, with less government funding for abortion and more laws requiring parental consent. Antiabortion forces have escalated from angry rhetoric to violence and terrorism, bombing clinics and terrorizing doctors. Nonetheless, young women still perceive abortion as a right. As in all other modern industrialized societies, young women in America continue to take for granted the control of their own reproduction and their sexual and financial independence.

Adoption

A more traditional and socially acceptable solution for unwed pregnant women is to give up their child for adoption, and it still is a choice for single women who do not want an abortion, although it is less common than before abortion was legalized in the 1970s. What has changed are the options available to birth mothers, now allowing them to tailor the adoption to their terms and to do it more openly.

The one woman I interviewed who mentioned adoption and changes in it in the past twenty years was Bellinda, 22, a full-time secretary and part-time student (and the sister of Pat, a member of the four Austin couples profiled). When Bellinda was 20, she gave away her daughter for reasons similar to those that lead women to have an abortion: she wanted to continue her education and knew that she could not afford a child. While this decision has been immensely painful, especially on her daughter's birthday, she still is glad she made this choice. She did not feel comfortable with her mother's suggestion of abortion, as she had some hopes that she could raise the child herself. She also was influenced by her Catholic background and felt an instant bond with the pregnancy. Finally, she did not accept her father's suggestion of marrying the child's father, an ex-boyfriend whom she knew would make an irresponsible father.

As the founder of an Internet support group for birth mothers, Bellinda is a keen observer of differences between the generations. She observes that the major change for young birth mothers is more openness, through their pregnancy and afterward. "It's not so hidden," said Bellinda. "You don't necessarily send the birth mothers off to some little girls' home or to your great aunt in Michigan. My mom didn't want my grandmother to know about it. But other than that, I think most of my aunts and uncles and cousins know about it. And I talk to people about it. So I think it's more open than it was." Because they have less shame and there is a greater demand for adoptions, the young mothers on Bellinda's e-mail list also have more leverage than did past generations in selecting the type of adoption, such as regular meetings with their birth children to a yearly letter and pictures from the adoptive parents (her arrangement). As testimony, a framed picture of her laughing daughter at her second birthday party sits on her desk in her residence hall at the University of Texas at Austin. It is both a painful and affirming reminder of her decision.

But Bellinda also sees that birth mothers have a long way to go, pointing out a lack of information about their rights and options. She recognizes that birth mothers are historically an extremely isolated and weak group, who can only become stronger through organizing and awareness. As examples, she says they need better counseling about the process and should know what type of financial support they are entitled to during their pregnancy. Just as young women have taken control of their own sexuality, they also are deciding what they will do if they become pregnant.

Clearly, these diverse single living arrangements and options represent both gains and losses. Young American women have a wider range of choices than their mothers and grandmothers did, with less shame and more power to make them. But many young women also lament a major limit of this more individualistic and high-pressure society: severed relations with men. That is, they find fewer men who are willing and able to commit to others. Also, despite some gains in equality, more women make emotional demands from relationships and are less willing to settle for shabby treatment.

Conflicts with men have had the most damaging effect on women who have children. As a result, these women assume an unfair share of the burden of raising children and accordingly account for most of the poor families in America. Most of the nine single mothers I interviewed were angry about men's lack of support, even though none of them wanted to be married to their child's father. Some blamed society for not pressuring men to be responsible, if not by marrying them, at least by helping support their children. "In the olden days, you would see the father feel like he was obligated to help with the children. In this generation, a lot of guys feel it should be up to the mothers to do everything, take care of the child," said Vanessa.

"I think it changed because some guys grew up to be like that. They think it's cool that they should do that."

While looking to men for change, the women I interviewed also mentioned the role of communities and government, which have the power to help them become independent. Without men to support them, single women need pay equity, child care, health care, job flexibility and training, and fairer systems for securing government aid and child support from fathers. But many conservatives would argue for seemingly easier solutions, such as making women dependent on men, as was the case in the 1950s. In this modern society, however, there is no turning back. Women have gained and value independence, and besides, the current economy does not support one-income families and their modern standards of living. For better or for worse, commitments between women and men have weakened in the United States, as they have in every other industrialized nation. Just as women and men have more freedom and more choices than ever before, they also have less reason to rely on others. As a result, unlike their mothers and grandmothers, a great number of women today in their twenties and thirties are remaining single and discovering that it is both a liberating and often a necessary fact of life.

7. Lesbians and Bisexuals Out and Proud: "The Groping Generation"

When I told my parents I was gay, . . . they were concerned for me for . . . the problems that I was going to have with society. And I told them, I said, "I'm not going to have a problem with society. It's society who has the problem."

—Allison, University of Miami student on MTV's
Sex in the '90s documentary

I slept with a woman once and I thought, "Am I gay? Am I straight?" Then I realized I'm just slutty! Where's my parade?

—comedian Margaret Cho, from her 1999 one-woman show,
"I'm the One I Want"

It is Sunday morning in the Bible Belt. Like other churches in Dallas, the Cathedral of Hope is filled to capacity. Few spaces are left in its vast mall-like parking lot, and inside the cavernous sanctuary, there is standing room only. Upon entering, a visitor notices some subtle differences between this church and the others. The stained-glass front, in addition to a picture of a dove of peace and an Easter lily, includes intertwined pairs of the circular symbols for both women and men. Those lining up to accept communion stand either alone or in same-sex couples. Beneath a towering white cross on the back wall and in front of rows of pillars spelling out the word HOPE is a pink triangular marble altar in the shape of a well-known symbol of homosexuality. The minister, dressed in long white robes, calls out: "When the brokenness of the world threatens to break you, remember when He calls. . . . Once again we come here to receive from you, as you have given to us in the past . . . that we may go from your table as courageous people."

Like other churches, the Cathedral of Hope contains many symbols. But this one, the largest gay church in the United States, with more than one thousand members, goes further to provide unique testimony to the hopes and sensibilities of a new generation. The members of the Cathedral of Hope, like other gays, lesbians, and bisexuals, have gone beyond shame and self-hatred to feel a new sense of pride and entitlement to live openly and visibly. This means that they have new comfort entering, and transforming, such traditionally heterosexual and establishment institutions as the Christian Church.

The Cathedral of Hope, dedicated in 1993, is part of the Universal Fellowship of Metropolitan Community Churches (UFMCC), a denomination founded in 1968 in Los Angeles. Today, it has more than three hundred churches around the world, a majority of them in forty-seven U.S. states. The UFMCC sponsored the mass wedding at the 1993 March on Washington. Its dean, Mel White, is a famous former insider of the Christian Right and was a speech writer for such figures as Jerry Falwell, Jim Bakker, and Oliver North. His 1993 book, *Stranger at the Gate: To Be Gay and Christian in America*, details his years of repression, desperate marriage, and disillusionment with the Religious Right's escalating gay bashing.

The vast size of the Cathedral of Hope is understandable, considering the enormous cultural significance of churches in the South. It supports many aspects of the lives of its diverse members, such as constructing a nursing home for elderly gays and lesbians, a television ministry to help counter fundamentalist Christian views on homosexuality and religion, and a retreat and wellness center for homosexual teenagers rejected by their parents.

I visited the Cathedral of Hope after interviewing two of its loyal members, partners Annette and Crystal. As they discussed the significance of the church in their lives, they also revealed their generation's new struggles and successes in living openly in the mainstream. Annette, 30, a student at Texas Women's University, described breaking from her Catholic faith in her rural Louisiana town. This was the main problem she faced in coming to terms with her homosexuality, a conflict that plagued her for nine years. "For me, the struggle was that I was brought up in a Catholic family and community. It was like 'Oh my goodness, if this is true, if I'm one of *those*,' which is how I thought of it, 'Am I going straight to hell?' And so for the longest time I just kept questioning. I've always been spoon-fed that God puts you through tests, you know. So I thought, 'Oh gosh, this must be one of those tests they told me about. Why me? Why is He doing this to me? Why did He come down here in this little bog town in Louisiana and take me of all people?'. . . Finally I had to come to terms, and I guess you'd say teach myself in a sense, and separate myself from that issue of religion, that I was OK and that I could be indeed in love with a woman and still be OK and I wasn't going to hell and the whole nine yards. But I really seriously thought that for the longest time. And once I was with a woman, I had all these dreams about the end of the world." Today, ironically, Annette still considers herself a Christian. The same force, religion, which caused her so much pain earlier in her life, is now an important source of her community, support, and faith.

In our era, more young lesbians and bisexuals than ever before, like Annette and Crystal, have stopped living a lie. Instead, in every possible aspect of their lives—their families, schools, workplaces, churches and synagogues, and the media—they have come out. While much progress still needs to be made—with those in liberal urban communities enjoying the most freedoms and discrimination, though hate crimes are still being committed—the general range of life choices available to them is staggering when compared with those in the 1970s and 1980s. More cities, universities, and major corporations offer partnership benefits to same-sex couples. The media offer syndicated openly gay and lesbian columnists and TV stars (a record number of thirty gay characters were on network series in the fall of 1997) (Gay and Lesbian Alliance against Defamation, "TV Features More Gay Characters," *Chicago Sun-Times,* 18 August 1997, 38). Without fanfare, gay couples appear alongside the straight ones in the long-running MTV documentary series *Sex in the '90s* and the hit game show *Who Wants to Be a Millionaire?* At colleges, gay and lesbian studies classes and peer-education and activist groups are part of the landscape along with football games and homecoming floats. Reflecting this change in presence, polls show young people with new, if grudging, acceptance. According to a 1998 Gallup Poll, seven out of ten people aged 65 and older believe that homosexual behavior is wrong, but only five out of ten aged 19 to 29 have that view (Berke 1998).

Just a short time ago, without this visible and organized movement, gay women had very different choices. Although life for any single woman was difficult, living as a lesbian was virtually impossible. In the 1950s, police regularly harassed and arrested homosexuals when they gathered in groups. Psychologists branded them as sick and abnormal. Parents institutionalized their daughters if they showed such symptoms, in hopes of a "cure." Mired in shame and isolation, lesbians had not organized to defend their rights as individuals. The media offered few lesbian images outside pulp fiction or lurid confessional accounts, which mainly portrayed them as tortured, depraved she-men out to recruit innocent young victims. Except for limited bohemian enclaves, lesbians were forced to live completely closeted, typically marrying a man and repressing their true desires.

This movement for lesbian and bisexual freedom may be the greatest sexual revolution of the 1990s. More than any other sexual change described in this book, lesbianism represents young women's greatest sense of entitlement to conduct their sex lives on their own terms. These women certainly qualify as sexually aggressive "superrats." The more choices available for living openly lesbian, including membership in a gay church, new parenting options, and even special vacation-cruise lines, are possible because of a combination of factors unique to our times. In the 1960s and 1970s, socialist and activist movements laid the vital groundwork. The sexual revolution gave its blessing, especially to women, for sex not tied to reproduction. Specific homosexual sex practices and lifestyle arrangements, such as oral sex and cohabitation and single parenthood, became more common in the heterosexual population. The mood of the era encouraged sexual experimentation.

The gay liberation movement exploded after quietly beginning in the 1950s, when the first homosexual political organizations were founded: Mattachine, started in 1950 by five Los Angeles men who had been members of the Communist Party, and the first lesbian organization, Daughters of Bilitis, established in 1955 in San Francisco by Del Martin and Phyllis Lyon. In the more liberal 1960s, more militant groups, such as the Homophile Action League, were established, borrowing from the civil rights movement the techniques of boycotting and picketing. Mirroring black-pride slogans such as "black is beautiful," they chanted, "gay is good." They became more active after the first gay riots in 1969 when police raided the Stonewall Inn, a Greenwich Village gay bar, and they were buoyed by a new generation of educated, articulate young people who had higher expectations of how they should be treated.

The budding women's movement gave new power and status to lesbians. Through reforms in work and education, women gained new options for self-sufficiency and alternatives to depending on a man. Fostered by critiques of the current inequality of marriage, feminist ideologies also gave new social permission to women to live without a man. Feminists pointed to women's relationships with men as the cornerstone of their oppression, and some radical feminists even elevated lesbianism as a political act, as the truest form of feminism and absolute identification with and devotion to women. "I became a lesbian because the culture that I live in is violently anti-woman," wrote one of the most famous lesbian feminists, Rita Mae Brown, in 1976. "How could I, a woman, participate in a culture that denies my humanity? . . . To give a man support and love before giving it to a sister is to support that culture, that power system" (Faderman 1991, 207).

In the 1990s, building on this foundation and challenging some basic assumptions about lesbians, a new generation of sexual rebels emerged with their own sensibilities. Unlike lesbians and bisexuals in the past, who were faced with more oppression and fewer rights, these younger women do not have to choose between living on the margin or pretending to be straight. Taking their rights for granted, young gays, bisexuals, and lesbians are much more open than their predecessors. "There is no set thing," said Winsome Gayle, 21, a lesbian activist at Rutgers University in New Jersey. "The set thing, if there is a set thing, is to do what is best for you. That's a feeling that I'm getting from the movement now. There is no one shoving their views down other people's throats. It's just saying to whatever straight community that is out there, just saying to them that we deserve rights."

In the recent past, lesbians conformed to very strict roles in both behavior and appearance. In the 1950s, some working-class lesbians imitated straight gender norms by becoming either extremely masculine (butch) or extremely feminine (femme) in their fashion and personality. (This was partly a survival mechanism to avoid being recognized as a female couple in public.) In the 1970s, radical lesbian feminists were separatist and attempted to build their own politically correct Lesbian Nation. Like the 1950s butch/femmes, they adopted a strict code of dress and behavior, but theirs was a different type of conformity, to styles that defied the traditional female requirement of pleasing men. True to stereotype, many cut their hair short, denounced capitalism, wore "natural" unconfining clothes like jeans and natural fiber shirts, and celebrated "honest" working-class professions by working with their hands. They also downplayed their sexuality as defining their lesbianism, instead pointing out political and egalitarian angles.

The less rigid lesbian roles today can be seen in young women's fashion styles. Today's young lesbians are not divided neatly into butches or femmes or earthy granola woodswomen. Winsome Gayle, a "feminine" black woman from suburban New Jersey, made the same observation. She was dressed plainly, with a short bob and a plain Gap-type sweater and jeans. "There is no butch/femme thing. Some younger lesbians may do it to some degree, but it's maybe 10 percent. There's a dyke thing. It's in between. Just a strong woman. There is no code that you have to go by. That stuff is gone. As long as you're confident in yourself, as long as you're you. That's all that matters."

At the same time, young lesbian and bisexuals are more generally "out" and individualistic than were the activists in the 1980s homosexual rights movements. The older generation emphasized assimilating and reassuring straight people that they were just like them. They also started groups like the National Gay and Lesbian Task Force and the Human Rights Campaign Fund, two organizations that work closely with the government and politicians. In contrast, observed lesbian staff writer Achy Obejas in the *Chicago Tribune*, "the younger generation has filled up the ranks of ACT UP and Queer Nation [started in 1990], which rely heavily on civil disobedience and street theater to often mock government and politicians" (1993, 6). While the older generation pushed for civil rights legislation, the younger one is making more radical and personal demands, such as for gay marriage and adoption rights.

The more aggressive and open sensibilities of young lesbians and bisexuals is evident in the recent transformation and adoption of the word *queer*, a term that the older generation of gay activists shunned as an insult because it signified their differences from the majority. It also drew attention to their sexuality, which gay activists have tried to downplay. But younger people have proudly reclaimed this word and others, including *fag*, *fairy*, and *dyke*. Accordingly, many campus groups have recently renamed themselves as "queer," partly also as a way to unify the many new publicly acknowledged orientations, such as bisexuals and the transgendered (people who do not live according to the gender of their birth). For example, at the University of Chicago, the Gay and Lesbian Alliance changed its name in the 1990s to Queers and Associates.

Four Friends

The women I interviewed who best represented these modern trends are four working- and middle-class friends (three lesbians and one bisexual) who live in Denton, Texas, a small city that recently became part of the northward suburban sprawl of Dallas. Three out of four, including Annette and Crystal, gave me permission to use their real full names, a decision that they said reflected their strong views about their right to be visible.

"We each have a T-shirt that says 'Freedom of expression: if you don't like it, don't look,'" said Annette, speaking with a lilting and slurred Louisiana accent. "That's where I'm coming from. Yeah, I do think I have a right to show affection in public to refer to her [her partner] as who she really is to me and not have to cover it up. And I do think that I have a right to that just being a citizen of this country. And in using my full name . . . I'm going to be myself. As long as we stood back and remained within the closet, that is where we were going to stay."

Crystal, also a student at Texas Women's University, added that this open attitude contrasted with the greater inhibitions of older lesbians. They had less ambitious goals of just being tolerated and not persecuted as they lived their sexual identities in secret. Crystal described this attitude as "keep it in the bedroom or keep it in the house. Don't hold hands in public. There's no need to go out and run and tell everybody that you're gay. Just kind of know it within yourself. Whereas the younger generation, they're very out, they're very proud, and they want equal rights. I see that a lot." When I asked her for an example, she mentioned seeing older lesbian couples on campus. "It's like they're in their own little bubble and they don't want to touch each other. Whereas younger people walk around campus holding hands; they grope at each other." "The groping generation," joked Annette. "Yeah, the groping generation," said Crystal, 20, who wore a white T-shirt with a pink triangle.

Another difference from some older feminist lesbians is that this generation does not have a political ideology but sees the gay liberation movement as more visible in and relevant to their lives, addressing such issues as bans in the military. As a result, unlike many radical lesbian feminists in the 1970s, these women are lesbians for purely personal, not political, reasons. "In my view, a lot of the older lesbians had bad sexual experiences with men, got totally wrapped up in the women's movement, and turned to women for their sexual expressions," said Crystal. "But they didn't truly love women, love women for women . . . love what they looked like, what they felt like, what they smelled like. And the younger generation of lesbians truly love women. I mean they look at women and they love women, and that's why they're with women. . . . I think the older generation of lesbians are more conformist." "Conformists to their own norm," added Annette.

Openly mixing into the mainstream and less political than some feminist lesbians, Crystal and Annette also feel comfortable getting married. They already had set a date for their church commitment ceremony, which they will consider a bona fide marriage (though no state except Vermont legally recognizes gay marriages). They had just bought rings, which are set with each other's birthstones and interlaced with diamonds. In the next three to five years, which they consider a test of the stability and endurance of their relationship, they plan to have kids. "I think the marriage between us two is going to be just like it would in a heterosexual relationship," said Crystal.

"Bills are going to be shared. Money is going to be shared. If I get insurance, I am going to get an insurance company that covers my spouse. And I will make sure that the spouse will cover Annette. And that's the thing with gay rights. I want to be able to put her on my insurance and call her my spouse. And that's what I want . . . I plan to do everything the same."

Just like the heterosexuals I interviewed about marriage as a partnership, Annette and Crystal will not have rigid roles in their marriage based on "female" or "male" jobs. Instead, they will be themselves. "Say if it has to do with loading the car or doing 'Mr. Fix-Up' things," said Crystal. "Sometimes I take on that role and sometimes I pick on the role of also doing the dishes and doing the laundry. And it's more of whoever is in the position to do whatever needs to be done. If I'm sick and I need to be taken care of, she'll take care of me. And I'll do the nurturing as well. It's almost a male and female role inside each of us. I mean I could be masculine, and I can be feminine, if that's what you want to label it."

But before Crystal and Annette and their friends reached this level of peace and belonging, they endured many years of turmoil. Their struggles represent the common journey of young American lesbians to discover communities where they are able to find themselves. This process can be the most painful for women like them, from conservative towns and families without a visible lesbian presence. Still, they had an easier time than did the older generations, who usually never found such affirming communities and either never left the closet or came out much later in life. All four Denton women learned of this alternative to living as they really are only after moving to Denton, the home to two universities and a small gay community. Lisa, 24, a graduate of Brigham Young University who was raised in a strict Mormon household, remarked that her religion would still prevent her from considering having children and exposing them to her lifestyle. Stacie N., 24, from a small town in Indiana, did not come out until she was 21: "I couldn't find who I was until I came out here. I was around a friend that was gay, and then it was like, God, this is it. This is what I wanted."

Along with Annette's discussion of her struggle with Catholicism, Crystal described her sacrifices and conflicts in the most detail. She lost two of her close female friends from high school when she recently came out to them. She is not out to her family, who regularly denigrate gays in their conversations. "She [her grandmother] said she never would have voted for Clinton if she knew that he was really serious about lifting the ban of gays in the military. And she went off on a tangent about how they ought to be exterminated and things like that. . . . And my uncles and my father, who are all 40 and above, have a hard time with it [homosexuality]. They are like, 'They shouldn't flaunt it,'" she said, laughing softly. "They don't know about me."

In fact, before they found this Denton community, Stacie N. and the fourth friend, Lisa, all were engaged to men. Right after high school, Crystal, a petite blonde with a tomboy spirit, actually married a classmate who was being sent overseas in the 1991 Persian Gulf War. She explained that because she was living with her grandmother at the time and unsure about her future, she wanted the security and social validation of marriage. "I was infatuated with the label," she said. She lived with her husband for only two days at his naval base in Norfolk, Virginia, before he was shipped out for six months. Without his company, she sought to fill the void with college. Vaguely thinking about becoming a police officer, she enrolled at Texas Women's University. After three and a half months, during which she came to terms with her long-felt lesbianism, she called her husband and asked for a divorce. "He says, 'Are you having an affair with another man?' And I was like '. . . no,'" emphasizing her tentativeness. "And he goes, 'You're having an affair with a woman.'. . . When I told him, he threatened to kill me. . . . And then he calls my mother and he tells my mother. He says, 'You'd better keep her away from me, because if I see her, I will kill her.'"

Crystal explained that he was especially angry because of his traditional views. "For one, he's in the navy. Two, he's a very macho man. Very traditional. You know, 'the wife stays at home and I'll go out and earn all the money.' You know, 'you cook me dinner and I'll sit and watch football with the boys while you clean the kitchen.' He's that type of man. I'm not that type of woman. I'm the type of woman to be in the living room watching the football game while the dishes are sitting in the sink, gathering whatever dust they want to gather." But she and her ex-husband have finally made some peace with each other. "I received a letter from him saying that he doesn't regret marrying me," said Crystal. "He tries to remember the fun times we had that he'll always love. By that, you know, basically just knowing the type of man that [he] is, he's let go. . . . I also think that he's met someone else."

Today, Crystal says that she knows she made the correct decision. Like other lesbians and bisexuals (and straight people) I interviewed, she knows that being true to herself is the highest ideal. "When I finally got to college when I was 19 and I came out, I felt a peace and serenity inside myself that I had never felt my whole life. Alcohol, drugs, nothing has ever given me the sensation. When you come out, when you admit to yourself that this is OK, this is what I want, I felt so peaceful." She said that she has a personal connection with Annette that she was never able to achieve before. "It's just being able to look at each other in the eye and know what the other person is thinking. . . . I mean it's what I call 'the look.' When I look at Annette and I look in her eyes, it's like I can feel her inside of me. I can feel her emotions. And that's something I was never able to accomplish with a man. Never." The sex was also better. "With sex with a man, I grit my teeth and pray that it's over real quick," she said. "With a woman, I want it to last forever."

Bisexuality as an Option

Young women today are also more comfortable with bisexuality. In the 1970s, radical lesbian feminists often railed against bisexuality as political treason against women, and the gay and lesbian community often condemned bisexuals as confused and in denial about their sexuality. But today, ironically, as a result of the feminist and gay rights movements, which questioned rigid gender norms, young people more readily accept these differences. Less political about their sexuality, more of them insist on their personal right to live their lives according to their own, often shifting, orientation.

Bisexuality naturally fits this generation's strong individualism, which defines morality personally instead of according to outside ideologies. Bisexuality also reflects these young people's sensibilities that were formed growing up in a popular culture designed to appeal erotically to both sexes. Bisexual characters in the 1990s became more visible, including those in the TV series *Roseanne* and in many films, such as *Chasing Amy*, *High Art*, and *Three of Hearts*. The late Kurt Cobain of the music group Nirvana announced that he would have lived as a bisexual if he had not been married to his wife, Courtney Love. Michael Stipe of REM told *Newsweek*, "I've always been sexually ambiguous in terms of my proclivities. I think labels are for food." Fans of the folk-rock phenomenon Ani DiFranco follow the twists and turns of her romantic life with women and, most recently, with a man. In the activist world, some major lesbian figures are now claiming to be bisexual. In 1997, attracting some criticism from lesbians, longtime lesbian rights leader and *Lesbian Sex* author JoAnn Loulan, began dating a man (Cotter 1997).

Bisexuality has only recently become an acceptable identification. I was surprised to interview three women who said they were bisexual but whom I had assumed were straight. (One was married to a Boston computer specialist, and the other two were students interviewed with groups of straight friends.) Crystal, Annette's partner in Denton, reflected this view of inclusiveness when discussing her support of Alfred Kinsey's 1940s theory of a sexual continuum, which argues that people are one of six different degrees of homosexuality, with completely homosexual people on one extreme and completely heterosexual ones on the other. Another recent change is young women who may sleep with people of different sexes at different times of their lives and who may never use any label at all.

As evidence that this "sexual flip flopping" has reached the mainstream, *Glamour* magazine featured an article in January 2000 about young adults who started out as either gay or straight and then changed. The magazine gave examples of high-profile celebrity mates who made the switch, such as Anne Heche, "who was happily hetero prior to meeting Ellen DeGeneres in 1997," and Julie Cypher, who left her husband, actor Lou Diamond Philips, to be with singer Melissa Etheridge (Tager 2000, 86). In my interviews, three feminist activist women in Austin emphasized the difficulty of labeling one's sexuality. Cheryl, 31, labeled sexuality as "a conversation," an evolving process in one's life. "Nobody is going to have the same conversation over and over their whole lives for the same reason," said Cheryl, the executive director of a nonprofit legal organization for women. "Thinking that biology informs whom we have sex with, I think, is like thinking biology informs whom we have conversations with and where we go to school and whether we like tall people or short people. Human behavior is far too complex to be instinctive, and sexual behavior is more complex than most human behavior."

In the past decade, many student groups have been renamed to include bisexuals (and the transgendered), including "B"s and "T"s among the "L"s and "G"s in their names. In references to the homosexual community, a common shorthand is the acronym LGBTQ. The "T" is for transgendered, which has become a widespread term only since the mid-1990s but is not yet as well known as the larger category of bisexuals. Of all these gay subgroups, the transgendered—people who are born physically as one gender but identify as the other—are the most "politically incorrect." In other words, they don't fit into neat categories. For old-school feminists, someone born as a man saying that he is really a woman can be problematic.

I saw this generation gap played out in person at the 1995 National

Women's Studies Association conference. One of the featured speakers was Leslie Feinberg, a gender rights activist and frequent university guest lecturer, who grew up as a "butch dyke" (according to her/his bio) and looks like a man. Feinberg's 1993 book *Stone Butch Blues* and 1997 book *Transgender Warriors* are classics in this cause for "transliberation." At the conference, I saw support for Feinberg split almost completely according to generation. When she/he came up to speak, the young women applauded thunderously from their groups in the audience while the older ones generally sat still, befuddled. During a meeting session, some of the older women voiced doubts about accepting someone living as a man in women's activist spaces.

Life for the transgendered is a pioneering experience, for even bisexuals still feel like gender outlaws. In the group of Denton friends, Lisa discussed some of the common challenges of living as a bisexual woman in America. She discovered her bisexuality only when she was in her early twenties when her fiancé, an air force pilot, was away. (These stories of women coming out when their men were away help explain why lesbian subcultures had small renaissances during both World War I and World War II.) "That's when I fell in love with my best friend named Diana," said Lisa. "We had been friends for a year and a half without anything sexual going on between us. At the beginning of my second year [of law school], she broke up with her girlfriend. And I started to have dreams about her, sexual dreams about her. And I pursued the relationship. And I fell in love with her, hard and deep. And we dated for two and a half years."

Like other bisexual women, Lisa complained about the difficulty of not belonging to one well-defined group, either gay or straight. "I have had experiences with both men and women, and I could see myself in the future dating either a man or a woman. So I really can't define myself, and that's one of the most difficult experiences. You don't relate fully with lesbians because a lot of lesbian partners do not want a bisexual partner. . . . Men don't want a bisexual partner either." Lisa noted that she also is bothered by accusations that her bisexuality is less "natural" than lesbianism or being straight. "In a way, it's not a choice. I did not choose to be sexually attracted to men and to women. You do not choose to be attracted to women. Straights didn't choose to be sexually attracted to the opposite sex. I mean I find women beautiful. I love their smell, their touch, the whole bit. But I enjoy men too. I mean I love the way a man looks, his muscles, a certain way he carries himself. Sex with a man, I love that. I love sex with a woman too."

Creating Diverse Images

Grateful for their supportive communities, these Texas women pointed out other important sources of social approval. They appreciate the new realistic images in the media of lesbians and bisexuals, who were invisible just a decade earlier. Following the conforming "fitting-in" ideals of the 1980s, even now visibly lesbian singers Melissa Etheridge and k. d. lang did not officially come out until the 1990s. Worse, most of the outwardly lesbian images were purely pornographic, created by men for titillation. With this invisibility during their formative teen years, the Denton women found role models where they could. Like the other gay women I interviewed, they mentioned singling out nonlesbian but independent women, such as Kristy McNichol of *Family* and Jo of *Facts of Life*.

But in the 1990s, not only did lesbian and bisexual women come out in the media, but they also took bold new steps to create their own images of themselves. As a result, the images available are more diverse than ever, reflecting the real individualism of the LGBTQ community. They also better reflect the many dimensions of lesbian/bisexual life, ranging from the serious to the lighthearted, including sex. An example of this very new phenomenon is *Curve*, a best-selling lesbian magazine, which has a large readership of women in their twenties and thirties (the average reader's age is 26). The original name of the magazine was *Deneuve* (after the publisher's first lover, as she revealed to me). But in 1996, the name changed to *Curve* after a lawsuit from the not-so-amused Catherine Deneuve. In 1999, the magazine's circulation rose to 200,000 (with a paid circulation of 68,400), more than twenty times that of the first issue in 1991. Attracting support from advertisers, *Curve*'s readership is affluent: 89 percent are college graduates, with a median household income of $46,100 (compared with the U.S. average of $32,789). Publisher, editor in chief, and founder Frances Stevens witnessed this dramatic groundswell of support from the beginning, when she started the magazine at the age of 23 in her apartment. A graduate of San Francisco State (which she terms "the land of young lesbians"), she discovered the need for a general, professionally executed lifestyle magazine for the school's diverse population of lesbians. Not one to sit and complain, she put up a flier advertising for contributors in A Different Light Bookstore in San Francisco's gay Castro district. In the next month, she received three hundred calls. A year later, the first issue hit the stands and sold out in six days. Almost a decade later, many of her original staff are still on the job.

The glossy, well-written magazine is distinguished by its mainstream sensibilities and reach. In the 1970s, lesbian publications such as *The Ladder* and the still surviving *Off Our Backs* had a more low-rent separatist approach, were usually published on newsprint, and had a low circulation and a defiantly unpolished image. But Stevens said that she sees value in this professional product. "I think that the quality is important, and it's about time that women have something that they can be proud of and happy to take off a shelf and leave on a coffee table, and think, 'This is really good quality and I'm worth that.' It's true; we are."

Another example of young lesbians creating realistic images of themselves for a widespread audience is the hit 1994 film *Go Fish*, the first lesbian movie written and produced by young women. Like *Curve*, the creators of this movie told me that they wanted to provide new role models for young women. These goals are made clear in the beginning scene of the movie, set in a classroom, which focuses on the problem of lesbian invisibility. The professor asks the students to name famous lesbians in history:

"Eve," the first responds.

"Sappho."

"Margaret, the neighbor of Dennis the Menace."

"Marilyn Quayle?"

"Peppermint Patty."

"Endora on 'Bewitched'?"

"The entire cast of *Roseanne*?"

From that point on, the film's characters seek to rectify the situation. With boldness and honesty, director Rose Troche and her cowriter, Guinevere Turner, tell the story of a diverse web of friends and lovers, whom no one would ever mistake as straight. Like *Curve*, the particular subculture of lesbians portrayed in this movie has a distinct Generation X sensibility: streetsmart, sexy, and out.

Chicago native Troche, 29, and Turner, 26 (in 1994 at the time of our interview), first met in the Chicago chapter of the HIV/AIDS activist group ACT UP. In 1991, they decided they wanted to do the unprecedented and document the reality of their own subculture in the bohemian Wicker Park neighborhood. Three years later, *Go Fish* opened at the 1994 Sundance Film Festival. The film immediately made headlines. Samuel Goldwyn bought the worldwide distribution rights, making it the festival's first film to land a deal. Marketers touted it as the first nationally released film about lesbian couples and as a "possible" crossover to mainstream audiences. *Vogue*, the *New*

Yorker, and the *New York Times* reviewed it, and *Rolling Stone* named Troche as the year's "hot director."

From the beginning of our interview, Troche and Turner made clear their intentions for the movie. They had not plotted to "cash in on this whole ridiculous 'lesbian chic' thing," Troche asserted, and added that the notorious 1993 *Newsweek* cover on lesbians came out during the film's production. Turner also stressed that *Go Fish* was targeted to a lesbian audience and was not meant as a public relations piece. "We don't want anyone to think that we made this movie for straight people to feel comfortable with lesbians. It comes off that way to a degree, just because it has [done that]. People have said to us," she said, taking on a mock Valley Girl voice, "'It's so universal, like you guys go on dates just like us. You're so normal!'" Besides featuring the right to be different, the film portrays sex as a major issue, not an afterthought. Roommates constantly question others' dating progress. "Did you slip her some Spanish fly?" roommate Daria asks Ely. When teacher Kia (T. Wendy McMillan) oversleeps and misses her class, she tells her lover, "That's it. No more sex after midnight." The end of the movie features a montage of nubile women's bodies in various stages of heated entanglements.

In keeping with *Go Fish*'s realism, its portrait of the lesbian community and lesbians' lives isn't all sugar and spice. Troche also tackles more controversial issues concerning lesbian identity, contradiction, and judgment. In a haunting dream sequence, Max, dressed in a wedding gown, discusses her ambivalence about not getting married to a man and having a "normal" and safer life. In another surreal scene, Daria, played by Anatasia Sharp (a waitress discovered at a local restaurant by Troche and Turner), faces a tribunal of lesbian peers after she sleeps with a man. In contrast, in past movies about lesbians, such boldness was taboo. Other touted lesbian movies, such as *Claire of the Moon* and *Desert Hearts*, ignored this side of life to avoid making waves.

The Activists

Reflecting *Go Fish*, a major push of young lesbian activists involves increasing dialogue about sexual desire, one of the most historically feared public topics of the lesbian community. In the 1970s, while gay males had no qualms celebrating and even reveling in the erotic by seeking meaningless and quick sexual gratification, women held back. The out lesbians of the day, who were often feminists, concentrated on the political parts of their identity, partly because of the urgency of addressing women's lack of equality. Lesbians in the 1970s had grown up under an even stronger double standard, which had only given men permission to be aggressively sexual. These women, however, often emphasized the gentler and egalitarian parts of sex, such as hugging and affection, and associated baldly erotic self-centeredness with men. In the conformist 1980s, lesbians and gays together, seeking society's acceptance of their cause, often refused to talk publicly about sex, knowing that this was the aspect of their lives that defined them and branded them as different.

This focus on sexual desire was evident at the 1993 Third National March on Washington for Lesbian, Gay, Bisexual Rights and Liberation (as it was officially called). Revealing the generational splits in the movement, the older and younger planners disagreed with each other over which causes should take priority. According to Achy Obejas in a 1993 profile of the generations in the *Chicago Tribune,*

> The organizing group, packed with younger gays and lesbians, wrote more than 50 planks in the march platform, some addressing issues such as equal rights for "transgendered" persons, universal multilingual education, and acceptance of polygamous relationships. The older generation, which started and owns most of the community's newspapers, has consistently editorialized in favor of the march, but against the platform as too strident. (6)

An example was a band of fifteen very young women carrying a large banner reading "LABIA: Lesbians and Bisexual Women in Action." They said that this was now an officially recognized student group at Rutgers University. Most stood in couples, leaning affectionately against each other. Of course, my first question was about the name. They explained that they were "taking back the erotic" and "trying to get rid of the idea that lesbian sex is gentle sex," that this attitude denied their sexuality as powerful. They told me that their name often causes confusion on their campus, especially among men who do not know that the "labia" are the outer parts of the vagina. "Guys have gone up to us and said, 'What's labia?'"

Months later, when I was in the New Jersey area, I met with and learned more from LABIA president Winsome Gayle on campus at the annual gay and lesbian coffee house on National Coming-Out Day. She took the stage and told the large crowd present about her own frightening experience telling her college friends about her identity. But she was most nervous about what was to come over the looming Thanksgiving holidays: telling her parents. Afterward, we sat down in a student lounge, and she discussed her personal convictions about the particular importance of lesbians' coming out. LABIA was founded two years earlier by women from the university's gay and lesbian alliance, which was then dominated by men. "It's important even on campus to let people know that there are lesbian and bisexual women and that we do have fulfilling lives and to let them know that we're not nonsexual beings, as usually the theory is," she said. Gayle added that the name directly forces people to "come to grips" with that aspect of lesbian life. "A lot of people have a hard time seeing women being sexual, especially women being sexual with other women. . . . If they see women being sexual with each other, it's usually in a *Penthouse* and [a man] is invited in. We're saying, 'No, you're not invited. It's just between us. Live with it.'"

The group itself has been influenced in spirit and ideology by the greater lesbian sex-radical movement, which emerged in the 1980s as a reaction to politically correct 1970s antiporn feminists. One of LABIA's more recent programs was showing the video "Safe Is Desire," produced by Blush Entertainment, which also published the controversial and influential lesbian sex magazine *On Our Backs*. The film challenges all past notions of lesbian sexuality as tame, unlustful, egalitarian, and relationship oriented. The plot is about a couple who visits a lesbian sex club to learn about safer-sex techniques. They observe members of the sex club indulge in their own orgies, featuring adventurous sex acts previously associated with male-oriented power plays, such as S/M accompanied by leather harnesses, whips, multiple piercings, and dog collars. Also defiantly imitating men, many in the elaborate entanglement of bodies use dildos, strapped on or inserted by hand.

The reaction to the film was mixed. Gayle said the older women in attendance were uncomfortable with the types of sex involving penetration that they associated with male dominance. She also said that the sex was too wild for most of the women's personal tastes, including hers. And political enlightenment was not exactly the main priority of some more voyeuristic persons there. She added, "One guy was in there and said, 'Why don't we have less dialogue next time?' And he obviously wasn't the right person for this film. But for the most part, it made safe sex look like fun." She said the showing was worthwhile in the end to emphasize the "importance of diversity" in the lesbian community.

Discussing differences and negotiating life between "the real world" and queer politics occupy many of LABIA's weekly meetings. Subjects in the fall of 1997 included the history of butch/femme roles, body image, and lesbian parenting. On campus, it helped sponsor World AIDS awareness week, an antidomestic violence rally, and many musical groups and political speakers, including Urvashi Vaid, former president of the National Gay and Lesbian Task Force. Some of these projects are carried out jointly with other queer student groups, which include RUGBI (Rutgers Union for Gay and Bisexual Men), LLEGO (Latino/a Lesbian and Gay Organization), LASA (Learning about Self-Acceptance), the LGBT Studies Section queer studies rap group, and RUST ("the educational, support and cultural group concerning body art, BDSM, gender play and other fetishes").

Campus Conflicts

Although many different groups thrive on campus, Rutgers is no queer utopia. In the fall of 1997, LABIA helped sponsor an antibias rally, which followed a series of antigay graffiti written in particular residence halls. Such tensions are especially evident, and growing, in places where gay/lesbian activism is new. Because the younger generation is more out, it is facing more harassment. According to Overlooked Opinions, a Chicago-based market research firm that specializes in gay and lesbians, in 1993 (the most recent data available), 53 percent of gay people under 25 claimed to have been harassed on the basis of sexual orientation, compared with less than 17 percent over the age of 54, and only a third of those in their thirties and forties.

When I was visiting campuses, I witnessed many conflicts with emerging lesbian groups, including one at Stephens College in Columbia, Missouri, in 1996. This school, the country's second-oldest women's college, founded in 1833, has a conservative, sheltered past. While academically strong and now somewhat diverse, it historically served as a finishing school for southern aristocrats' daughters. Its reputation is evident in the still popular major of equestrian science, with courses in horse riding and maintenance. But this veneer of southern-belle composure was recently chipped away by the newly officially recognized lesbian and bisexual group, QUES (Queer United Educated Sistas), which is actively striving for visibility. Before that, the college's lesbian presence, mostly underground, was much tamer, not heard and not seen. The one other campus lesbian group ever established on campus, which lasted for only the 1994/95 school year, was organized by a student counselor to provide emotional support. Now, however, these more confident women are ready to act. "You might go [to the old group] if you want to talk to somebody and maybe get emotional help. Now [QUES] is a place where we can be who we want to be for a little while and then go out and cause trouble," said copresident Scotte, 21, a junior, from a small town in Missouri.

From its beginning, QUES has been a source of controversy on campus. In October 1995, right after its founding, the group marked National Coming-Out Day with chalkings on main campus sidewalks, spelling out its name and writing quips about "heterosexism." Also in a playful mood, the group set up outside the cafeteria a "kissing booth," which handed out Hershey's chocolate kisses. Outrage immediately followed. "The kissing booth made everybody crazy," said faculty sponsor Tina Parke-Southerland, the coordinator of women's studies at the college. A lesbian's dorm room was trashed, and in the same residence hall, known to house a lesbian population, the gay symbol decorations on many doors were torn down. The QUES members also witnessed an "antichalking" of homophobic rantings on the campus grounds.

Parke-Southerland and the group became the target of angry attacks by an administrator, students, and faculty. She described a barrage of memos from an evangelical Christian Marxist professor. "The first memo that he sent me was that I was perverting students and promoting homosexuality to the great eternal damage of their souls. You could understand that I was a little angry about that," she said, laughing ironically. But QUES shows no signs of backing down. As at other schools, straight people like Parke-Southerland, who is married with children, have stepped forward as allies. A longtime feminist activist, she is steadfastly standing by the group, as she did in Alaska where for ten years she was an advocate of Native Americans. "This is what as a friend, a helper, a supportive person, can do," she said. "You can take the risks without risking everything. So I can be the point person. I can say the most radical things. Because people can get in my face, but they can't say I'm 'a pervert.'"

These conflicts represent growing sexual confrontations in American society. Even though the queer students are more out and defiant than ever, so are the fundamentalist Christians and other conservative forces who oppose them. The battles have just begun, with young people still facing resistance at work, at school, and as they make legal commitments and plan their families. No longer preoccupied with just quietly coming to terms with their own sexuality, young women like the ones described here are living openly and loudly challenging all preconceptions of them, whether or not society is ready.

IV

Getting to "Her Way": Social Movements for Power and Permission

8. Education and Jobs, the Sexual Revolution, and the Women's Movement: The Foundation

If there is going to be a breakthrough in human sexuality—and I think that such a breakthrough might be in the wind—it is going to occur because women will start taking charge of their own sex lives. It is going to occur because women will stop believing that sex is for men and that men (their fathers, their doctors, their lovers and husbands, their popes and kings and scientists) should call the shots.

—Barbara Seaman, *Free and Female*, 1972

I am not a pretty girl.
That is not what I do.
I ain't no damsel in distress
And I don't need to be rescued.

—Ani DiFranco, title song from *Not a Pretty Girl*, 1995

Until relatively recently, women in the mainstream society did not always conduct their sex or family lives on their own terms. Rather, because they lacked power, they were dependent on male authorities such as husbands, clergy, psychologists, and doctors, who prescribed and proscribed their proper places, often within a submissive and self-sacrificing female framework. These men, previously as women's only sources of official knowledge, enforced their own sexual agendas, telling women only what they thought they needed to know. But for the past four decades, various interconnected social forces have converged to give more women more authority over their own lives and to create and propel the sexual evolution. This effect has followed a greater pattern that sociologists have documented: *the people possessing the most power in society also enjoy the greatest sexual permissiveness* (Reiss 1986, 97, 126–27).

First, social movements emerging in the 1960s and 1970s provided a foundation. Women gained economic power and greater social status by entering the labor force and becoming better educated in greater numbers. The ensuing sexual revolution helped weaken the double standard, which had confined sex for women purely to procreation, not recreation. On a more organized and political level, the women's movement reframed sex from a woman's point of view, giving women more power and control, and securing equal rights in the home, in relationships, and in the family.

Second, boosted by these social movements, young women have overcome the most restrictive sexual authority of women: organized religion. American culture has traditionally allowed men to define religion and morality on their own terms, and women have always been expected to take the role of follower. Now, however, taking the lead of the spiritually seeking boomer generation, young women are redefining religion and are becoming their own moral authority.

Third, the information age, accelerating in the 1990s, has had a profound effect on women making their own sexual choices. With better and more accessible information and safer-sex campaigns, women are now less isolated and know more about sex, thus making them less reliant on and more critical of male "experts."

Work and School: The Bottom Line

The basic source of women's control over their sex lives is their financial independence. As some of the most prominent feminist writers of the past century predicted, financial power, assisted by education, raises women's expectations and abilities to do things their own way, as well as shaping their views of men, marriage, family, sexual satisfaction, and romance. As Simone de Beauvoir wrote in *The Second Sex* in 1952:

> It is through gainful employment that woman has traversed most of the distance that separated her from the male; and nothing else can guarantee her liberty in practice. Once she ceases to be a parasite, the system based on her dependence crumbles; between her and the universe there is no longer any need for a masculine mediator. (755)

When my interview subjects talked about sex, they frequently brought up their work and education goals. This was especially true for Stacie S., 27, who kept returning our conversation to the topic of money.

She isn't rich. But her job as a social worker, her small sales business, and her graduate degree give her a sense of independence that governs even the most personal aspects of her life. She has surpassed the economic and educational reach of her mother, a postal worker with a high school education. She just bought a small condo in a modest low-rise in a middle-class Chicago suburb and hopes some day to have a summer home, as her older coworkers do. "[Money] gives you power," she said. "It gives you freedom. You know, if I want to go somewhere, I go. If I want to go to Jamaica in November, I'll go. If I want to go to Cancún in January, I'm going to go. I'm not going to ask anyone. As long as my bills are paid, you know, I can do what I want to do."

Stacie repeatedly insisted that she is looking for a man who can be her companion, not her meal ticket. She makes more money than do most of the men she dates and doesn't need them to take care of her. Her financial independence also enables her to leave a relationship. "I don't need them to pay my mortgage, or I don't need them to pay my car note, or I don't need them to give me money to get my hair done, a manicure, my pedicure. That's why I go to work every day. . . . In the past, [women and men] kind of traded off. 'We'll give you sex if you give us the money to go to the beauty salon on Saturday.' What's up with that?"

Although poor women have always had to work, more middle-class and upper-class women are now in the workforce than ever before. In fact, working outside the home is more the rule than the exception for young women of all backgrounds. Three out of four women aged 25 to 54 were in the workforce in 1994, twice the proportion for this group shortly after World War II. In 1994, women accounted for 46 percent of the labor force, up from 24 percent in 1940. What has changed most in the past fifty years is women's steady long-term work patterns, which now resemble those of men. In the years immediately after the war, the majority of women workers were under 25, and most quit when they had children. Today, the greatest workforce participation is by women in their late thirties and forties (eight in ten are in the workforce) (Herz and Wootton 1996, 48). Their financial goals have also become more ambitious. Just a few generations ago, almost all women, even those with a college education, were relegated almost exclusively to the lowest-paying "female" jobs, almost never on a serious "career" track. When married middle-class women worked, it was often part time, and they were thought to merely be seeking "pin money" or extra change. Women's most dramatic employment gains have been in managerial and professional jobs, the occupational groups in which men and women are most equally represented, with women accounting for three in ten of these jobs.

Women began entering the job market in large numbers in the early 1940s, spurred by the war, which created labor shortages because of the loss of male workers and the need for increased production. As a result, 5.2 million more women were in the labor force in 1944 than in 1940, reaching a proportion of 36 percent. After the war, the percentage dropped slightly to 31 percent, which was still above prewar levels. In the 1950s, married women continued to work to support their families (Herz and Wootton 1996, 46–48). In the 1980s, women's labor force participation continued to grow, but at slower levels. In the early 1990s, it reached a plateau of 57.2 percent (Bureau of Labor Statistics 1997, 45), but in 1994, it started to climb, reaching an all-time high in 2000 of 60 percent of women participating in the labor market (Bureau of Labor Statistics 2000).

In general, today women also earn more than ever before. In 1963 women earned 59 cents for every dollar earned by men; today women earn 73 cents for every dollar earned by men. (This is widely understood to be the result of discrimination, which still keeps disproportionate numbers of women routed to and stuck in low-wage jobs with little opportunity for advancement.) However, this progress has not been shared by all. Gender differences are still apparent in the less elite occupations, with the majority of women working in low-paying clerical, sales, and service jobs. White women have gained more than black women, who are much more likely than white women to be stuck in low-wage service jobs. Women's overall career growth is also overshadowed by the general state of poverty for a substantial subset of women, mainly single female heads of families, who account for 14 percent of all households in 1993, compared with 9.4 percent in 1970. Half of these households are poor, compared with 10 percent of the general population (Gody, Andrews, and Harter 1990, 5).

Just a short time ago, college was a male pursuit and women were called *coeds*, reflecting their novelty and secondary status, but today the number of women has surpassed that of men on all educational levels (except the number earning doctorates). In 1998, the U.S. Census Bureau reported that for the first time, young women are completing both high school and college at a higher rate than are their male peers. According to 1999 statistics, in the past decade the annual number of women receiving Ph.D.s increased by more than 50 percent, now accounting for about 40.6 percent of the total (Wyatt 1999, annual study by the National Opinion Research Center). As their entry into the professions indicates, women have made particularly great gains in securing degrees in traditionally male fields. In the thirty years between 1961/62 and 1991/92, women's share of all business degrees sextupled, and their share of biology degrees almost doubled. By 1991/92, the number of women who received dentistry degrees had nearly tripled from 1976/77. The number of women receiving degrees in medicine and law more than doubled over that same time. In computer and information sciences, engineering, and the physical sciences, however, women remain significantly underrepresented (Costello and Krimgold 1996, 279, 276).

This greater amount of education is a powerful force in shaping women's sexual attitudes and behavior. The authors of the University of Chicago's 1994 National Health and Social Life survey point out that education is an especially significant variable for young women, determining their level of recreational sexual exploration. They discuss this issue most directly in a section about same-sex partners. Although educational level is not a variable for males for homosexuality, it does correlate strongly with lesbian behavior. The women college graduates surveyed were eight times more likely than high school graduates to claim a homosexual or bisexual identity and were more than twice as likely to have had same-gender sex since puberty. The Chicago survey noted other nontraditional behaviors that are more common among highly educated women. Sixty percent of women who had attended graduate school reported having masturbated in the past year, compared with 25 percent who had not finished high school. Women with at least some college were 40 percent more likely to have received oral sex than were women with less than a high school degree, and women with graduate degrees were 40 percent more likely to have had anal sex than were women with high school degrees (Laumann et al. 1994, 83, 105, 98, 99).

The 1993 *Janus Report on Sexual Behavior* also found that educated women had greater sexual options:

> They report much greater gratification in their sexuality, are aware of the sexual double standard, demand parity in initiating sex rather than playing the traditional passive female, have had the most premarital sexual experience, and report being the most sensual. Women in the more highly educated groups were more easily able to assert their sexual opinions and preferences and to maintain a greater level of control over their sex lives. (312)

In addition, the *Janus Report* found a related variable, career, to be such a strong influence on women that it divided women into two categories: homemakers (those not employed outside the home at all) and career women employed outside the home. (Data on part-time workers were not specifically tabulated.) These two groups were "two distinctly different populations" regarding sex life and lifestyle in general. In fact, the *Janus Report* found that "one of the most striking indications of our data" is the similarity of agreement between men and the career women (55 to 56 percent). Educated women also have sex later and are more careful. The 1994 National Health and Social Life survey discovered a positive correlation between education and delaying sex and using birth control as a teenager (Laumann et al. 1994, 324, 332). In addition, the odds of becoming an unmarried mother fall sharply as education rises and opportunity broadens. Almost 50 percent of births to high school dropouts occur out-of-wedlock, whereas among college graduates, the proportion is just 6 percent, according to U.S. Census Bureau statistics. In contrast, by the time they reach thirty, about 10 percent of the less-educated women, compared with 30 percent of those with a college education, still did not have a child, according to the Chicago survey (Laumann et al. 1994, 466).

Young women today are more aware of this connection between jobs and gaining power in their relationships. The social critic Florynce Kennedy, 77, an African American attorney and activist, described the main difference she had observed over the years: "I think they don't believe so much in men. They used to be so round eyed about men and relationships. I think now they're not. I think women are much more skeptical that their romances are going to be all right. . . . The fact was that they were fixed on romance because that was the way you hooked a guy, so that you can get him to pay the rent and everything. But now that women are better educated and can pay their own bills, they don't have the same need for romance. What they thought was romance was really the need for economic arrangement."

The Sexual Revolution: Erasing the Double Standard

As women left home and joined the workforce in the early 1960s, they began laying the foundation of the sexual revolution. The expansion of pink-collar service and clerical jobs drew more women to the cities and helped contribute to a new urban singles culture. More women also were going away to college, ready to experiment with sex (Ehrenreich, Hess, and Jacobs 1986). Birth control pills first became available in 1960, giving women more confidence in avoiding pregnancy than with the less effective and obtrusive diaphragm (often restricted by doctors to married women). Hugh Hefner, founder of *Playboy* in 1953, helped glamorize the swinging single life for men, who were waiting in the wings from their martinis- and modern art-stocked bachelor pads for their female counterparts to emerge. But men knew that for the sexual revolution really to begin, women still needed cultural permission, as premarital sex was still frowned on.

The tide started changing in 1963 with Betty Friedan's book *The Feminine Mystique*, which exposed many married women's feelings of suffocation. Helen Gurley Brown's *Sex and the Single Girl* in 1962 had already put a new spin on the single life. (Of all the writers of that period, Friedan and Brown, both radicals, particularly influenced exactly how future generations of women would shape their married and single identities and expectations.) Challenging traditional images of the single woman as a pathetic spinster or a neurotic leftover, Brown portrayed her as complete, fulfilled, and not necessarily in hot pursuit of a husband. She also put a large dent in the double standard, reducing women's shame for having sex outside marriage. "Perhaps you will reconsider the idea that sex without marriage is dirty. . . . You inherited a proclivity for it. It isn't some random piece of mischief you dreamed up because you're a bad, wicked girl," she wrote (Brown 1970, 262). She then widely promoted these beliefs for the next thirty years as editor in chief of *Cosmopolitan* magazine, which has both enhanced other women's magazines' sexual content and carried her beliefs to future generations of women.

In another influential and emblematic best-seller, *The Sensuous Woman*, published in 1969, the anonymous author, "J," continued this discussion. As Brown did, "J" begins her book discussing the actual benefits of sex for women outside marriage, namely, to obtain pleasure and to snare a man. In fact, she devotes an entire chapter to assuring readers they have nothing to feel guilty about:

> Now I know a few people are going to try to beat you down and force you into a corner marked "shame," if you don't play the virgin role. But you don't have to abide by their rules. . . . Our world has changed. It's no longer a question of "Does she or doesn't she?" We all know she wants to, is about to or does. Now it's only a question of how tastefully she goes about it. (54)

The mass media first discovered this sexual revolution or "new morality" in the mid-1960s, culminating with a *Time* cover story on January 24, 1964. In 1963, *Time, Mademoiselle,* and *America* also referred specifically to this "sexual revolution." This term won out over other popular labels such as the "morals revolution" (*Newsweek*, April 6, 1964), the "moral revolution" (*New York Times*, May 7, 1965), and the "sexplosion" (*Christian Century*, January 29, 1964) (Smith 1990, 415). Today, despite reports that the sexual revolution is dead, it continues to influence women's lives and choices. But its legacy is mixed. On the one hand, we now have a "sexualized marketplace," the result of society's greater openness about sex. Sexualized pictures of women are everywhere, used to sell every product possible, but in a market still dominated by male tastes and defining female sexuality as what is attractive to men. On the other hand, women now have more control over their sex lives because of their better access to sex education, erotica, and information about their bodies.

For many traditionally oriented women, however, the sexual revolution has meant a loss of power because sex is no longer a bargaining tool for a long-term commitment. In the past, not having sex until marriage merited a big reward: being supported for life by a man. But after the sexual revolution, when sex was given freely, it became a less precious commodity. Just as many men lost their financial bargaining power with women as women started to earn their own money, many women lost their sexual bargaining power with men. But the most sweeping criticism of the sexual revolution was that it was conducted entirely according to men's rules. Women still knew little about their own bodies and how they could have an orgasm, as sex was still being defined in men's terms. Women continued to have little protection against pregnancy because abortion was illegal. Moreover, women no longer could say no without being labeled as repressed or frigid. They also had no defense against forced sex; date rape, sexual harassment, and sexual abuse. In other words, even though women's behavior had changed, society had not. Now many women felt trapped in another role, that of sex object.

The Women's Movement: Organizing for Sexual Control

When the women's movement began in the late 1960s (in what has been called "the second wave" of feminism), these problems were at the top of the agenda. Some of these early feminist activists were inspired by their work in the civil rights and antiwar movements, in the process of which they were made aware that they were second-class citizens themselves. Despite the rhetoric about the importance of equality and of ending oppression, their supposedly enlightened fellow male activists often didn't take them seriously as peers and relegated them to a strictly sexual role.

"I think the 1960s sexual revolution was really a way where more women were supposed to be available to more men," said longtime leader Gloria Steinem in an interview, describing women's experiences in the New Left. "It wasn't about autonomy. It was about you ran the mimeograph machine and you were sexually available."

Steinem remarked that the first issue of *Ms.*, which she cofounded in 1972, featured an article entitled "The Sexual Revolution Isn't Our War." The author, Anselma Dell'Olio, while affirming women's right to sexual pleasure and rejecting the double standard of the past, talked about the "sexual revolution" as a male invention, a "more free sex for us revolution." She wrote that the revolution neglected, however, to address women's sexual pleasure and orgasms, along with women's infinitely greater risks, such as pregnancy and unreliable contraception.

Women's activism for change began with the powerful process of consciousness raising, talking to one another about their own experiences. The slogan that emerged from such discussions was "the personal is political," referring to no longer seeing individual problems exclusively as personal, random, or idiosyncratic but as related to the greater systemic oppression of women. The more conservative feminists concentrated on gaining more work and education opportunities, whereas many radical feminists explored the intimate sphere of life to which women were restricted and in which so many of women's oppressions were rooted. They recognized that questions of sexuality and reproduction were not just private matters but concerns that determined women's freedom and status. Issues like abortion, rape, welfare for single mothers, child care, marriage, heterosexuality, motherhood, and women's sexual pleasure didn't take place in a vacuum but were shaped and influenced by the greater male-dominated culture.

These insights into "sexual politics" provided the spark for women organizing as a group to take control and start to change attitudes. As a result, feminists of the 1960s and 1970s had a powerful impact on future generations of women's being able to conduct their sex lives "her way." They redefined sex and sexual freedom from a woman's point of view, broadened women's knowledge of their own bodies, secured reproductive rights, and began to expand freedoms for lesbians and minorities. With new rights in education and the workplace, women were able to become independent, by either remaining single or divorcing, and to better control every aspect of their sex lives. Much of this work continued in the 1980s and beyond, as the women's movement became more firmly established in American culture. Even though the media repeatedly report that we are in a postfeminist age and that activism is dead, feminists are continuing to push for change, which often comes gradually and behind the scenes.

Minorities and Organizations Expanding Rights

In the late 1980s and early 1990s, women of color started organizing their own groups to address their basic physical needs, such as sexual health and self-determination. Their work includes the Black Women's Health Project, founded by Byllye Avery in 1981, and in 1994, the project published *Body and Soul: The Black Women's Guide to Physical Health and Emotional Well-Being*, the black counterpart of *Our Bodies, Ourselves*. By that year, the project had organized 150 local health support groups and many education initiatives, such as teaching women about cancer and infant mortality and helping homeless women. Hundreds of other groups for women of color have also been formed since the 1980s, including the National Latina Health Organization in Oakland, California, in 1986, and the Native American Women's Health and Education Resource Center in South Dakota in 1988.

Feminist criticism from minority women has also had an impact on broadening the agenda of the larger women's health movement. Women of color have expanded white middle-class women's interest in keeping abortion legal and birth control safe to make these services also affordable and accessible. They are especially concerned about the needs of poor and young women, whose right to abortion has been restricted by state parental consent laws for teenagers and the Hyde amendment, first passed in 1976, which prohibits federal Medicaid funding for abortions. A term popularized in the 1990s to address this wider focus is "reproductive rights," which refers to the full spectrum of women's choices regarding their reproductive lives, including basic medical care, housing, child care, and access to abortion and family planning. Reflecting this shift, the National Abortion Rights Action League changed its name in 1993 to the National Abortion and Reproductive Rights Action League.

In the 1980s, nongovernmental organizations were established in almost every city in the United States, providing support for women's sexual rights. These organizations include domestic violence shelters, health advocacy groups, rape crisis centers, women's studies programs, displaced-homemaker programs, and political action lobbies. Feminist organizations also are now a part of campus life, with the latest directory of college women's centers for the National Women's Studies Association listing more than 360.

Acquaintance Rape

Many feminist organizations deal with violence against women and unwanted sex. Just as feminists in the 1970s helped affirm women's rights to sexual pleasure, they demonstrated in the 1980s and 1990s that a woman's right to say no to sex was just as important as her right to say yes. In the past thirty years, the women's movement's battles against violence have affected both personal attitudes and the legal system. Since the early 1970s, feminists have founded hundreds of organizations to raise the awareness of and to fight all forms of sexual coercion, from assault by a stranger to coercion from family, husbands, lovers, and coworkers.

The crime of *acquaintance rape* (or *date rape*), a relatively new term, first came to light in the 1988 book, *I Never Called It Rape*, by Robin Warshaw, and it is now part of the popular vocabulary. In 1988, the annual UCLA Cooperative Institutional Research Program poll of college freshmen began including a question about date rape. The men and women surveyed overwhelmingly refuted the traditional assumptions about women "asking for it" and forfeiting their right to say no. The gender gap supporting the statement "Just because a man thinks that a woman has 'led him on' does not entitle him to have sex with her" narrowed from 15.7 percent in 1988 to 10.5 percent in 1996.

By the 1990s, awareness of the problem at colleges had grown, with almost every major campus sponsoring antirape education. In 1992, the first national college conference was held at the University of Pennsylvania, and in 1994, the first campus network, Speak Out: The National Student Coalition against Sexual Violence, was formed. In 1998, the group held three student conferences across the country, and about a third of the people attending them were men, reflecting the movement's desire to target them for change. As testament to the success of this movement to stop rape is the backlash that it has created. That is, in the 1990s, many of the magazine articles about acquaintance rape took the angle of "date-rape hype," questioning the extent and even the existence of the problem.

One of the leaders of the date-rape hysteria charge was 25-year-old Katie Roiphe, author of the 1993 book *The Morning After: Sex, Fear and Feminism on Campus*. Her theory is that feminist activism against date rape confuses young women into mislabeling as crimes a wide array of normal though often unpleasant sexual experiences. She argues that the battle against date rape is a symptom of young women's general anxiety about sex. A central target of Roiphe and others is a major survey by University of Arizona Medical School professor Mary Koss, published in 1987, sponsored by the Ms. Foundation, and financed by the National Institute of Mental Health. One of the study's major findings was that 27.9 percent—or, as most often quoted, "one in four"—of the college women surveyed reported having been the victim of a rape or attempted rape, with a majority having known their assailant. About 15 percent of those sampled reported completed rapes (Koss, Gidycz, and Wisnieski 1987, 168; Warshaw 1988, 11).

Roiphe's and others' criticism ignores, however, the large body of unbiased research proving the existence and harm of acquaintance rape. This includes the 1995 federally funded National Survey of Family Growth, which reported that of the 10,847 women interviewed, 20 percent said that they had been forced by a man to have intercourse against their will at some time during their lives. Eight percent said that their first intercourse was not voluntary (tables 22 and 21). The National Health and Social Life Survey, released in 1994 by the National Opinion Research Center, found that since puberty, 22 percent of women had been forced to do something sexually by a man, and 30 percent of those by more than one man (Laumann et al. 1994, 337; Michael 1994, 225; also see Kamen 1996).

Nonetheless, despite the backlash, the campus and community antirape movement is growing even faster. Take Back the Night Marches are proliferating across the country. In 1996, the Association for Student Judicial Affairs produced a training video for adjudicating cases of sexual assault, and universities have just started to expand date-rape education to include dating abuse and violence. During the 1996/97 television season, date rape was a plot theme on the most highly rated shows, such as the struggle of a promiscuous woman to be believed as a rape victim on *NYPD Blue* and the trauma of a young woman given "roofies" (a date-rape drug) on *ER*. And on September 23, 1996, NBC dramatized date rape in a full-length movie, *She Cried No*.

The "Sex Wars"

At the same time that they have fought against rape, feminists have also questioned degrading images that objectify women. No discussion about rape awareness would be complete without mentioning the antipornography movement, which began in the late 1970s, as awareness of and outrage over sexual violence mounted. Radical feminist Robin Morgan provided the theoretical impetus, writing that "pornography is the theory and rape is the practice." Feminists formed groups to outlaw pornography, which they saw as antiwoman propaganda, reflecting society's hatred of women and perpetuation of violence. The two leaders of this movement were activist Andrea Dworkin and attorney Catharine MacKinnon, who devised legal strategies in the 1980s to ban porn. These included city ordinances—which were, however, ultimately struck down as being unconstitutional—allowing women harmed by porn to sue the makers and distributors for discrimination. Although these radical feminists attracted much publicity in the past twenty years because of their extreme antisex and sensational views, they represent only one, and recently shrinking, school of feminist thought.

The radical feminists' impact has been to raise provocative questions about pornography's possible harm. As Andrea Dworkin pointed out in an interview with me, antiporn feminists have challenged pornography's most fundamental and destructive messages about women's sexuality: "The whole notion of pornography is that every woman is available for sex all the time. That presumption, that a woman is there and she wants to be used by whatever man is around her, that's part of what we attack when we attack pornography. That's part of the reason pornography and rape are so closely related in women's experience. So I think we've had an enormous impact, because we've been able to articulate in ways that women then know and understand that 'no, we don't want to be raped. That's wrong.'"

Whereas young feminists made the most headlines in the early to mid-1990s protesting acquaintance rape, they later became just as active trying to expand women's sexual expression. Beth Freeman, a graduate student who was teaching a gender studies course at the University of Chicago, countered that antipornography attacks on sex and natural desire ignored the greater social forces oppressing women. "I think that taking your clothes off in front of the camera is not in itself an intrinsically degrading act," said Freeman. "[But] it's an act that can be done under incredibly degrading conditions of not being paid enough, of not feeling like you have choice, or of doing it under the threat of being raped, or doing it because you don't have a place to live. It's the conditions that need to be addressed and not the fact that people are taking off their clothes." She added that despite opposing censorship of any kind, she does not support the misogynist brand of porn that involves hatred of women. She personally uses and appreciates lesbian-made pornography, such as that from the recently revived and influential San Francisco magazine, *On Our Backs*. As a lesbian, she appreciated the information about exactly what lesbians do in bed and the alternative to male-defined images and sexual frameworks. That is, instead of limiting the sexual images of women, anticensorship activists like Freeman seek to broaden the range available while improving its quality and depth by pioneering new woman-friendly erotic books, films, and products. While procensorship feminists decry pornography's role in aiding male masturbation, the prosex feminists actively encourage women to join them in such self-exploration and fantasy.

The wide range of feminist pornography now on the market is reflected in the inventory of woman-oriented sex toy and pornography stores, which include A Woman's Touch in Madison, Wisconsin, founded in 1996, and Eve's Garden, the original founded in 1974 in Manhattan. The most famous is Good Vibrations, with stores in San Francisco and Berkeley. It is part of Open Enterprises, which includes Down There Press, a publisher of sexual self-help books, the Sexuality Library catalogue of books and videos ("Knowledge is Pleasure" reads the inside cover), and a booming mail-order business started in 1985. Since its founding in 1977, Good Vibrations has enjoyed steady growth. The Mission District store is twelve times the size of the original spot of 200 square feet. Sales from the stores, published ads, and mail-order catalogue combined to generate more than $4.5 million in revenue for fiscal year 1995.

A visit to the San Francisco store revealed the open, prosex philosophies of these businesses. The place's attractive consumer appeal stands in striking contrast to the male-oriented, shadow-filled strip clubs in the neon-lit Broadway neighborhood across town. With its plentiful windows, slick displays, and inviting and helpful sales staff, the Good Vibrations store resembles an upscale Pottery Barn or Crate & Barrel outlet.

On the day of my visit, sunlight streamed in through the windows, giving the room a pure, Reaganesque "morning in America" glow. It spotlighted the goods, including books, videos, and vibrators, which were attractively displayed on tables. One featured a gift registry: "Wedding or commitment gifts are one of the most fun aspects of having a ceremony. Now you can request that double-headed Hitachi vibrator (built for two!) or those hand-made leather restraints that you've been craving, instead of just another casserole." I watched a member of the sales staff army candidly answer the questions of a couple wondering which dildo best fit their needs. They walked out with their product in a paper bag, the only sign of self-consciousness in the store, labeled "plain brown wrapper."

Like other women's sex stores, Good Vibrations is active in providing community education. Fliers on the counter included "Enjoying Good Vibrations," a guide to masturbating; "About Safer Sex Supplies"; "Your PC Muscle and You"; and a calendar of in-store events, including speakers and an "erotic reading circle." The rows of books filled with women's erotica also revealed a significant trend of the past decade. This genre has grown and received new respectability. Boosted by women-oriented books, the number of erotica books published quadrupled between 1991 and 1996, according to the Subject Guide of Books in Print (in contrast, the overall number of all books published increased by only 83 percent) (Brotman 1997). The most famous are the Herotica and Best American Erotica series edited by Susie Bright, the Bay Area sex guru (and former employee of Good Vibrations).

Also for sale were woman-oriented pornography videos, from the instructional to the exotic. According to the 1997 catalogue, best-sellers included *Carol Queen's Great Vibrations*, a guide to using vibrators; and the *Complete Guide to Sexual Positions*. Many of the dramatic videos are part of an emerging genre for couples or female audiences. A notable feminist director and producer featured is Candida Royalle, who specializes in women's erotic self-discovery. While male-created and focused pornography is still dominant and hard-core work still flourishes, more women than ever are seeking these turn-ons. In fact, according to *Adult Video News*, a trade magazine for retailers, 40 percent of all video rentals are now to women.

High Expectations and More Choices

Young women as a whole and those in my sample have been profoundly influenced by the past forty years of feminist organizing. Ideas that used to seem radical are commonplace today, and young women have higher expectations than ever about their sexual rights. In the 1960s, it was radical for an unmarried woman to use birth control; thirty years later young women on college campuses are passing out condoms to one another. In the 1970s, it was radical to not blame a woman for rape, even if the perpetrator was a stranger. Now, young feminists are moving the debate to the next level, labeling it rape even if the assailant is an acquaintance or family member. Women used to have trouble being accepted in the workplace at all; now they are addressing issues affecting the quality of their work lives, such as sexual harassment. In the 1970s, considering lesbianism was radical; in the

1990s, lesbians are fighting for their rights in marriage, the family, and the workplace.

The older women I interviewed also recognized the younger generation's greater sense of entitlement, from how they are treated personally to how they define their career paths. "What encourages me is that my students and the young people I meet on college campuses have a much better self-concept," said Sarah Weddington, 50, who teaches law at the University of Texas. "They feel more self-confident than I ever was at that age. And I think part of that was I was raised in West Texas, in a little town with people . . . in the community often saying, 'Women don't, women can't, women shouldn't.'. . . So if they're starting far ahead of where I was, I think they can make a longer, a better race than I did." In an interview, syndicated sex columnist Isadora Allman described the greater variety of life choices: "When I was growing up, a woman was married with children, or not yet. Those were the only choices. If you weren't married, clearly you were a left-over. If you didn't have children, it must have been God's will, not a choice. And if you didn't marry or have children, then you were something weird, like Marion the Librarian. If you were a career gal, sexless, peculiar. Nowadays a person can be a nurse or an astronaut, male or female, can be monogamous or not, be with a person of the same sex or not, marry several times, not marry at all, have children whether you're married or not. There are more choices for making a life that's personally more rewarding."

Mary Ann Hanlon, 54, who raised five children while her husband worked, said the lesson of the women's movement was that "women had a value. We had a right to a job, equal pay with men. We didn't have to sit home and wash dishes." She added that young women also demand better treatment from men, willing to get divorced if they are not satisfied. "Women feel we're not to tolerate certain forms of behavior. Whereas in the past, in my generation, or my mother's generation, it just went with the turf." Hanlon now appreciates these effects, although she was not a supporter of the women's movement in the 1960s when she was at home raising four children. In fact, after she read Betty Friedan's *The Feminine Mystique* in the 1960s, she hurled it across the room in disgust because she viewed the book, a critique of women's compulsory housewife role, as a "put-down of what I did."

As Hanlon suggested, another challenge for the new generation is to raise the value of women's various choices. As the women's movement matures, it is becoming more sensitive to differences in race, class, and sexuality. If their goal is to be inclusive and to attract broader support, young feminists must avoid making and enforcing a list of requirements of what it means to be a feminist. Accordingly, they have largely abandoned the heated feminist arguments of the 1970s and 1980s about what a true feminist is. This defiance of strict rhetoric is the legacy of young activists, known as the "third wave" feminists. They are freer to explore gray areas and apparent contradictions such as bisexuality as opposed to lesbianism or heterosexuality, making and using pornography but also being critical of it, and looking at the dark side of abortion as well as its necessity.

Many of the young feminist activists I interviewed for this book voiced this hope for more flexible and open dialogue. Instead of viewing feminism's purpose as telling young women what to think, they value it for teaching young women how to think critically. A prime example was the small group of feminists at the University of Illinois, Sluts Against Rape, who dress in lingerie during their protests. But despite the sexiness of their look, Sluts Against Rape, founded in 1991, have more than fashion on their minds. They seek to drive home the message that women have a right to control their sexuality no matter what, no matter how they dress or how promiscuous they are. Current organizer Dawn Flood told me that the group started to add some "sexual fun" to the more staid annual campus Take Back the Night March, an antirape protest. Some chants include: "We are straight, we are gay, we are wearing lingerie," "We are gay, we are straight, we fuck on the first date," and "Yes means fuck me and NO means fuck you." A manifesto written by founder Kirsten Lentz (later a graduate student at Brown University), elaborates on the Sluts' consciousness-raising goals: "When female sexuality does become visible, when we put on a sexy dress and say naughty things, we are seen as colluding in our own oppression (read: we invite rape). We participate in the Take Back the Night march to protest rape. But we will not erase our own sexual adventures, our own sexual displays."

The Sluts Against Rape group represents a culmination of the past forty years of feminist organizing for women's sexual control. It reflects organized drives to expand their range of choices, including rejecting unwanted sex and exploring historically forbidden sexual desires. The group challenges the old confining sexual model of a woman's being either a virginal "good girl" who follows the rules or a promiscuous "bad girl" who forfeits her right to be protected from rape.

To attain sexual self-determination, all women must also face another overall struggle, an inner one. Planning one's life requires active attention to one's needs and desires and a willingness to create new roles instead of passively following old ones. After the influx of women into the labor force, the sexual revolution, and the women's movement, we are living in a more democratic society than our mothers and grandmothers did, and even though we should not complain, life can still be tough. "It is easier to live through someone else than to become complete yourself," wrote Betty Friedan in the 1963 *The Feminine Mystique*. "No woman in America today who starts her search for identity can be sure where it will take her. No woman starts that search without struggle, conflict, and taking her courage in her hands" (326, 363).

9. Redefining Religion and Morality: Overcoming Traditional Male Authority

i found god in myself/ & i loved her/ i loved her fiercely.
—Ntozake Shange, *For Colored Girls Who Have Considered Suicide /
When the Rainbow Is Enuf*, 1976

I am not petrified of sex, consumed with guilt, or convinced that gays and atheists will go to hell. I don't think the Pope is perfect, and I find nothing wrong with birth control, as long as it works.
—Tish Durkin, quoted in "Why I Am a Catholic: What's a 20th-Century Girl Like Me Doing in a Church Like This?" *Mademoiselle*, March 1995

As a single mother, Ivy was seeking spiritual support. Her marriage had fallen apart after almost four years of constant financial and family health crises. After her divorce, her husband, stationed in Germany with the U.S. military, had stopped paying child support. Ivy's mobile home and all her belongings in Kileen, Texas, had been repossessed. Not able to pay all the bills with her waitress and then telemarketing jobs, she sent her two children to live with her family in Puerto Rico. She said that she felt she could no longer turn to Catholicism—the religion of her family and her Hispanic culture—because of its opposition to divorce. So she switched to an evangelical Protestant church, which, contrary to stereotype, allowed her to be herself.

"I'm pretty lucky with the people I have met, because I'm not being judged," explained Ivy, a small woman whose worn face ages her beyond her 25 years. "I'm being accepted for who I am . . . I go to church and I'm a totally different person, because I'm free of my sins." In broken English, she voiced her criticism of the Catholic religion by recounting a story from the Bible, of God creating Adam and then making Eve from his rib, signifying a woman's second-class status. "I believe that 30 years ago . . . that's the way

I would accept it. If the woman [has a problem], it was like she is wrong and the man is right. Today this generation is so completely different. Today, you know, now every woman is changing their culture."

Megan, 22, has similar complaints about her family's Catholic religion. But instead of abandoning her faith, she has decided to follow it according to her own conscience. Megan, an insurance company administrator in the Boston area, disagrees with the church's fundamental teachings about women's place in society and, even more, with its limits on sexual behavior. In college, she slept with many different men, without feeling very guilty. Unlike her fiancé and family, she is decidedly prochoice. After all, to Megan, religion is primarily a matter of personal faith and private practice, not of doctrines and ritual. "It comes down to people believing that there's someone watching out for them," Megan explained. "But going to church every Sunday doesn't mean that you're a Catholic. I mean you could sit in a room and say a prayer for ten minutes with all your heart and that will not mean that you're a Catholic."

This personal view also influences how Megan sees sexual issues. Although she believes that premarital sex is wrong, as the church teaches, she thinks what matters is "to be conscious of it. . . . I don't see it as a mortal sin." She also disagrees with the church about abortion rights. "It's more up to their own personal belief," she said. "I know that talking to my mom, she's completely against abortion. She won't hear it. I mean, if we ever sat down and had a discussion on it, she'd leave the table. . . . I can't picture myself as being as close to the church as my mother was. . . . Sometimes parents put more emphasis on it than you want to hear. I think it has to come down to you wanting to go to church, wanting to do it for yourself, not because your parents want you to."

After years of searching, Cheryl also has learned to look to herself for answers about sex: "I looked to the church, but there was no place for me because I became sexual very young," she explained. "I looked to my family. The messages that they tried to give us were really healthy, but there was an underlying sense of shame. So I knew that wasn't right. I looked at television, and every act of sex was portrayed as a violent act, and I knew that wasn't right." And so in the end, Cheryl, 31, a lawyer in Austin, Texas, decided that she had to rely on herself to define morality. "So what informs my sexuality is that I ditched every cultural influence I could possibly ditch, and I have a constant fight within myself to remain free and to look at my feelings as they come up and acknowledge them as they come up and make informed decisions about my behavior after that. And I think there are a lot of people doing that now because the generations before us did not do sex right. They did not get it right."

As women's power has increased over the past several decades with careers, education, and feminism, the power of male clergy and organized religion to regulate women's individual behavior has declined. When discussing moral standards, the dominant belief of the many various women I interviewed was the importance of being true to themselves. Although religion is still an important and influential force in young women's lives, forming the foundation of their moral beliefs, the ultimate authority for making their sexual decisions is now their inner authority.

This is one of the main differences between young women today and previous generations. Whereas their mothers tended to define sexual limits according to the teachings of their religion or other institutions, young women today are much more likely to view morality as a personal matter. This is a significant shift because organized religion has historically been women's most sexually restricting social force, controlling their behavior, reproduction, and conscience.

Statistics show that while young women still consider religion meaningful and influential, they follow only some of its teachings. For example, in a September 1997 *Glamour* magazine survey, 67 percent of the respondents said that religion was "very important," and only 3 percent said that religion was "not important." Eighty-four percent believed in God, and only 16 percent did not. At the same time, 46 percent said their parents were more religious, and more than half had stopped practicing their parents' religion because they disagreed with its social and political stances. Fifty-four percent of those in that category said that the church's rituals left them spiritually unfulfilled, and 36 percent had dismissed the religion's doctrines as "illogical and untenable" (231). And concerns besides religion actually control behavior. In a 1996 study of college virgins, the sixth most common reason given by women was "[Premarital sex] is against my religious beliefs," after fears of pregnancy, AIDS and STDs, and not feeling personally ready (Sprecher and Regan 1996).

Even if it doesn't ultimately control their sexual behavior, religion still is a source of young women's inner struggles concerning sex, a fact often ignored by many secular and feminist critics. When discussing sexual issues, the women I met brought up no other topic more often than religion. They mentioned religion as a factor in how they were dealing with almost every sexual issue, such as homosexuality, premarital sex, abortion, openness when discussing sex, the family, and especially sexual pleasure and guilt. Those women most preoccupied with religious issues were the ones raised as Christians, a majority of those I interviewed (and 80 percent of the country). Particularly affected were Catholics and evangelical Christians, faiths that rigidly define women's sexual roles. In contrast, none of the several Jewish women whom I interviewed mentioned their religion as a factor in their sex lives. By all accounts, Jews (representing only 2 percent of the total U.S. population) are the most educated religious group and thus the most sexually liberal. Furthermore, unlike Catholicism, Judaism is not opposed to contraception.

Moral and Spiritual Values

American women have seldom viewed morality as a personal matter. Rather, the assumption has long been that men are naturally corrupt and lustful and that it is therefore the responsibility of the naturally more virtuous woman to keep them under control. Accordingly, women are supposed to sacrifice their own sexual fulfillment and to try to prevent men from going too far. Though rooted deeply in American culture, the ideals of self-discovery and spiritual fulfillment enjoyed a great popular resurgence in the 1960s among men and women alike. In *A Generation of Seekers*, religion professor Wade Clark Roof notes the individualistic shifts of the 1960s baby boomers, who set the pattern for the next generations. As a group, people in their twenties have always attended church less often, but the boomers and those succeeding them were even more likely to distance themselves from their religious institutions during their entire lifetime, to question religious institutions, to design their own styles and patterns of worship, to switch religions, or to drop out.

Also defying the established churches in the 1960s, the courts paved the way for more personal freedoms. Between 1965 and 1977, the U.S. Supreme Court, in opposition to religious doctrines, confirmed the constitutional right to sexual or reproductive autonomy, or privacy. This began with the *Griswold v. Connecticut* decision for "marital privacy" for birth control in 1965 and culminated in *Roe v. Wade* in 1973, which established women's constitutional right to abortion.

For women in particular, the influence of education has been a liberalizing force, giving them new critical skills to evaluate sexist doctrines. Educated women are exposed to more secular ideas. For example, young Catholic women are less sheltered in their education today, whether or not they attend a Catholic college. Moreover, at the College of St. Catherine, the largest Catholic women's college in the country, which I visited in 1996, only a minority of the students and faculty were Catholics. "I went to university in the early 1960s," observed Frances Kissling, president of Catholics for a Free Choice, Washington, D.C. "The idea that somebody, a Catholic, would go to a non-Catholic college was almost shocking. 'Oh, she's going to a non-Catholic college! She's going to lose her soul!' would be sort of what we would be afraid of and what we were taught to be afraid of. Now, Catholics are all over the place. Not only are Catholics going in record numbers to non-Catholic colleges, non-Catholics are going to Catholic colleges in record numbers, so you don't have this kind of ghettoization of young Catholics that existed when I was growing up, and young women and young men are exposed to other ideas much easier."

Another particularly strong force affecting women's spiritual growth and sexual control has been the women's movement, operating both inside and outside religious institutions. In the 1960s, women started organizing within all major religions to make them more woman friendly and also to expand their own participation and power. At the same time, they actually transformed many religions to emphasize individual conscience and self-authority, which gave women more sexual freedom. More than anyone else I interviewed, Rev. Kathryn Ragsdale Hancock, 38, an Episcopal priest in the Boston area, personifies these changes. One of the first generation of female clergy, she has seen the gradual change in women's power and influence in the church. (The Episcopal Church, which ordained women as priests and bishops beginning in 1976, was the last of the Protestant denominations to do so.) In addition, she recently was the president of the Religious Coalition for Reproductive Rights and so represents women's religious movements for choices and personal decision making.

Hancock stresses that the change has been slow, with women now just at the entry level and power "still pretty much in the hands of the guys." Some feminists point out a "stained-glass ceiling" that prevents them from reaching higher posts. However, Hancock also sees women transforming religion by creating new models of leadership, which certainly applies to how they counsel women about sexual issues. "The whole notion of whether it's appropriate for the church to be telling you, to be answering your questions for you—as opposed to you answering your own—has, I think, really been changed by women in the priesthood or the ministry," she said. "What's different about that and the old model is that I now help the person sort through all those things to make her decision, rather than using my experience, my knowledge, to tell her what the answer to her problem is: you should or should not have an abortion. No, let's instead look at all the implications and help you make an ethical decision." This feminist style has also influenced how male clergy guide women. "I don't see as many guys acting that [old] way anymore either. Partly because they've been enlightened, and partly because they can't get away with it because people have seen that that's not intrinsic to the job," Hancock remarked.

New Priorities for a New Generation

As a result of this criticism of organized religion, young women—also following the boomers—have changed what they expect from religion itself. They define their religiosity less strictly according to traditional doctrines, such as those dealing with sexual behavior. Rather, they consider themselves as religious if they are spiritual or are part of a religious community.

Major surveys of young Catholic women confirm that beliefs about social justice are far more important bonds than the sexual rules. In a large survey for *A Generation of Seekers*, more than two-thirds (68 percent) of the Catholic women polled denied that one must obey the church's teachings on abortion to be a good Catholic, and 85 percent agreed that one could be a good Catholic without going to church every Sunday. But only 19 percent said that one could be a good Catholic without being concerned about the poor (Roof 1993, 232, writing about a survey conducted by an independent polling firm of 2,620 households in the United States in 1988 and 1989).

Claire, 25, who teaches at a Catholic school in Los Angeles and secretly lived with her fiancé before marriage, agrees with this philosophy. And because she disagreed with the Catholic Church's view of women and didn't want the church to restrict her sexual choices, she has decided to leave it eventually. She said she was still committed to religion, however, and planned to join a more egalitarian Episcopal church. Claire valued religion most for "the sense of community, the sense of needing to help people, the sense that you need to go there every Sunday so that you can keep on working on being a good person." She added that in "a big city like Los Angeles," finding community through religion was especially important.

The most articulate exponents of this individualistic attitude whom I interviewed were the students I met at the College of St. Catherine. Even though this school is more liberal than most Catholic institutions, these women typified the nonobedient views tracked in large-scale polls of both

Catholic women and the broader population. (Specific conflicts among Catholics are explored in a later section.) Influenced by an education that encourages critical thought, they are more likely to question their religion, and hence its sexual restrictions, than their mothers were.

Two good friends and student leaders, Taunya, 22, and Jessica, 21, subscribed to the prevalent views on campus about major controversial sexual issues. Both were prochoice and supported gay rights. "I don't necessarily agree with their activities," said Taunya, talking about lesbians, "but I'm accepting of other people's lifestyle and I'm not going to judge them." In contrast to their mothers, they both said that they don't even equate birth control with guilt. "I don't feel guilty at all, at all, at all," said Jessica. "I don't even think about it," agreed Taunya.

How did they define sexual morality—according to either what the church taught or what they thought independently? Jessica answered that she had learned about sex from the church but that she made her decisions independently because of the gray areas the religion does not consider. "My morals kind of come out of the church in a way because they have been strained through my grandparents down to my parents and finally to me, but they're not as strict or black and white. They're more fuzzy gray. It's situational. I'm not going to let a church decide what could be important to me. What I should decide is for myself as an individual—and what I decide is whatever I think is right about sex. What I think is that you should think about the reasons why you're engaged in this act of sexuality and then think about whether or not you're going to get pregnant. Think about: are you ready to handle the responsibility if something is to happen? And are you mature enough to understand what it really is all about? That kind of comes out of the church, but it's not limiting to me as far as ideas you have to do it after marriage, or it's just for procreation. There's a lot of gray when it comes to sex. And I think there is so much emotion that is involved that the church does not hit on. It's very black and white: 'It's after marriage, it's for procreation. You do it. It's submissive. You're passive.' Whatever. Don't talk about how fun an orgasm is—*oh no*."

Taunya mirrored many of Jessica's views, although she still considered herself a Catholic. I asked her whether there was just plain right and wrong, which couldn't be questioned. She agreed but said that sexuality specifically demanded investigation of the gray areas. "I think morality is individual. And I think that morality is you search and delve into yourself and know what you want and what you need and what is good for you. If you do something and you don't have a problem with it, and that's what you want to do and you know that's right for you, then how can that be immoral?" However, Taunya added that she had felt guilt, evidence of the still strong impact of her religion. Like other Catholic women I interviewed, she gave stunning examples of coping rationalizations, which had subsided with age. "But I also remember, intercourse was sex. I could do *everything else*, everything else besides intercourse and it wouldn't be wrong. That's how I would rationalize it. And when I did have sex, I had to rationalize it, well, he put it in a little bit, so that's not really sex. It wasn't sex until it was *full-fledged* sex. . . . And maybe I had to rationalize it that way because I don't want to feel guilty. And maybe I still am doing that. I don't know. Who knows? . . . I had the hardest time when I lost my virginity. I cried for two weeks. I thank God that I had a supportive boyfriend that could listen to me cry about it."

Other Moral Guidelines and Loopholes

Taunya's guilt reveals that traditional religious standards nonetheless still define morality. The ultimate moral ideal, combining traditional and modern beliefs, is to limit sex to a committed relationship. Thus the traditional injunction "that good girls don't have sex outside marriage" has changed to "good girls don't have sex outside relationships," said New York City marital and sex therapist Shirley Zussman, quoted in a *Glamour* article on women's sexual ambivalence (Jacoby 1993, 259). Studies reflect women's remaining standard connecting sex and love—for instance, that college women's support of premarital sex is highest when the couple is in love or engaged (Wilson and Medora 1990).

Jenn, from Austin, Texas, was cynical about this dictum. "We haven't changed any more attitudes about sexuality. We still, you know, may acknowledge other kinds of relationships besides marriage. We acknowledge living together. But we still require some sort of a marriage context. Some sort of a heart connection for sex to be acceptable in our society." Reflecting this standard's wide support, even the most conservative women I interviewed said they could live with it. Laura, a fundamentalist Christian student at Texas Women's University, said that she is personally waiting until marriage. But, she added, "I don't look down on people who are in monogamous relationships and having sex. I think it's wonderful that they have a relationship. I wish that I had a relationship right now."

Another moral standard for casual sex is the "mutuality" of the sexual encounter, that is, whether the woman is having sex voluntarily. This is a strong feminist influence, the result of the growing movements against acquaintance rape and nonconsensual sex. University of Maryland sociologist and sex researcher Ilsa Lottes told me that in addition to securing protection against disease and unwanted pregnancy, this is a standard that defines the morality of an encounter, and she often discusses it with students.

Occasionally, people set their college years apart from others, as a time when such behavior can be justified as a time when sexual experimentation is expected. Shelly, a Miami high school teacher, said that casual sex was more permissible in college, but not as much for women of her age, the mid-twenties. "If I didn't have a boyfriend now, I wouldn't be promiscuous, by any means," she said. "But I wouldn't be waiting six months to sleep with someone, either." Also reflecting common norms, Shelly and her friends, fellow high school teachers, admitted that they disapproved of teenagers having sex, for reasons of disease, pregnancy, and emotional immaturity. This is a common American belief, even for those who had sex in their early teens, as Shelly did. One study found that men and women students more harshly judge behavior by those under 18 (Sprecher 1989). This contrasts with the prevailing belief in Scandinavian countries, where sex for teens aged 15 to 19 is regarded as a normal part of growing up, Lottes added, in an interview. As a result, sex education in those countries is more thorough, and condoms and birth control for teens are more accessible.

The Ethic of Social Tolerance

Tolerance is a related social value that challenges old-fashioned religious practices—whether or not rooted in the actual doctrine—of condemning women who do not follow traditional sexual roles. Even though it is not always the actual practice today, the concept of sexual tolerance is a much better articulated ethic of our social climate, such as in the workplace and at schools. This tolerance varies somewhat by gender and by issue. Thus women are much more tolerant of homosexuality, but men are more tolerant of extramarital sex and casual sex (Smith 1994a, 85).

When discussing the benefits of regarding religion as a personal matter, Kris, 22, an office manager in California, stressed tolerance. "I think everyone needs something to believe in, but we all need to shut our mouths and believe to ourselves and not dictate to other people. I mean the importance of a religion is practicing and believing what you want to believe, but also giving the people around you a practice and a belief that they want freely."

In turn, many of the more conservative women also indicated their tolerance of those who had made other choices. Leslie and Mark, both 24, a devoutly Christian married couple in Santa Barbara, California, who waited until they married to have sex, noted that they don't judge others who have made different choices.

"I can't say which is right," said Leslie. "All I know is for us, waiting until we got married was right."

"Right for us," emphasized Mark.

Catholic Dissent on Sexual Issues

Also following the boomers, young women are comfortable disagreeing with their particular religion's teachings on sex while remaining in that faith. Again, perhaps no group of women better exemplifies the impact of resistance to church authority than do young Catholics. The shift to following one's conscience over the church's male hierarchy has become pervasive. Young Catholic women define a "good Catholic" more liberally—that is, less according to sexual behavior—and are much less likely to feel guilty. Those I interviewed were the most likely to disagree with their church and to leave specifically because of its doctrines on women and sexuality, and they were also by far the most likely to discuss religion as a source of personal sexual conflict.

Part of the reason for my so often hearing about this dissent is that Catholicism was the most common denomination of my respondents, who were typical of the U.S. population as a whole (and represent about a quarter of the population). But a more significant reason is probably that the Catholic Church's doctrines on sexuality are among the most strict, confining, and unrealistic. Sex defines a person's goodness or purity, with the Virgin Mary's immaculate conception as proof of her virtue. The most revered members of the Catholic community, the clergy, are celibate. In contrast, young Catholic women's sexual behavior and attitudes fit squarely in the mainstream, with surveys showing that they aren't having any less premarital sex or using less birth control than other Americans do. In fact, studies show that Catholic attitudes toward abortion match those of the American population, including those with no religion. As a result, they are likely to confront the issue of religious guilt and reconcile the split between dogma and practice. (Conversely, evangelical Protestant women are the most uniformly conservative in behavior, and mainline Protestant women have less conflict with their more moderate religions.) Catholics are also split down the middle as traditionalists or progressives, resulting in half of its followers being active dissenters from official doctrines (*Diminishing Divide* 1996, 9).

Two separate large-scale studies of church-going Catholic women, the first conducted in 1979 of the boomers and the second in 1993 of the post-boomers, reflect similarly defiant sexual attitudes, a dramatic change from the pre-1960s generations. Writing in the journal *Conscience* in 1994, William D'Antonio summed up these postboomer patterns:

> Church leaders cannot count on docile laywomen. . . . These young people as a whole have pretty much rejected church teachings on contraception and divorce, and are ambivalent about morality of premarital sex, abortion, and gay/lesbian relations. Yet, they frequently engage in premarital sex, want abortion to remain legal (at least in a range of circumstances), and support some gay/lesbian rights even if they deem homosexual behavior immoral. (39, 40)

Such sexual conflicts between women and the Catholic religion are not new. But young women today, as did the boomer women, are more likely to question the church's authority. They more commonly blame church teachings, and not themselves, as wrong. Those who don't feel comfortable with dissent often leave. The young Catholic women I interviewed volunteered how they had disagreed with the church's stands on sexuality and women, and as a result, most had either left the church or distanced themselves from it, such as by pledging not to raise their children as Catholics. Some sociologists, such as Father Andrew Greeley, argue that the decline in Catholic commitment that started in the 1960s was accounted for "almost entirely by a change in sexual attitudes," along with attitudes toward the papacy (Greeley, McCready, and McCourt 1976, 304).

In the 1960s, the Second Vatican Council introduced reforms emphasizing the importance of the individual conscience in faith. But then in 1968, the church issued the infamous *Humanae Vitae*, the encyclical affirming traditional views banning birth control. This confused many Catholics, who had been optimistic about the recent reforms heralding future changes. The encyclical also triggered doubts about the church's views on divorce, abortion, remarriage, and the ordination of women. Among the most alienated groups were the more educated and affluent, the most likely to question Catholic dicta on sexual and gender matters.

Francis Kissling, president of a leading dissent group, Catholics for a Free

Choice, noted the difference between generations: "I think that Catholic women who generally might be classified as pre–Vatican II, Catholic women who were growing up and reached maturity prior to 1970, tended to have more of a belief that you had to accept everything that the church taught, or you had to separate yourself from the church. I don't think that one would find a very strong difference in what they believed about these issues, but I think that what you would find is that older Catholics believed that they were out of sync with the church. Younger women have a greater sense and have been more readily, more easily, taught that they have the right to evaluate moral situations on the basis of their own experience and to apply their own conscientious reasoning to these situations, to use their conscience rather than to automatically accept the teachings of the church. And I think that is indeed what they are doing."

Another older, but more conservative, Catholic, Mary Ann Hanlon, 54, the earlier-mentioned mother of five who leads religious "pre-canna"—premarital counseling sessions—in her home, had the same observation. "The teachings have not changed one iota, really. But you're no longer told every day that you're going to go to hell because you didn't go to mass. So people marched to this drummer because they didn't want to pay for it in the afterlife." As a result of women's relying more on their consciences than on church authority, Hanlon said, "I think there's a lot less guilt. We had a religion of guilt. Because the decisions lie within you, you can make these decisions."

Protestant Religion as a Guideline to Sex

No matter what their religious backgrounds, young women also become their own sexuality authorities by viewing their religion as offering a guide, not an absolute command, to how they should lead their sex lives. In many ways, mainline Protestant women best represent this attitude. Those I interviewed rarely mentioned a clash with their religion and sexuality, and relied on their conscience to guide their decisions. In contrast to evangelicals and Catholics, and like the small number of Jewish women I interviewed, the Protestants were the most greatly influenced by and open to the spiritual, therapeutic, and feminist movements of the 1960s. Most did not see a conflict between their religion and their sexuality, because mainline Protestant clergy were much less likely than evangelical Protestants to speak out about sexual issues. In fact, as Episcopal priest Kathryn Ragsdale Hancock asserted, most of her congregants don't seem to know about their church's generally positive stand on sexuality. Hancock explained that speaking positively about sexuality is more difficult for clergy than is condemning it. In taking a pro-choice or pro–gay rights stance, for example, she risks offending the more vocal conservative factions in her church.

A few of the mainline Protestant women I interviewed discussed their practice of sex under their religion's often unspoken guidelines. They pointed out that their religion succeeded primarily in making them more conscious of sex, not to make them take it for granted but to help them appreciate and see its spiritual dimension. The result was not complete permissiveness, but neither was it utter restraint and docility.

Sarah, a Washington, D.C., law student, told me that at the age of 23, she was finally able to look back and understand how her religious background "shaped my sexuality in more ways than I realize." Her father, a Lutheran pastor, made it clear that he thought premarital sex was wrong. "I wouldn't say that my parents are strict, but they gave me a pretty good idea of what they thought was expected, right or wrong type of thing." But her parents are also children of the 1960s, very open about talking about sex with her. They emphasized the importance of spirituality and told Sarah that "your faith is very personal." As a result, she observed, "I think about sex more thoroughly. I don't think of myself as conservative as far as sex goes, but I guess maybe some people would."

Sarah defied her parents' teachings about premarital sex without guilt but also with the high degree of consciousness that they instilled in her. She has had sex with two different people, both boyfriends in relationships that lasted about eight months. In the first, she waited to have sex after four months, and the second, after six weeks. She was in love with one of her boyfriends, and she describes the other relationship as "maybe I thought I was in love but really wasn't kind of thing." Sarah resolved issues of sexual morality by looking into herself. "It's not necessarily the fact of whether this goes against my values. Because to me, I think it really comes from the fact that if I feel good about a situation, if I feel good about this person, I communicate with this person and they understand where I'm coming from and I understand where they're coming from, then there's not a moral question for me." When her first relationship started, Sarah felt comfortable enough to tell her parents that she was considering having sex with her boyfriend. "I was very open with my parents. I said, 'Look, I spend the night there all the time.' At that point, I wasn't sleeping with him. . . . My dad wrote me this letter and said that whatever decision you make, I trust you to make the right decision because I really believe that you have a really good idea of who you are and what your beliefs are as far as this relationship."

Seeking Alternatives from Liberal Churches

In the past, with less mobility and fewer choices of religion, women would probably have had to follow the one religion of her family or community. But today, with increased mobility in society, they have more freedom to choose more egalitarian faiths and institutions. "There's no grand authority. There's no tradition that you have to hold on to. And of course, with any cultural change, it's got to be more pronounced in the younger people," said Rev. Hancock, the Episcopal priest in Massachusetts. "I think you find much more denomination hopping than you used to. People move, and instead of finding an Episcopal church again, they find the nearest compatible church, regardless of denomination. It's kind of interesting to know what the church teaches about this, that or the other thing, but no one feels compelled to believe it just because the church teaches it. I think that's a very widespread phenomenon."

As a result of this mobility, many women search more actively to find a denomination that reflects their sexual beliefs and lifestyles. For example, Ivy, interviewed in the beginning of this chapter, moved from the Catholic Church to an evangelical one that gave her more personal support and tolerated her divorce. Two of the three feminist activists in Austin whom I interviewed in my core sample group, both friends, described their move to the Unity Church, a "New Thought" church founded in the late nineteenth century as an outgrowth of Mary Baker Eddy's Church of Christ, Scientist.

Jenn, 27, the executive director of a nonprofit group in Austin, explained this switch from her family's conservative Lutheran church. "I remember being 13 years old—I hadn't even kissed a boy, and we were driving home from church one day. And somehow they started talking about premarital sex. And my parents informed me in the car on the way home from church at the age of 13 that if they ever found out that I had sex before I was married, that I would be disowned. And as I got a little bit older and got into college and felt more independence from my family, I just completely abandoned religion and wouldn't go. And I thought the whole thing was a plot by the devil to make us all feel bad about ourselves. But just recently I've been feeling like I need some spirituality, so I've been doing some more searching and I've found a church now that I feel like helps me to relate to sex as a spiritual act, instead of as a physical act. . . . They basically recognize all religions as cogs in the wheel and don't have a doctrine that says if you don't come to our church and say these words, then you aren't going to be in touch with God. It's pretty much we're here to support you as you find your own way, to be right with yourself. And a lot of the literature that I've picked up at the church bookstore and things like that really helped me get in touch with the fact that sex is not just a physical thing. It's not just an emotional thing; it has to do with your spirit and your mental attitude. It's a soul connection between two people. And God is there when you're having sex, too. It's been really good for me to find a place that supports the attitudes that I'm seeking."

A growing number of women are finding that they don't have to leave a conservative faith for sexual acceptance. Aimee, 23, another student at the College of St. Catherine, has found a liberal Catholic Church that tolerates her sexual views and history. As a single mother and a bisexual, she had thought that she couldn't find a place in that religion. But a few years ago when seeking a community and religious values for her daughter, she decided to return to the church. Today, attending services every Sunday, she is an active member on several boards. While her particular church is unusually tolerant and she has a more challenging sexual history than most, her arrangement is one that would not have existed twenty years ago.

Beyond "Wifely Duties": The Fundamentalists

Many women, however, do accept their faith's teachings on women's sexual restraint. For fundamentalist Christians, the word of the Bible is more than a guideline; it is irrefutable law. To them, individual conscience is clearly second to religious doctrine and obligation to the church. These women are probably the least individualistic in behavior and opinion. They are less apt to question their religion's interpretation of Scripture, which rigidly prescribes the proper place, time, and sequence of sexual acts. The Bible is widely interpreted as portraying women's sexuality as the "gateway of the devil," and thus evangelicals are more likely to regard women's proper sexual place as passive and subservient. Unlike mainline Protestants, evangelical churches commonly openly discuss sexual issues, but in a commanding way, mandating women's proper roles and actively organizing against sexual freedom and information, such as with campaigns condemning abortion, gay rights, and the media.

In the past thirty years, however, in often subtle ways, American culture has altered the way that even the strictest fundamentalists view and speak about sex. As a result, a common view among evangelicals is that sex is a positive and important force—as long as it is confined to marriage. Among the most influential boomer forces was an upsurge in education, and as a result, evangelicals have made a more dramatic shift than even that of the immigrant Catholic population. Its members are no longer on the rural fringes of society but instead now represent mainstream American society. They have moved from rural areas or small towns to cities and suburbs. Moderate evangelicals are now better educated and pursue careers like those of the rest of the population (*Diminishing Divide* 1996, 10).

Laura, at Texas Women's University in Denton, follows this pattern of being traditional, but on her own terms. On the one hand, she describes her sexual views and those of her fundamentalist Christian friends as conservative. They are putting off having sex until they are married: "I'd like to be married as a virgin; I'd like both of us to discover love together." Laura also openly worries about the sinful effect of lesbian activism on campus and told me about a friend's trauma of having been stuck with a lesbian roommate. Yet some of Laura's views are independent, reflecting the majority American culture and not all consistent with her strict Methodist religion. For example, she is prochoice, which she admits is "a strange view for me to have." I asked her about how she reconciled that view with the Bible. "It says 'thou shalt not kill,' but I feel like if you cause a woman—like in Louisiana, they were wanting to restrict all abortions—to go to term with a baby that's going to kill her, that's the same thing." I asked her about cases in which the life of the mother is not in danger, and her views sound more liberal. She would never choose abortion for herself but felt it was the right of others. "Constitutionally, I think that they [women] should have the right to choose. I certainly don't agree with it, and I wouldn't want my daughter knowing that she should have an abortion as birth control or something, but I feel constitutionally she should have the right. I wouldn't want someone else telling me that I couldn't."

Despite their frequent condemnation of things secular, even the most conservative churches have subtly adopted individualistic ways of perceiving morality. No matter what the denomination, the most basic messages of morality are expressed in personal, individualistic terms. People of a variety of faiths and religious commitments frame right and wrong in the same ways. "What matters is that people live good lives, that they try to live by the Golden Rule, and that they try to do the best they can," reports Wade Clark

Roof about his large and diverse interview sample in *A Generation of Seekers* (1993, 186–87).

But the Religious Right does have reason to be alarmed. To be sure, religious individualism's greatest threat to the status quo is to the religious establishment itself. Boomers and postboomers are seeking and demanding more authenticity from their churches and synagogues in order to unite the religious and the spiritual realms of their lives, which too often have been separate. This drive for spirituality and meaning is changing the institutions, forcing them to examine entrenched sexist beliefs and traditions and to become more dynamic and egalitarian and less condemning of women specifically as "sexual transgressors."

Whereas religion formerly molded young women, young women are now demanding to remold their institutions. Instead of allowing themselves to be judged, they are judging their religions as narrow-minded and oppressive. In their quest to live their sex lives on their own terms, they are demanding to be treated in the same way as men are. They seek to be defined apart from their sexuality—not primarily evaluated as people according to how well they conform to traditional gender roles and what they do in bed.

10. Women's "Locker-Room Talk," Safer-Sex Education, and the Media: New Information and Openness

Girls are getting better sex now than they did before, now that they can talk about it.

—Good-looking South Miami Beach guy on MTV's
Sex in the '90s documentary

When 20-year-old Darlene had sex for the first time (a few months before our conversation), with her first real boyfriend, she hardly fit the stereotype of a virgin as a sexually ignorant naïf. She knew about birth control. She knew how to make the experience more enjoyable physically. She knew she shouldn't feel guilty. After all, she had done her homework. Darlene explained her personal journey for sex information during much of our interview in her parents' Orange County, California, home. She was on summer break from Occidental College and was living in her old room, filled with objects from her teenage years. Tennis trophies crowded the small desk, and on the wall were movie posters, already curling around the edges with age.

While she was in high school, she couldn't depend on getting sex education in the classroom, as the fundamentalist Christians in her area had restricted the curriculum to lessons on abstinence. So she and her parents filled in the gaps. Years ago, they gave her a copy of *Our Bodies, Ourselves*, which became her central reference source. "When I was a teenager, I was in that stage: 'That's gross, Mom and Dad. Don't talk to me about that. I'm not into that stuff. You don't have to worry about me.' And so I didn't read it. And recently, a week ago, I was like, 'Gee, I wonder,' and I pulled it out and was reading certain sections. I think I read the section on masturbation. It was decently helpful." A major source of information has been her friends; she has received emotional support from those closest to her and practical technical advice from others. "A couple of my friends that know me well enough analyze why I have certain guilt about certain things. They have insight into that. But with other friends . . . it's more superficial: 'Oh gee it hurts my back when I do this.'. . . The ways you could do it. It's just normal talk. It's like if I said, 'I'm building this thing, and I don't know. I don't know how to build a bench.' And they say, 'Well, try doing this, and it will work.'" Darlene also took a human sexuality class in college, which provided more details and included topics such as AIDS and women's sexual response. "But we got into this section at the very end and she [the professor] talked about the three types of orgasms that women can have. She went through all of this stuff and really educated me. I had no idea."

Like Darlene, millions of American women are overcoming a competing onslaught of sexual censorship, such as that imposed by the Christian Right on her high school, by plugging into a wide range of other channels. With friends and family and in the schools and in the media, they discuss sexual subjects with new frankness. Darlene represents a generation of women raised with an unprecedented level of sexual openness and access to information. This opportunity was made possible by the social movements that set the stage in the 1960s and 1970s: jobs for women gave them consumer power to seek information; the sexual revolution gave them permission and created a "sexualized marketplace"; and the women's health movement, a separate branch of feminism, advocated that women take control of their bodies through personal and political awareness. At the beginning of a new century, the constantly expanding technology of the information age has accelerated this flow of communication. Its effects have been mixed. On the one hand, we observe the negative and cheapened side: the proliferation of male-manufactured, profit-driven, degrading, violent, and sexualized images of women that now litter our landscape. Yet we young women of the information age also should be grateful for the empowerment that has resulted from this sexual openness. Despite its negative aspects, this climate has enabled women to conduct their sex lives their way.

A Generational Divide

Growing up in this more liberal climate, young people are more likely to dismiss old-fashioned notions that talk about sex ruins romance, is always tasteless, or leads to promiscuity. Studies reveal that the generation gap in sexual knowledge, like that in sexual behavior and attitudes, is greatest between the boomers and their elders. In a Kinsey survey of sexual literacy, the lowest scorers were both men and women, 45 and older, who grew up in very different environments. Women aged 18 to 44 and men aged 30 to 44, which included both boomers and the younger generation, scored higher than did the other groups (Reinisch and Beasley 1990, 20, from a 1989 statistically representative survey of 1,974 American adults). The authors of the 1993 *Janus Report on Sexual Behavior* also discovered dramatic differences in knowledge between the oldest generation and their children:

> Our research unearthed some gothic fears and beliefs that were widespread among today's grandfathers when they were young and uninformed—none of which was mentioned by any of today's young male respondents. The most deplorable were "vaginum dentatum," a belief that the vagina had teeth and could bite the penis, and "penis captivus," the power of a female sex partner to "clamp up" and hold the penis captive in the vagina. (36)

Other surveys of young women reveal not only the demise of such myths but also a new sexual openness that surpasses even that of the boomers. This includes support of the most mundane and unsexy information about sexual health, which is now readily available to the middle class. A marketing newsletter about women consumers, the "EDK Forecast," reports on young women's particular receptiveness to advertisements of feminine hygiene products. In "The Tampon Taboo: The Period Goes Public," it reports that women's main complaint about advertisements is that they insult their intelligence with "outdated notions of modesty":

> Women think ads for feminine hygiene products are stupid, but not offensive. They don't consider sanitary protection a badge of shame. It's just part of everyday life for them, and those around them. The older a woman is, the more uncomfortable she is likely to be with those ads; 32 percent of women aged 40–50 say these ads shouldn't be aired, compared with only 5 percent of women under age 30. Older women are also more apt to say that women get embarrassed when a sanitary protection ad pops up in the middle of their favorite TV show (31 percent versus 16 percent of those under 30). (1995, 4)

The generations also differed on the subject of AIDS-prevention messages. According to a 1996 Kaiser Foundation survey of Americans' views of AIDS and HIV, 87 percent of the respondents aged 18 to 29 years strongly supported open communication about the disease and were the most likely age group to support condom advertisements on television, compared with 71 percent of all Americans and only 52 percent of those 65 years and older. Sixty-two percent of those aged 18 to 29 were also more likely to agree with distributing condoms in high schools. In contrast, only 46 percent of all Americans and 29 percent of those 65 and older agreed with this practice.

Others have personally noticed these changes. Sarah Weddington, a lawyer in Austin, Texas, who successfully argued for abortion rights in the 1973 *Roe v. Wade* case when she was in her mid-twenties, said that she notices more women supporting one another through personal crises. When she was in college at the University of Texas in 1967, she had a dangerous and illegal abortion in Mexico, an experience made even more harrowing and shameful by its secrecy. Even though she became famous arguing for abortion rights in public before the U.S. Supreme Court, she never told any of her friends about this experience. Now she notes, "I think with close friends, there's much more openness now and much more support. . . . I think that also means they get more support through the experience and making the decision. It's a healthier environment."

Women Versus Men as Seekers

Young women now know more about sex than do their male peers, contradicting the stereotype of women as sexually ignorant and men as experts. The Kinsey sexual literacy test attributed the higher scores of women aged 19 to 29 than those of men of that age range to their "growing belief that they have a *right* to sex information and accessible publications about women's health."

This difference in men's and women's desire for sexual information was confirmed in my interviews. Many of the men said that they were too embarrassed to ask friends or get information in books. Rather, they were much more likely to name "experience," "the street," and pornography as their primary and exclusive sources of information. When seeking sexual knowledge, then, the old double standard has actually been reversed: young women feel free to search for sexual facts while men hesitate to discuss sex, except in pornographic terms with their friends. The reasons are numerous. First, information about women's biology and sexual response is less commonly discussed in the media and thus requires more active seeking to discover. Also, if they are ignorant, women have to suffer more consequences, including unwanted pregnancy and sexually transmitted diseases, with the latter often more harmful to women's health than to men's. According to the Kinsey sexual literacy survey, women knew more than men did about sexual health and contraception, and men knew more about the occurrence of certain sexual behaviors, such as anal sex, masturbation, and extramarital sex.

The women I interviewed recognized this evolving sexual openness as enhancing their sexual development in the 1980s and 1990s. When asked about the central difference between their mothers' generation and their own in directing their sex lives, they often discussed openness, mainly in the media or when talking about sex with their parents. (This was the third most common answer, surpassed by having more sexual choices and then by dealing with the threat of AIDS.) This openness was apparent in their frankness when talking to me. When I asked them about their primary sources of sexual information and openness, they named (in almost equal numbers) sex education from parents and schools, the informational media, and "locker-room talk" with friends. (They had more mixed opinions about the entertainment media, which generally offer limited and often degrading sexual images of women.) Studies reveal these sources of information as typical. A 1996 Kaiser Foundation survey ranks parents as the top source of sex and birth control information, mentioned by 72 percent of those surveyed. Sixty-nine percent of the teens surveyed mentioned teachers, school nurses, or sex education classes; 60 percent cited their friends (other than boyfriends or girlfriends); and 53 percent named the media, such as TV talk shows or movies (Kaiser Family Foundation Survey on Teens and Sex 1996).

In a single generation, reliance on parents and schools has replaced hearsay from "the streets" as the principal source of sexual information. But even though parents and schools are increasingly more likely to give children the information they *should* know, other sources provide more of what they *want* to know, such as information about sexual pleasure, maintaining relationships, and detailed instruction on protecting themselves.

Young Women's "Locker-Room Talk"

"In college, one night there were six or seven girls, our same age, good friends, sitting in a bar and really talking, I mean just how we have orgasms," said Janine, 24. "And this happened to be a masturbation conversation. In the middle of the bar. There were millions of people around us, laughing and learning. It was unbelievable. I guess that's how we figure things out." This Florida high school teacher and two of her friends again discussed this topic together in detail. One of them, Tammy, admitted that she had never had an orgasm. "They told me how and now I can. I'm healed . . . ," Tammy announced. "It's comforting to know that people have experienced similar things or that your friends know and that they understand that it's OK. I guess it's good to know that you're OK." Even though Tammy's parents were so progressive that they regarded sex as a positive experience, their conversation stopped short of discussing the erotic details. "My mom is totally ignorant as far as that is concerned," said Tammy. "She is a highly educated woman and we're very close to her. As far as sex, she's from the Midwest. She was with my father. That was the only person. . . . So we don't talk about it. . . . I would never tell my mom, 'I can't have an orgasm. I don't know how.'"

As these friends demonstrate, women's locker-room talk today can be both edifying and trashy, therapeutic and ego fanning. One's girlfriends are often a constant presence influencing sexual relationships in many roles: cheerleader, referee, Internet listserve, crisis hotline, absolving priest, Greek chorus, sister, mom, aunt, RA, RN, MSW, reference book, shameless voyeur, and, sometimes, feminist advocate.

As the rules about sex have changed, so have the rules for talking about it. Feeling less guilty about being sexual beings and taking advantage of strong and sharing friendships, women have opened their channels of communication. Instead of remaining silent and serving only as subjects of conquest for men's "locker-room talk"—as was the standard in the past, by all accounts— women are even more likely than men to talk about sex and in more vivid detail and more critically.

The pervasiveness of locker-room talk among young women of all backgrounds reflects the particular feminist legacy of the baby boomers. They opened the doors to free communication about their most intimate concerns and made women's friendships into a nurturing, empowering force. The early personal consciousness raising of the women's health movement in the 1960s and 1970s has now become a part of mainstream life. To understand the impact of the boomers, we need to look at how women in the general population related to one another before them. Before 1960, women usually didn't talk frankly about sex. Meanwhile, the men talked about getting laid. Documentation of these differing traditions can be found in Alfred C. Kinsey's 1953 *Sexual Behavior in the Human Female*. Kinsey and his coauthors noted that women's traditional silence about sex inhibited their behavior and knowledge. For example, they wrote that the women they surveyed who did masturbate typically discovered it entirely on their own. In contrast, most of the men (75 percent) that Kinsey had surveyed earlier had heard about it from others, and 40 percent had actually observed it. As a result, the men had usually begun this practice, a "basic training" for sex, ten to twenty years before the women. The authors observed:

This provides striking evidence of the ignorance which is frequent among females of sexual activities which are outside of their own experience, even though they may be common in the population as a whole. . . . It is obvious that neither younger girls nor older women discuss their sexual experiences in the open way that males do. (1953, 138)

Summing up the studies by Kinsey and by other social scientists through the mid-twentieth century, Sharon Thompson wrote in her 1995 book *Going All the Way,*

Talking romance is a female adolescent tradition; talking sex is not. In the 1940s, sociologist August Hollingshead observed that a "conspiracy of silence" surrounded teenage sex; Kinsey noted the "covert culture" in the 1950s. As recently as the 1960s, young college women reported that they didn't even tell friends about having sex unless they could represent it as a sign of progress in love. (Thompson 1995, 7, 8)

Accounts from the news and the entertainment industry offer a glimpse into the world of the modern-day woman. In one of the most explosive news stories of the century, Monica Lewinsky, following the open spirit of her generation, told at least ten friends about her relationship with "the creep." As is often the case with women's locker-room talk, Lewinsky's accounts of every aspect of the affair were explicit and thorough enough to satisfy the demands of a FBI probe, launch an investigation, and lead to impeachment hearings.

Likewise, book authors offer sex advice based on women's conversations, giving them the same weight and authority that "experts," such as doctors and psychologists, had in the old days. Popular books about sex written by young women start with accounts of women's locker-room talk. In her 1995 *Mindblowing Sex in the Real World,* Sari Locker discusses the influence of her Cornell University friends' "sexually graphic conversations in the hallway of my dorm some time between the midnight pizza and the 4 A.M. laundry" (2, 3). Former *Details* sex columnist Anka Radakovich entitled her 1994 book after its first chapter, "The Wild Girls Club." It describes the semiannual meeting of her friends with the admitted agenda of dishing the dirt about men in their lives. "What makes our gatherings different from the boys' night out is that nothing is too personal to say. And nobody drinks ten beers and throws up," she writes (4).

Television's greatest hits of the past decade also included locker-room talk. The 1996 season premiere of the highly rated sitcom *Friends* involved a conflict between Ross and Rachel in which Ross feels betrayed when he realizes that Rachel has told her friends about his sexual fantasy about Princess Leia of *Star Wars*. Rachel doesn't apologize, explaining that this sharing is standard; after all, "women tell each other everything." Ross answers that men instead only brag about exploits, without details, bringing up such sensational feats as a date with a stripper or doing it "on the back of the Staten Island ferry." Writing about HBO's popular *Sex and the City*, about a group of high-style, single, thirtysomething friends in New York City, *Entertainment Weekly* noted the show's foundation in "aural sex": "These women jabber with eyebrow-raising frankness about every subject under the *Kama Sutra*: oral sex, threesomes, romance-killing farts, cradle robbing, and anal sex, to name a few" (Jacobs 1999, 33, 34).

In the popular culture, women's music and videos provide possibly the most revealing view of what goes on behind the scenes. In Dolly Parton's 1993 music video "Romeo," she, Mary Chapin Carpenter, and others candidly discuss how the sight of Billy Ray Cyrus turns them on. "That sexy little body beats all I've ever seen. I ain't never seen a cowboy look so good in jeans," Parton sings. That year, young upstart Liz Phair became a media wonder with her frank dirty talk and bravado. Her song "Glory" from her debut album, *Exile in Guyville*, is a tribute to a man's cunnilingus skill: "He's got a really big tongue, it rolls way out," she describes. One of the top-rated and best-selling albums of 1998, *The Miseducation of Lauryn Hill*, is a paean to women's locker-room talk, even featuring bits of conversation among women between songs. Hill delivers her own worldly advice about men and relationships in "Doo Wop (That Thing)": "Girlfriend, let me break it down for you again. Don't be a hardrock when you're really a gem. Babygirl, respect is just a minimum."

Perhaps the ultimate women's locker-room song is Salt 'n Pepa's "Whatta Man," from the 1993 *Very Necessary* album, sung with En Vogue. These women sing in vivid detail about the pleasures of a man who gets it right.

"He's not in a rush. He loves me good and touches me in the right spot. See every guy that I've had, they try to play all that ——— (beeped out in song). But every time they tried I said, 'That's not it.' From 7 to 7, he's got me open like a 7–11."

In the 1990s, technology opened up a vast new frontier of women's locker-room talk: the Internet. While the sites are too numerous and constantly changing to list here, one revealing portal to this world (at the time of this writing) is the www.chickclick.com, started by two California twentysomethings, which features links to many young women's sites. The home page lists many open sexual conversations to visit on sister pages, such as one on the safety of Depo Provera on www.estrogen.com and another on sexual modesty on www.hissyfit.com.

Growing Instead of Bragging

In their quest for improvement and sharing, women are pursuing the "higher" goal of self-development. While many women exaggerate as much as the guys do, they also focus on the *quality* of their sexual experiences more than men do. Their conversations include more criticism, ambivalence, and emotional disclosure. While women are socialized to share, men are conditioned to concentrate on the score. Men's locker-room talk seems limited to bragging, often couching their conquests in battle terms. And it can be cruel; I associate its darkest side with the boyfriend of a friend in college whose fraternity gave out a "tuna award" on the day after the dance to the guy who had brought the ugliest date.

Former *Penthouse* sex advice columnist Susan Crain Bakos is an accomplished inside observer of this type of talk. In *What Men Really Want*, she sums up what happens behind the scenes:

Manspeak is usually spoken in places where women are not: within groups of men or written on pages sandwiched between photos of nude women. It is not meant to explain or demystify sex. Manspeak is penis talk, and the penis only knows up from down. It is the voice of bravado, the black humor of the soldier who tosses out expletives in the hope that "him" rather than "me" will be consumed by the opposing side. This is something women seldom understand. Manspeak is penile cheerleading. (Bakos 1990, 5, 6)

Academics also note this gender gap in locker-room talk. Ohio State sociologist Timothy Jon Curry, employing eavesdropping researchers, found out that men's locker-room talk is a loud performance centered on women as objects. Discussion of ongoing intimate relationships was quieter, often taking place behind rows of lockers and more subject to ridicule (Nelson 1994, 84). In contrast, according to Cynthia Begnal, a lecturer in speech communication at Pennsylvania State University, whereas women may often start out talking about men as objects, "the discussion eventually rolls around to how they're being treated by that man and what they want out of a relationship." She adds that women frequently talk about the values of men they have just met, and that men are more likely to restrict that type of conversation to their wives and girlfriends (Teegardin 1993, F17).

The most revealing interview I had about locker-room talk was with the three Florida friends, all high-school teachers enrolled in graduate school at Florida International University. Their open relationship, and its function in their own sex lives, was the topic that occupied most of our hour-and-a-half interview. Janine and Tammy grew up together in Miami and were used to telling each other everything. Tammy said that their boyfriends didn't mind, expecting that close friends would talk about men. Then Janine added, "Yes, but I also don't think they realize *the extent* of what we talk about." She explained that instead of talking about the expected female topic of love, they discuss the technical and detailed aspects of sex. They are cynical about love, seeing it as a rare occurrence, unlike sex, which is more common. "We see ourselves as different from most girls. We don't go around talking about love and relationships and flowers and doves singing. We don't do that." They also don't talk about the emotional aspects of a relationship, as they regard them as too intimate and personal. Shelly, the third friend, said that such information would invite judgment about the quality of their boyfriends and relationships. For instance, she would not tell her friends about a fight she and her boyfriend had about his getting drunk too often.

Sharing comes naturally to these friends. They all are seekers of information, buying stacks of self-help books. On the floors and shelves of Tammy's room were columns of books combining insights from New Age spiritual, therapy-based, and feminist movements, including *The I Ching in Ten Minutes, Care of the Soul, Soul Mates, The Road Less Traveled, Women's Bodies, Women's Wisdom*. When she was having trouble with her boyfriend, she had him buy *Men Are from Mars, Women Are from Venus*, which they read together.

Shelly, who met Janine and Tammy in college and who is in her third long-term relationship, serves as the teacher for the group. Janine is still dating a guy she met in high school; their eight-year relationship was interrupted by a two-year breakup in college, during which she experimented more casually. Tammy, who has had one sexual relationship, with her college boyfriend, is the recipient of most of the advice. Their talk has few limits, except that it must have value, either educational or supportive. For example, said Shelly, "You wouldn't talk specifically about your boyfriend's anatomy or anything like that, but you can talk about sex in general and 'Has this happened to you?'"

Shelly also gave her friends some new ideas. "Like the one thing with the sushi. My boyfriend and I got take-out sushi. It's a very sensual food, first of all. And I was describing to my friends what we did once we got home with the sushi. Kind of put it on the body. And they were like 'Oh wow' and wanted to try it. And some of them did."

Sometimes the talk revolves around more weighty topics. Janine said that she first consulted her friends in college when she feared that she may have contracted a STD. Other women I interviewed also commonly remarked how friends had helped them deal with the negative consequences of sex. Kris and Dionne, two friends in Anaheim, California, discussed Dionne's comforting Kris before her abortion. "I had nobody to turn to except my partner. I needed someone else, so I went to Dionne. . . . The first night, I had guilt because I had nobody to talk to. I needed a second opinion." "There is nothing to be ashamed of," said Dionne, still supporting her friend. "It's an option. And nine times out of ten, I would probably say it was the right choice. I've never been in that situation, but I have to say if it were to happen today, I'd do the exact same thing."

The two students from the College of St. Catherine in St. Paul, Minnesota, emphasized a more personal function of helping each other recognize their own values. "It helps us work through our actual feelings, towards what we want and what we believe in. Our beliefs are still kind of forming about what's right and what's wrong about sex, or if there is any right or wrong of sex. . . . Are you moral when you follow strict religious views, or are you moral when you're being true to yourself and what you want for yourself? I mean where does that morality lie?" asked Taunya, 22.

Even though talking about men has become more acceptable and candid, one topic that women brought up as still difficult to discuss with friends is masturbation. Although more than a dozen people I interviewed (such as the Florida high school teachers) said that they discussed it with friends, several of them said that this was one of the last sexual subjects they had tackled. After mentioning the taboo of masturbation, another woman I interviewed, law student Jeanne, admitted that she was not able to talk with her friends about her sexual feelings about women. "We can never talk about, 'I was attracted to a woman. She's beautiful. She has a great body. She has great breasts.'" Indeed, lesbianism, or even just feelings of attraction to other women, is stigmatized partly because it has nothing to do with men.

Safer-Sex Movements for Openness and Control

Without doubt, one reason that women feel freer to consult one another today is because of the work of safer-sex activists, enabling society to explore sexual information more openly, though the progress isn't always apparent. While discussion of a killer disease would seem at first only to kill sexual appetites, in practice anti-AIDS activists encourage more acceptance of sexuality while also discouraging shame.

I witnessed a sample of this now commonplace dialogue one rainy April afternoon at Northeastern Illinois University in Chicago. While most students on this commuter campus sat silently listening to lecturers, others were having more fun. In another classroom, a sign on the door welcomed visitors to a "safe-sex party for ladies only." This marketing strategy has proved successful. The previous year, an organizer told me, this program was advertised as a "health education" event, and no one showed up. One woman asks about the chances of getting pregnant during menstruation. Someone else asks her how to eroticize condoms. "I know prostitutes who use their tongues to put them on," she answers. "Men don't even notice what happened." At this school, as in the broader society, messages about safer sex have an impact beyond just encouraging condom use. These public campaigns, conducted at schools and in the media, are a particularly radical source of openness and information for women, encouraging them to challenge traditional roles of passivity and silence and to actively and unapologetically take charge of their safety.

Symbolizing this acceptance of safer-sex education is the condom, now a fixture in residence halls and even college orientations. Only in the past decade or so, the message of this latex accessory has changed from negative to positive. Today, condoms lack the immediately chilling, sleaze-ridden antipleasure symbolism of their recent past. Even as late as the 1980s, when their use was not as common, men were frequently insulted by the suggestion that they wear one.

In fact, safer-sex messages sometimes make sex *less repressed*. In the 1960s and 1970s, with the advent of the Pill, people didn't really have to talk about sex, as this form of birth control made conversation between men and women unnecessary. I recently saw a late-night public service announcement on MTV that drove home this message. A man complained about using condoms, saying, "Now, you really have to talk to someone before you sleep with them!" This basic human gesture, talking about sex with a partner, though still very difficult for many, is now more commonplace.

Messages encouraging openness and communication, along with women's empowerment, are central in safer-sex literature. This is a radical prescription for women, who have traditionally been encouraged to be passive and polite in sexual encounters. An example is the standard and widely distributed brochure "Women and AIDS," first published in 1990 by the American College Health Association in Baltimore:

> Sometimes it can feel less awkward to have sex than to talk about it beforehand. Discussing past drug use and sexual activity as well as safer sex may make you feel vulnerable or worried that your partner will be turned off or leave. However, you need to talk with your partner so you *both* can agree on what safer sex practices you will use. Your feelings are valid—do not let someone else's lack of concern intimidate you or make you feel that you should not insist on safer sex.

Many other safer sex campaigns I have witnessed, especially those by gay and lesbian groups at college campuses, are actively celebratory and nonjudgmental about sex. A particularly bold example is the pamphlet "Safer Sex Handbook for Lesbians," which I picked up at a literature display at the bustling Community Pharmacy on the campus of the University of Wisconsin at Madison. The introduction outlines the philosophies of the San Francisco Lesbian AIDS Project, encouraging creativity and imagination:

> Fantasize, fetishize, imagine your most desired scenario and integrate gloves, plastic wrap, latex barriers, clean sex toys, and implements. Have sex in a way that is powerful and fulfilling, as well as thoughtful about your health and the health of your partner(s). Your hand as well as your mind is a sex toy.

Many such safer-sex messages widen the dialogue about sexuality, including explicit information about high-risk sexual acts. This includes the most traditionally secretive and forbidden, especially anal sex. Some safer-sex literature, such as the lesbian handbook, also includes an unabashed discussion of a panoply of the most mysterious and sophisticated acts to be performed on a female, including oral sex techniques and the use of fists, dildos, and butt plugs.

In the third decade of HIV/AIDS, many new safer-sex messages have become less alarmist. In the 1980s and early 1990s, educators were likely to push more absolutist behavior for "*safe* sex," not "*safer sex*" and failed to differentiate between highly or only slightly risky behavior. They warned that even if both partners tested negative, they should still act as though the threat were present, that is, never to have intercourse without a condom, refrain from oral-anal contact, and use latex during every act of oral sex. But such absolutist warnings can be self-defeating. People may begin to see all acts as equally dangerous and, in frustration, ignore all precautions.

Glamour and Gynecology: Women's Magazines

For most American adults, the media are the main source of information about AIDS and other sexual concerns. In my interviews, young women commonly mentioned the informational media as they described their own sexual pasts. Sometimes I could detect the influence of specific types of mass media, mainly women's magazines.

Just before I met Kris and Dionne in person, I heard them laughing in the next room. I had just walked into the empty after-hours waiting room of a doctor's office, where Kris worked as a manager. When I looked through the glass panel of the receptionist's room where they were sitting, I saw them hide a magazine from me.

They came into the waiting room and said they were embarrassed that they were taking the notorious *Cosmopolitan* magazine quiz, which they dismissed as "a joke." But later, when I asked them about the influence of women's magazines on their sex lives, they were more positive. Dionne, 23, a junior at Fullerton State Junior College and part-time model for a bridal expo, said she appreciated *Cosmo*'s "legitimate surveys on sex and dating," which report on readers' experiences. She cited an example of an article about women's first sexual experiences, which let her know that what she had experienced as a teen was typical.

"You're not alone," said Dionne, explaining its message. "You're not the first person who felt that way. Personally, my first sexual experience was a nightmare . . . so it was like OK, it wasn't just me. It's pretty much the norm. . . . I look at my relationship with Tim, whom I dated for six years. . . . We lost our virginity with each other, and it took time for sex to get good with us. You know? So I think you learn from the magazines and surveys that that's OK. It's OK for things not to be right now, for you to feel this way and that way."

She added, "If you didn't read it here, where are you going to read it?"

"I couldn't even talk about sex in front of my family even today," agreed Kris, "so I needed my friends, I needed my books, I needed my television, and I needed my own experiences."

Kris gave a specific example of information not available elsewhere: "If I didn't have these magazines, I wouldn't know what an orgasm is," she said.

Dionne agreed. "I'm not going to run to my mom and say is it an orgasm when this happens? Is this true?"

Despite their mocking of women's magazines' clichéd and contrived nature, Kris and Dionne recognized the more serious purposes of some informational media. Tailored to a female audience, such media sources reduce guilt, expand choices, and relieve isolation. In addition, they offer sexual health facts about a variety of topics, including birth control risks, not available from friends. Also, read in private, they answer questions with confidentiality.

Cosmopolitan represents the best, and the worst, of the glossy women's magazines. The eleven largest—*Cosmopolitan, Glamour, Self, Mademoiselle, New Woman, Family Circle, Woman's Day, Ladies' Home Journal, McCalls, Redbook, Good Housekeeping,* and *Better Homes and Gardens*—have a combined circulation of more than 42 million. According to a 1994 Louis Harris survey, more than one-fourth of women aged 30 to 49 reported that magazines were the source on which they usually relied for information about birth control (second only to health care professionals). And according to a 1997 Kaiser Foundation survey, Men's Role in Preventing Pregnancy, 87 percent of women aged 18 to 24 considered magazines an "important" source of information on such topics as birth control, sexually transmitted diseases, and HIV/AIDS. The magazines' influence starts early in life. Another 1997 Kaiser Foundation study, by Kim Walsh-Childers, found that fashion/beauty magazines, particularly the ones targeted to teenagers, are a vital source of information about sex and its consequences. Of the seven in ten teenage girls who reported reading magazines regularly,

51 percent said that the magazines were an important source of information about sex, birth control, and the prevention of sexually transmitted diseases, and a majority (69 percent) of all teenage girls said that this was often information they didn't get elsewhere.

Women's magazines are largely based on sex. In fact, Betty Friedan's 1963 *Feminine Mystique* includes an extensive study of how this singular focus revealed women's lack of greater life choices in the 1950s. Ironically, women's magazines stand out from men's magazines—often condemned for their overt sexist objectification of women—by their obsession with sex. While young women's magazines such as *Cosmo, Mademoiselle,* and *Glamour* are consumed with sex, men's publications still generally treat it as only one of many topics covered, one component of the whole man. Even those men's magazines that seem to be centered on and defined by sex, such as *Playboy,* cover it much less thoroughly than expected, perhaps only with an advice column and one or two features on naked women and self-help.

In an interview, former *Playboy* adviser James Petersen sounded like Betty Friedan in condemning women's magazines' single-minded obsession with sexual improvement: "I think we talk about sex exactly the right amount. It is a small part of the whole man, and you have to remember it's the whole man making love, not just [his] dick. And women's magazines use information to create anxiety because anxiety sells cosmetics. And *Playboy* does not seek to create anxiety, and that's a major difference. And one of the ways we do it is at a certain point [we] don't talk about sex; [we] do it. There's a huge emphasis on pleasure and romance and quality and fantasy and all these other things [in men's magazines], and yes, there's information, but by and large we trust our readers to have a grasp of the topic, which to my mind, women's magazines don't treat their readers that way." He echoed the opinion of the young woman I interviewed who was most critical of women's magazines. "It's so degrading," said Tammy, the high-school teacher in Miami. "It's like, my God, you would never see a male magazine about how to get a girl to commit. It's always how to rise to the top of your company. You, to dress for success. Him, how to start your own company. You never see that in *Cosmo.* It's how to tell if your man is cheating. Who the hell cares?"

Another major gripe is the magazines' mission to sell products through advertising, which shapes their sexual content. Like other critics, author Ellen McCracken shows how advertisers covertly influence editorial content, for example, by demanding that beauty columns promote their products or by inserting "advertorials" or ads that resemble the regular features (which became more common in the 1980s). In her book *Decoding Women's Magazines*, McCracken points out how ads often counteract any positive messages of the magazines, such as those in an article promoting a positive body image and self-acceptance. As a rule, such articles are surrounded by pages of ads featuring only skeleton-thin models, with computer enhancements that even the most stringent diet regimen couldn't replicate.

The four major magazines for young women, *Mademoiselle*, *Glamour*, *Essence*, and *Cosmopolitan*, each have demonstrated, to varying degrees, an ideology of sexual autonomy for women. Although the editors would not agree, the first three young women's magazines are strikingly alike and attract a very similar audience. This similarity is immediately apparent on the covers of two recent issues, the January 2000 *Cosmo* and the February 2000 *Glamour*. Both are pink, with the magazine's name at the top in almost the same sleek, whitish typeface. They both feature twenty-year-old, brown-haired models with almost the same shoulder-length haircut, both with parts on the right side and wearing almost the same hot pink, low-cut, silk-slip dresses. The two magazines are also strikingly alike inside the covers, both sharing the same editors in recent years. *Glamour* is second only to *Cosmo* in circulation of women's magazines, both with a readership of more than 2 million. *Mademoiselle*, also published by Condé Nast, is often described as a slightly younger version of *Glamour*. But at least for a decade, *Glamour* stood out from the rest with its overt feminist politics, a result of focus groups in 1988 (Warren 1993). A decade later, however, such market research had the opposite effect. Responding to reader surveys, the magazine introduced horoscopes and dropped its "Women Right Now" column, which had covered political activity regarding women's issues (Kuczynski 1999).

Essence distinguishes itself from the others profiled here in many ways, including its status as "the magazine for contemporary black women." With a circulation of just over 1 million and spanning many age groups, it is also known by readers, including a few I interviewed, as "the black women's Bible." While many of its sex articles are similar to those in other magazines, the quantity and tone are different. Most noticeable, in *Essence*, sex and self-improvement are a minor focus, treated as only part of a woman's entire life. It has one advice column, "Mind/Body," by Dr. Gwendolyn Goldsby Grant, and I couldn't find a single sex article in the March 1997 issue, which instead featured "The Flap over Ebonics" and "Career Power Moves: Where the Jobs Are."

Compared with all other women's magazines, *Cosmo* distinguishes itself as being synonymous with young women's sexuality. It is the most successful young women's magazine ever and has been the best-selling magazine on college campuses for at least the past two decades (according to an annual magazine survey by the College Store Exchange, based in Westbury, Long Island). It has the greatest reach, with twenty-nine international editions. *Cosmo* also has the most active libido: the cover models are trashier, the necklines lower, the skirts tighter, the heels higher, the perfume cheaper, the diets crueler, the men buffer, the gossip juicier. *Cosmo* and its founding editor, the now retired Helen Gurley Brown, serve as a lightning rod for explaining why our culture has absorbed only certain parts of feminism and sexual liberation. At first, it may be hard to find any redeeming social value in its glossy and breezy pages. Indeed, *Cosmo* is the most politically incorrect of women's magazines. In a television interview, Gloria Steinem stated a basic criticism: "[Editor in chief Helen Gurley Brown] just never seemed to be convinced that there was a form of power for women that wasn't sexual."

Cosmo's editorial content and tone was shaped by Brown, a former successful Los Angeles copy writer, who herself did not marry until the then ripe old age of 37. In 1965, after writing her best-selling *Sex and the Single Girl*, Brown took the helm of *Cosmo*, a foundering conservative lifestyle magazine, and raised its circulation from 700,000 to more than 2 million, becoming the most profitable editor in magazine history. Both her book and the magazine feature italicized words and gushing, fanciful personal anecdotes and confessions. In 1997, the Hearst Corporation replaced Brown with Bonnie Fuller, who made mostly minor changes in the direction of blandness. (Fuller later moved to *Glamour*, also stripping it of any personality and making it a *Cosmo* clone in look and content.) But even more than ever, sex still permeates every page of *Cosmo*. Indeed, the profitability of Brown's ironclad formula for success, centered on all kinds of desires, will perhaps serve as its greatest insurance against change.

Despite these differences, these four magazines are generally unabashedly prosex for women. Their lack of shame in speaking candidly about a wide array of fears, experiences, and pleasures delivers a strong message to readers. The effect of such confident articles is ultimately to fight the age-old double standard for women. They give the message to readers both directly, by telling them they shouldn't feel guilty, and indirectly, by talking about sex without apology.

Women's magazines demonstrate this philosophy most convincingly by taking it completely for granted. The editors assume that their audiences, primarily single women, are sexually active and seeking information. In fact, these magazines decontextualize sex, or demystify it by discussing it on the same level and in the same candid tone as other types of information. They cover the minutiae of sexual relations along with the minutiae of other daily tasks, such as practical "news you can use" sections, usually in the front of the magazines. The March 1997 *Glamour* "Health & Fitness" section is typical. The most prominent blurb of the three on the page is about dressing properly for nighttime jogging. Below, on the left, is another story, "Which IUD is for you?" picturing two T-shaped devices. It includes two matching columns comparing the copper and progesterone IUDs for size, failure rate, replacement schedule, and cost. The last blurb on the page, "Steps to better healing," shows how to take care of a cut or burn.

Many articles address the double standard head-on. *Cosmo*, the most militantly prosex magazine, has the most direct commentaries, shunning guilt and promoting the sexually aggressive woman. Sample articles, just from 1996: "Who Says You Can't Enjoy Sex without Commitment?" (January), "Coping with Shame" (March), "Who Says You Have to Have Just One Lover?" (August), "The Appeal of a Sexually Aggressive Woman" (November), "The New Good Girl: The Many Faces of Sexual Guilt," and "Anatomy of the Sexually Aggressive Woman" (December).

The magazines also provide support and bring sex down to earth by making "ordinary" women into experts and not putting authorities with degrees on pedestals. They strongly urge women to consult one another and to value themselves as their ultimate authorities. In "Hotter, Happier Sex," in the September 1995 *Glamour,* writer Sara Nelson specifically states the value of nonscientific information: "We talked to experts who specialize in sexuality issues and women who've *become* [italics in original version] experts in their own bedrooms."

Like this one, many articles rely primarily on comments from ordinary women. From 1986 to 1996, this use of the "woman on the street" increased 30 percent, to at least one account per sex article in the twelve major women's magazines. (This is the same as the proportion of articles quoting "experts.") (Childers, Treise, and Gotthoffer 1997). The comments of such women are the foundation of the round-up survey, a collection of quotations concerning a particular topic, such as embarrassing first dates. (Kris and Dionne earlier cited these articles as special sources of support and validation.) *Cosmo* most commonly uses this format, such as in the March 1997 feature "Your First Night Together." "If I get anything out of a *Cosmo* or *Mademoiselle*," said Kris, "it's the sex surveys, because you're reading them and you're hearing what other people have experienced. I'm going, 'Cool. Next time my sex drive is down, I'm going to try this.'"

These writers also go beyond the clinical in discussing sexual acts, taking a female-centered perspective ranging from what goes on in the bedroom to what gives women pleasure. Women's magazines commonly explore women's orgasms, masturbation, sexual variety, lesbianism, and even anal sex, all of which are out of the traditional realm of sexual intercourse and reproduction. According to the 1997 Kaiser women's magazine study, of all sex articles not relating to health, the most commonly covered subject was general sexual activity, which accounted for 36 percent of such articles. (Next covered was monogamy, representing 18 percent, and sex appeal, at 17 percent.) (Childers, Treise, and Gotthoffer 1997).

Women's orgasms in general are a staple subject in young women's magazines; they are what "easy-chicken recipes in under one hour" features are to *McCall's* or the *Ladies' Home Journal*. Columns explore every facet of the anatomy of an orgasm, from finding the G spot (*Mademoiselle*, May 1995); to learning how to relax and, when on the brink, to avoid losing it (*Mademoiselle*, March 1997); to the ethics of "faking it" (*Glamour*, October 1993; *Mademoiselle*, January 1994); to biological research on women's varying sexual responses (*Glamour*, January 1994).

Men are often not in the picture at all. Other related stories discuss the importance of masturbation, which was the subject of 6 percent of non-health-related sex articles in women's magazines (Childers, Treise, and Gotthoffer 1997). The February 1997 "Sex Q&A" column in *Mademoiselle* featured a question by a woman about how she could make her boyfriend more comfortable when masturbating in front of her. "First, why not masturbate in front of him and let him watch you?" answers columnist Blanche Vernon. "'This has always worked for me,' my friend Carolyn confided. 'Lots of guys love to watch a woman self-serve, and if he sees you being so uninhibited with your own body, he'll probably be less inhibited with his.'"

A related topic is oral sex on women, also reported from every conceivable angle. The tone is always enthusiastic, as in a characteristic May 1997 *Glamour* feature, "Good News about Your Sex Life," which cites findings that "a majority of men say they enjoy performing oral sex." Also encouraging self-gratification, another common subject is sex toys, used either alone or with partners. The tips are how to use and maintain them. The March 1996 *Cosmo* article "Tools for Love: AKA Sex Toys" muses: "Fur-lined bondage cuffs, peacock feathers, waterproof vibrators . . . with the wealth of pleasure props available, why *not* sample one or two?"

In the past few years, I have started noticing articles about anal sex. In the July 1999 *Glamour*, under the heading of "Alterna-Sex Dilemma," a reader asks: "My boyfriend has always wanted to have anal sex. How can I be sure I'll enjoy it?" And in response to a June 1998 *Mademoiselle* reader's request for more information on sex toys, columnist Sandra Hollander recommends "anal stimulators." She describes a particularly adventurous device, the Ultra Triple Stimulator, which fits on the penis and includes "a curved length of plastic that slides into your anus during regular intercourse."

Lesbian sex is another standard topic, accounting for 12 percent of non-health-related sexual topics in women's magazines (Childers, Treise, and Gotthoffer 1997). They explore the subject in an affirming and often enthusiastic tone. An example from the January 1996 *Glamour* is "The Lesbian Episode: It Is More Common, and Enlightening, Than You Think." With a more sensational headline, "I Left My Husband for An-other Woman," the September 1995 *Cosmo* gushes, "Finally, *finally* . . . no more averting my eyes whenever I spot a female I think is sexy, no more ignoring the breathtaking loveliness of half the world!" The photo illustration, of two thin models chatting on a dock with their legs dan-gling, is a *Cosmo* standard and helps "normalize" its content, fitting it in seamlessly with the other articles.

Yet nowhere do these magazines go out of their way to advocate hetero-sexual marriage. Rather, they affirm the life of the single woman and *do not* state that women's ultimate goal in life should be roping in a man. *Cosmo* advice columnist Irma Kurtz assures a reader not to compare herself with married friends and to feel pressured to follow them (March 1996). *Glam-our* extols the singles life in "Single Life: Enjoy the Adventure" (April 1995), as does *Mademoiselle* in "Single and Loving It" (October 1996).

While decidedly prosex, the magazines also are candid in pointing out the possible negative consequences of sex, essential information for women's control of their sex lives. According to Childers, Treise, and Gotthoffer's 1997 Kaiser study of women's magazines, the leading sexual health issue in women's magazines is pregnancy, accounting for 10 percent of all sex arti-cles in 1996. Half these stories are about unintended pregnancy, an increase of 50 percent from 1986 to 1996. Next is contraception, at 9 percent; HIV/AIDS, at 6 percent; and abortion, at 5 percent. In fact, women's mag-azines have been exposing the dangers of contraceptives since 1967 when the *Ladies' Home Journal* published Barbara Seaman's exposé of the long-touted and unquestioned birth control pill.

A more controversial topic concerning women's choices is abortion, which women's magazines cover candidly and with a prochoice view, as separate features or as part of round-up and advice sections. *Glamour* and *Mademoiselle* are especially daring in regularly addressing abortion without shame or apology. A *Columbia Journalism Review* study of the twelve major women's magazines ranked these two publications at the top in their coverage of abortion, accounting for half the articles written on the subject. From 1972 to 1991, *Glamour* ran thirty-seven such articles, *Mademoiselle* twenty-eight, and *Vogue* nineteen. *Cosmo* ranked sixth with nine (Ballenger 1992). A prime example of routine coverage is the December 1996 *Mademoiselle* "Sex Q&A" column, which explains how long a woman must wait to have sex after having an abortion.

Magazines also provide regular and comprehensive coverage of the morning-after pill, high doses of birth control pills used as emergency contraception. With sparse coverage in the mainstream media, women's magazines have become the main source of information about this controversial resource, which doctors have known about for at least twenty years. In fact, women's magazines covered the morning-after pill long before the FDA officially approved its use in February 1997. *Essence* devoted an article to it in the March 1995 issue, and *Mademoiselle*, in its April 1994 and August 1995 issues.

Despite the magazines' wide coverage of sexual territory, readers find limits. A series of focus groups conducted by Deborah Treise for the Kaiser Foundation in 1997 said they wanted more coverage of abstinence, STDs, and condom negotiation. Like my sample, the younger women surveyed wanted more realistic, non-fantasy-driven images and portrayals of "regular" women's lives. Women's magazines clearly offer women a mixed bag, just as do other informational media. Women's magazines endorse sex for single women, in defiance of past social norms and often on women's terms. Yet they generally do not transcend the depth and values that the corporate culture will allow, reflecting Helen Gurley Brown's proestablishment and always promen credo. This narcissism and superficiality is their real fault, not the explicitness of their sex information, a more common target.

Health Books: Owner's Manuals for the Female Body

After women's magazines, my sample group (such as Darlene, interviewed at the beginning of this chapter) mentioned books as their primary media sources of sexual information. Sex books have additional reference value, since they are available on the shelf to answer sex questions as they arise. The most common nonfiction book cited, as mentioned, was *Our Bodies, Ourselves.* This mammoth reference book (the 1998 edition numbering 754 pages) set the standard for women's health books as owner's manuals for the human female body covering topics as broad as body image, holistic healing, violence against women, and childbirth.

The 1998 edition of *Our Bodies, Ourselves for the New Century* is updated with on-line resources; more discussions of disability, class, and race (which influence how women experience their sexuality); and expanded sections on the wide spectrum of female "gender benders" in society, such as transgendered "drag kings." Also in contrast to women's magazines (which feature only slick and skinny models), its chapters include quotations from and pictures of "real women," who add to its refreshing authenticity. Because *Our Bodies* has no products to sell, unlike the women's magazines, it can deal more in gritty reality than in enticing fantasy. "It is distinct," said Laurie Williams, 25, a nursing student working with the Boston Women's Health Collective, the group that produces the book. "It is one of the first books written by and for women. It really challenged a lot of what was thought of as collective wisdom, challenged ideas. It also showed us just how much we didn't know and how much we had to find out." I met Williams at the Collective's office in Somerville, just outside Cambridge. I also talked to one of the original authors, Judith Norsigian, who told me that since its first newsprint edition was distributed in 1970, it has been a regular target of school boards for censorship. "There are always three issues that cause the most trouble," she said. "One of them is masturbation. One of them is lesbianism. One of them is abortion."

But despite this opposition, the book is widely available and accepted. In 1973, when the Collective couldn't keep up with demand for its stapled booklet, Simon & Schuster took over its publication, and since that time, it has sold more than 3 million copies and has become a fixture of dorm room shelves and mall bookstores across the country.

The original coauthors first met at a workshop at a 1969 conference sponsored by Bread and Roses, a grassroots socialist and feminist group. Over the years, they have never lost or watered down their political focus. Like *Cosmo,* the book has remained remarkably consistent in its many editions. In this tradition, the 1984 edition starts with a poem by English suffragist Christabel Pankhurst and a feminist poem, "Our Faces Belong to Our Bodies." All sections contain a cultural analysis of how sexism has shaped body issues, such as the menstruation section which outlines historic taboos. The section on abortion traces the history of feminists fighting for its legalization and talks about future political challenges. The chapters end by listing additional resources, such as feminist nonprofit groups, books, and periodicals. In recent years, this book has spawned a series of others, such as Dr. Christiane Northrup's *Women's Bodies, Women's Wisdom*, and the *Harvard Guide to Women's Health*. Health newsletters also have become more popular over the past decade, numbering more than thirty in 1995, compared with five or six a decade earlier. Among those are the *Harvard Women's Health Watch* and *Health Wisdom for Women* (by Northrup).

In sum, for more young women than ever before, the information age has transformed sex from a private, isolated experience to one of support and knowledge. Taking the lead from the most radical feminists of the 1970s and influenced by young "third wave" feminists and safer-sex activists, women today can speak and read in detail about the erotic or self-pleasing aspects of sex, including criticism of men. As expected, the most affluent have benefited the most because they are the most likely to have access to the best-quality, woman-produced and -defined sources, such as *Our Bodies, Ourselves* and Internet sites. They also have the requisite resources and education to create their own media, such as web sites and 'zines. Poorer women receive less sex education in their schools and are more likely to rely on hearsay and free sources, such as superficial television features.

Furthermore, young women's sexual information still lacks some of the empowering potential envisioned by second-wave boomer feminists of the 1970s. Mainly following therapeutic and spiritual growth models and reflecting an increasingly individualistic generation, conversations among friends and media features typically begin and end with themselves. They fail to see the bigger political picture of how all women's experiences are related and why they should organize together to influence the whole. For example, while affirming one's right to have sex, women's magazines and even 'zines like *Bust* frequently still fail to discuss practical steps to take to protect such rights. Women's magazines' commitment to such political issues is limited, based on the whims and fluctuations of focus groups. Safer-sex activists often are limited in scope, focusing on personal change through the use of condoms and appearing mainly on more affluent high school and college campuses. By concentrating on the broad general population, which is at low risk for AIDS, the government has neglected those most specifically at risk, including minority women in the inner cities (Bennett and Sharpe 1996, A8). These women, who usually are infected by drug-using partners and have very little power to negotiate protection, represent the fastest-growing group of victims (Altman 1997).

Finally, much of young women's information about sex is still centered on pleasing men, not on women pleasing themselves. Young women's locker-room talk, sex education, and media have only begun to explore the complex topography of female desire and sexual acts not revolving around male partners. In many crucial areas, the true consciousness raising has only begun.

Conclusion: Beyond Becoming Like Men, Becoming Like Ourselves

The original idea of feminism as I first encountered it, in about 1969, was twofold: that nothing short of equality will do and that in a society marred by injustice and cruelty, equality will never be good enough.
—Barbara Ehrenreich, in *The Worse Years of Our Lives* (the 1980s), 1990

This book has described the sexual state of the union at the end of the twentieth century. But what about the next century? What are some steps we can take to really make sure that young women can conduct their sex lives "her way"? Many of the most dramatic sexual evolutions documented in this book involved women's acting and thinking more like men, such as having more partners and premarital sex without shame. The superrats, who by my definition are women who act in the same sexually aggressive manner as men do traditionally, exemplify these changes. Such shifts are significant because they create a new range of sexual choices for women. But when we consider what has yet to be done, becoming like men seems like the easy part. After all, what is traditionally male is still what is most valued in our society, and what is traditionally female is still suspected and feared as weak and inferior. This is why the sexual evolution, though making some important beginning strides, has not yet overturned the basic male definitions of sex or sexual freedom.

That is, despite women's many advances, we are still living in a man's world. This is why the 1995 dating guide *The Rules* was so popular: the advice about acting passive to attract a man *works;* it is a guide, in the end, to *men's rules*, which still define the courtship process. True, women are initiating dates and sex more often, but they still are most successful in the dating world when they let the male take charge and do not threaten him with any sign of aggressiveness or human weakness or need. The authors of *The Rules* thus advise women to act "happy and busy" and let men do the rest.

I myself have noticed this male paradigm as dominant even among my "liberated" friends. While I was writing this book, a few of them called me because they didn't understand why they weren't satisfied with their casual, uncommitted sexual relationships. One friend complained, "But guys do this. Why should I want more?" I long for the day when men call their friends, shake their heads in confusion, and mutter feebly, "Why don't I feel right making a commitment? Women often want them; that means *I must be wrong*." Male sexual norms and customs are still the standard, and if women feel the basic and rational human need of wanting an emotional connection with sex, potentially the most intimate physical act between two people, then they feel as though they must be weak.

Other evidence of this male-defined reality is evident in studies of sexual practices. For example, women still experience an "orgasm gap"; that is, they are much less likely to have orgasms during heterosexual sex than men are. Of course, having an orgasm is not the only indicator of sexual fulfillment; there is the closeness, the affection, and so on. But this orgasm gap shows that women's physical gratification and entitlement are still secondary to men's. If a woman has an orgasm, it is considered to be an added benefit, not a defining moment of the experience (see Douglass and Douglass 1997).

One of the sources of this problem is evident in another gap: women's lower levels of masturbation. Only about 10 percent of women aged 18 to 29, compared with about a third of men that age, say they do this once a week (Laumann et al. 1994, 82). Masturbation represents basic comfort with and knowledge of one's own sexuality. It also provides important "basic training" for partnered sex, allowing a woman to learn what types of stimulation do the trick. If she doesn't know what will stimulate her, then her partner is bound to be even more clueless.

For women to have sex on their own terms, "her way," society must take some very difficult steps to validate a whole new realm of female-centered choices. As a bumper sticker put it, "Women who strive to be equal to men aren't ambitious enough." We have only just begun to understand female sexuality, to define sexual freedom in women's terms, to connect sex to the mind and to the spirit, to create a new range of sexual imagery and expression, to challenge false either/or sexual choices, to raise society's consciousness of how its culture influences our sex lives, and to organize on behalf of the reproductive rights of the least fortunate. The dialogue about the particular strengths and contributions of female sexuality must continue. What sets it apart from male sexuality? Which parts of female desire are socially constructed, and which are real? What can female energy add to male-defined heterosexual sex? What "male" or "female" sexual energies do we each possess within ourselves?

Awareness and appreciation of the female experience also challenge heterosexual sexual scripts. In all the books that I have read on the topic, none explains the possibilities more explicitly and enthusiastically than the 1997 *Are We Having Fun Yet? The Intelligent Woman's Guide to Sex.* Authors and sisters Lisa and Marcia Douglass pick up where Shere Hite left off in the 1970s to show how paying more attention to the clitoris transforms the practice of heterosexual sex. They demand more recognition of the specific acts that trigger orgasm, such as stimulating the clitoris with the hands. (Pointing out that this central sexual activity doesn't even have a name, they call it "clittage.") But redefining sexual freedom in women's terms has only just begun. Just as women have gained the important right to have meaningless sex in the way that men do, they must also feel entitled to inject it with emotion, spirituality, and moral and religious significance. To repeat, sexual freedom means more than promiscuity, or making one's self more available to more partners. The traditional male view of compartmentalizing sex, of disconnecting it from other realms of human experience, has limits. With connections to trust, sharing, passion, acceptance, and the human spirit, sex can take on new dimensions and authenticity. In the past, using a male-supremacist lens, such sexual meanings and connections have been mistakenly equated with female weakness and sentimentality.

This reconfigured view of sexual freedom has other radical implications. When women give meaning to sex, they sometimes end up limiting it for men. Young women have been particularly insistent on their right to say no, even if they are dressed "in a certain way," have a "sexual past," or invite a man to their room. This is why such a movement for women's sexual freedom has met fierce resistance and endless media ridicule. Such feminist efforts against sexual violence, date rape, and harassment are often misunderstood as antisex, prudish, Victorian, and "sexually correct."

According to the old models, giving meaning to sex meant associating it with women's guilt and shame. Real sexual freedom, though, is recognizing the potential power and consequences of sex without imposing antiquated societal stigmas on women. We need to discuss legitimate but seemingly outdated issues like morals, responsibilities, commitment, and values without making sex seem dirty and without controlling or judging or shaming women. At the same time, we must make morality a male issue also. Women are no longer willing to be the exclusive guardians of moral order. The old system of women's assuming all the sexual sacrifices and responsibilities and men's having all the rights has collapsed. But instead of seeing that collapse as signifying a moral decline, we can see it as a sign that *both men and women* are assuming sexual responsibility.

Other efforts to broaden women's sexual choices include a wider variety of media images and expressions of female sexuality. Instead of trying to censor already existing images, a much more challenging effort is for women themselves to expand the range of sexual expressions available. One of the most debilitating parts of growing up in our society is the lack of realistic images of women enjoying sex. Also, the women in the media who are sexual are almost always portrayed as objects, not as subjects; they are the ones being consumed, not the consumers.

Other changes to enhance women's sexual freedom are philosophical. When framing sexual choices, a traditionally male framework falsely views reality according to dichotomies, black and white reasoning, either/or logic. This, however, ignores the array of choices and realities between these extremes. The male model envisions a woman as either a virgin or a slut, each with her own set of baggage, and both identities defining a woman's entire being by what she has or has not done in bed. The male paradigm also falsely casts sex as either relational (done to please a partner, for love) or recreational (for fun), when most people have sex for both reasons. The male model demands that women either obey the dominant religion's sexual demands or be cast out of it. And the old models force women to choose between commitment and self-fulfillment, becoming either a homemaker or a career woman. While such life choices do indeed involve trade-offs (more personal demands in relationships do weaken commitments, and working outside the home does leave less time for family), the reality is usually more complex.

Consciousness Raising and Activism

Another mental shift for women is becoming aware of the politics of choices. As individualists, young women often fail to see how their culture shapes their sexual realities. (Some sources that have raised my own personal awareness are Shere Hite's *The Hite Report* [about sex] and *Women and Love* [about men], Sharon Thompson's *Going All the Way*, Gina Ogden's *Women Who Love Sex*, Ruth Sidel's *On Her Own*, and the Douglasses' *Are We Having Fun Yet?*) This blindness to social influences is especially evident in an extremely individualistic generation, as it causes women to unnecessarily blame themselves and thus to prevent further social change. If young women fail to have an orgasm, they blame their own inadequacies rather than finding out why their culture has hidden and suppressed knowledge of their bodies. If they are raped, they often still blame themselves, believing that they provoked the crime, instead of blaming woman-hating attitudes. If their boyfriend is distant and withholding, they blame themselves for being too grasping, not knowing that this is a standard power play for control. If they have marital problems because of financial pressures, they blame themselves or a lack of "family values," instead of looking at greater global changes and shrinking family wages.

This extreme focus on the personal is also a threat to women's hard-won sexual rights. Young women may believe in basic sexual freedoms, but they are not organizing to protect them. Young women passively believe in feminist principles of equality and justice, but they have failed to take an active stand and fight for the equality of other women. And young women believe in abortion rights, but they are not actively helping keep it legal or campaigning for RU-486, the abortion pill that has been available to European women for years. In contrast, the Religious Right, mentioned throughout this book, is well aware of the political dimensions of young women's sexual freedom and so is organizing swiftly and actively to limit their rights.

Those who will lose the most from this political blindness are the women with the least resources, mainly the young, poor, and minority. They lack sexual choices because they have fewer options for child care, job flexibility, abortion, prenatal care, and sex education. While elite universities spend thousands on anti-AIDS education, poor minority women in the inner city, representing the past decade's largest-growing group of AIDS victims, do not receive such messages. Even though abortion may still be legal, poor, young, and rural women have little access to it, with the number of providers reduced and parental consent laws multiplying. In no other culture are women expected to survive utterly independent of family, community, and state support, totally on their own. I'm not suggesting the creation of a communist state, but we do need some basic safety nets and more recognition of the interdependence of everyone in society.

Targeting Men for Change

Of course, those who need the most consciousness raising about women's sexual realities are men. Research reveals that men lag a generation behind women in challenging traditional roles. Not until the period from 1986 to 1990 did men arrive at the liberal/feminist/egalitarian attitudes that women held from 1970 to 1975 (Twenge 1997a, 41). Their slowness to change only limits women's sexual choices, in bed, in relationships, and in the family. Raising men's awareness therefore requires demonstrating what they have to gain. Even the most enlightened heterosexual women are doomed to frustration and loneliness if men do not follow. Yes, they may give up some power in the process, but men would also be unburdened of the pressure to be in control at all times and to live up to rigid "he-man" male roles. Some men already appreciate women's communicating their needs in bed, relieving them from having to do the impossible and read women's minds. Many men have already discovered the pleasures of taking a more active role as a father, even if it means sacrificing some career advancement.

This greater emotional role means expanding traditional notions of male responsibility. I keep thinking back to the comment of the nineteen-year-old anarchist philosophy major beauty-school student, Laura, also enrolled at North Texas University. Someone told her that men are now less responsible than they were in the past, pointing to the fact that fewer men are heads of households, and she commented: "I don't think men have ever been 'responsible.' I don't think that you can really say that [they were] being 'responsible' in the 1950s just because the men went out to work every day. I think it's responsible in a different way, but it's not responsible with everything. If they're letting their family go to shit or their life go to shit; just because they're functioning, that doesn't mean they're responsible. I think the base problems aren't really work or money, that they have to do with how people handle their relationships. If someone is a multimillionaire and abusing their kids, they're still fucked."

Toward Real and Lasting Sexual Power

Expanding all these sexual choices will lead to the greater goal of giving women *real sexual power*. I'm not talking about the transitory, superficial, traditional female sexual power that derives from women's ability to be a sex object for men. It is true that young and conventionally attractive women have always reaped many rewards. This is why the weight-loss and cosmetics industries are so powerful. This is why women's magazines sell so many millions of issues. As long as women count on deriving their social and economic power from their bodies, they will be faced with this never-ending undercurrent of anxiety. And even those who do manage to live up to these ideals can do so for only a short period of time. Counting on their looks for self-worth and status, such women are doomed to watch the value of their currency crumble as they age. It is a long and painful process, considering that women live most of their sexual lives beyond the nubile years of their teens and twenties. Also, in an ironic twist of nature, women reach their greatest levels of sexual awareness and self-comfort after those years.

As society is just starting to discover, a greater and more enduring type of sexual strength starts from within, based on self-knowledge, sexual awareness, and a sense of connectedness of sex to body, mind, and spirit. Instead of living up to the standards set by men, a woman with real sexual power lives up to those standards derived from within herself. She has the confidence and self-esteem to take precautions against unwanted pregnancy, steer sex toward her own satisfaction, and stand up for her rights in a relationship. Of course, sexual power is not only a matter of attitude. It is reinforced by outside forces, including support from men and a community of women, who provide validation, political consciousness, and greater knowledge of sexual choices. Furthermore, sexual power requires economic power, to make choices out of desire and not of desperation. When more women recognize these types of sexual power, they will experience a real sexual revolution.

Notes

p. xiii *With what I discovered*   In recent years, antifeminist books like Karen Lehrman's *Lipstick Manifesto* (1997), Wendy Shalit's *A Return to Modesty* (1999), and Katie Roiphe's *The Morning After* (1993b) and *Last Night in Paradise* (1997) have purported to express a generation's angst, even though the authors interviewed relatively few of their peers. Then, while useful as memoirs, the profeminist "third wave" books of the 1990s were limited to anthologies of young women recounting their personal experiences, such as Barbara Findlen's *Listen Up: Voices from the Next Feminist Generation* (1995) and Ophira Edut's *Adios, Barbie* (1998), on body image. These books contrast with the more research-intensive and political feminist books of an earlier era, like Shere Hite's *Hite Report* (1976) and Betty Friedan's *Feminine Mystique* (1963), which draw from hundreds of thoughtful in-depth interviews. (However, even Friedan has been accused of not interviewing a true diversity of women, limiting herself to affluent housewives.) For a satire on the lack of serious external research in nonfiction books on young women, see Toby Young's *Spy* (1997).

p. xiii *Even though my sample*   The interviews were detailed and ranged between forty-five minutes to one and a half hours in length. The women were born between 1960 and 1979 (the vast majority between 1965 and 1975). About a third were minorities: 13 percent black, 13 percent Hispanic or half Hispanic, and 4 percent Asian. About 10 percent were lesbians or bisexual, and 6 percent were disabled. Although the great majority were not interviewed on college campuses, more than half, thirty-six, were students, reflecting the large numbers of women getting higher degrees, often over several years. Twenty were undergraduates and sixteen were graduate students, most likely studying social work, teaching, or law. The majority of the students had either part-time or full-time jobs, and they also varied according to family status. The majority, thirty-seven, were single without children and had never been married. Of those, four were engaged. Another seven were cohabiting, and six were divorced or separated. Of the thirteen married women, three had children. The other nine who had children were either divorced (2), had never been married (5), or were separated (2). Although most of the women I interviewed were working or middle-class, I did interview some women from low-income backgrounds, including those at a shelter and group home in Orange County, California; a housing project in Austin, Texas; and a community outreach center on the Lower East Side of New York City.

p. xiv *To create more complete*   I chose my interview candidates in a way I thought would ensure as much honesty as possible, which is a perennial challenge for all researchers of sexual attitudes and behavior. I preferred not to rely on a printed solicitation, such as a magazine advertisement, because of the "self-selecting population" that results. Often those subjects who come forward on their own are more confident and self-assured than the norm and are from the narrow upscale population. I also didn't want to select complete strangers at random, such as from the phone book, because of the difficulty of gaining their trust and honest commitment to a long, detailed, and often irritatingly nosy interview.

p. xv *For a scientific perspective*   The data in the report are based on in-person interviews with a national sample of the 10,847 women, aged 15 to 44.

p. xv *Another major source*   The NHSLS is based on personal interviews in 1992 with 3,432 respondents from a random U.S. sample. Unlike magazine surveys, this has a high response rate, which scientists consider to be an indicator of accuracy: 80 percent of those approached agreed to participate.

p. xv *To compare college students'*   Each year, this study surveys 350,000 full-time, first-time first-year students at seven hundred colleges and universities. This series, initiated in the fall of 1966, is a project of the Cooperative Institutional Research Program (CIRP), a continuing longitudinal study of the American higher education system sponsored by the American Council on Education (ACE) and the Graduate School of Education & Information Studies at the University of California at Los Angeles.

NOTES TO THE INTRODUCTION

p. 11 *Polls reveal that*   This was the finding of the Pro-Choice Education Project's 1997 focus group research and 1998 nationwide survey of young women's attitudes toward choice ("New Generation of Women Recruited for Abortion Rights Battles," syndicated online by the Louise D. Palmer Newhouse News Service, 1 September 1999). For another example of this gap in consciousness, see "Debate Distant for Many Having Abortions," by Tamar Lewin in the *New York Times* (1998a). After interviewing women waiting for abortions at clinics across the country, Lewin reports that "a surprising number said they did not consider themselves 'pro-choice.' Some considered themselves 'pro-life'" (A1).

p. 16 *In fact, that was truer*   See the Associated Press report, "Freshmen Said to Have Conservative Views on Casual Sex, Abortion," 6 April 1999. It reports that in 1975, half the college students interviewed endorsed casual sex, while only 39.6 percent had that view in 1998. However, men's permissiveness has dropped more than that of women. According to the report, in 1974, 29.8 percent of women agreed "that sex is OK if two people like each other" (*American Freshman* 1997, 119), compared with 27.7 percent in 1998 (*American Freshman* 1999, 99). For men, that number in 1974 was 60.9 percent (*American Freshman* 1997, 89) and, in 1998, 53.6 percent (*American Freshman* 1999, 48). The headlines neglected to mention women in those years when their permissiveness actually rose, but when men's conservatism resulted in an overall drop. For example, in 1996, while headlines emphasized freshmen's becoming less permissive overall ("Fewer

College Freshmen Endorsing Casual Sex"), women's overall approval of casual sex was at 31.9 percent, more than in 1974 and up from 1995 (*American Freshman* 1997, 118–19). These differences in figures are very small but illustrate a willingness of the media to inflate any evidence that permissiveness might be diminishing and to ignore gender differences in data.

p. 16 *But a closer look*   Indeed, the actual figures tabulated in the survey reveal a different overall response for women than for men growing up with the threat of AIDS. In contrast to men surveyed, women of the youngest generation reported more partners under the age of 20 than their female predecessors. Recognizing this discrepancy requires actually adding up from Table 5.5 of the study the tabulations of those who reported two to four partners, and those who reported five or more under the age of 20 (Laumann et al. 1994, 198). This determines the total percentages of those with two or more partners under the age of 20. For men under 20, as reported, the total numbers of partners declined between the youngest two generations surveyed. Of men born between 1953 and 1962, 36.3 percent reported two to four partners and 29.8 percent five or more (making that a total of 66.1 percent with two or more partners). Of the men born between 1963 and 1972, 31.1 percent reported two to four partners and 30.6 reported five or more (a total of 61.7 percent with two or more partners).

But the columns for women reveal an actual overall increase in partners for women of the younger generation who are under 20. Of women born between 1953 and 1962, 36.6 percent reported two to four partners and 11.5 reported five or more (a total of 48.1 percent with two or more partners). Of women born between 1963 and 1972, 37.9 percent reported two to four partners and 13.3 percent reported five or more (a total of 51.2 percent with two or more partners). This increase is very slight, but nevertheless is an increase for the younger generation of women, denying the claim of the study that young people as a whole have fewer partners because of AIDS. This also reveals a continuing bias of male sex researchers still using males to represent the model sexual subject of the era.

p. 16 *And when men's publications*   For example, in a 1994 *Details* survey, when asked whether sexual correctness was a problem, 26 percent of the men responded yes, compared with 16 percent of the women ("Love Rules" 1994, 109). A larger-scale 1995 *Playboy* survey on sexual correctness revealed similar findings. When asked whether "political correctness kills spontaneity and fun," half of men agreed, compared with, again, nearly half that number, 27 percent of women. The study reported widespread male confusion about actually facing some limits: "Forty-five percent of the students, including more than half the men, said the focus on sexual harassment has made them fear being spontaneous with someone they find attractive" (Rowe 1995, 153).

p. 17 *This evolution toward women's*   "Rather than being an isolated phenomenon, these changes in sexual behavior, living together, and child-bearing have been part of broader social changes toward an individualistic rather than a family-centered society and toward modern rather than traditional roles for women," writes researcher Tom Smith in the *Demography of Sexual Behavior* (1994b), a report summing up the wealth of academic and government research on sex. "As such, the changes in American premarital and adolescent sexual behavior may result from the development of advanced economies, welfare states, and liberal governments in general rather than from any special situation peculiar to America" (19).

NOTE TO CHAPTER 1

p. 26 *Also, like a surprisingly*   Two others in my random core sample of seventy-two, including one I met in a homeless shelter (Mary) and another now working as a social worker (Tasha), had been prostitutes.

NOTES TO CHAPTER 2

p. 42 *Although the women were*   Consistent with other researchers, Lottes does report some differences in male behavior and permissiveness. The men in her sample had more sex partners; greater rates of masturbation, orgasm, casual sex, and acceptance of casual sex; and more positive reactions to first intercourse and to casual involvement with the first sex partner. Her study was of 411 undergraduates in the fall of 1989.

p. 43 *The 1995 National Survey of Family Growth*   It is important to note that the available research on sexual attitudes and behavior regarding race is often incomplete and biased. Critics observe that the black populations in studies are often poor and that whites are usually middle class. Also, different interpretations of the same results are possible. In a 1985 comparison of black and white college students, Philip A. Belcastro discusses how researchers differ in their individual standards of "permissiveness." For example, some may judge from his study that white women are more permissive by selecting only some of the findings, such as white women's higher numbers of partners (6.6 compared with 4.8 for blacks) and levels of giving (81 percent compared with 47.5 for blacks) and receiving oral sex (51 compared with 44 for blacks). He actually found, however, more similarities than differences in behavior, such as similar age of first intercourse (16.2 for blacks and 16.8 for whites).

p. 44 *Black women have sex earlier*   Hispanic girls have the added challenge of exceptionally high rates of dropping out of high school, substance abuse, and teen pregnancy, often rooted in cultural forces—such as a lack of birth control information and stigmas about its use, and a strong tie to motherhood as defining women's roles. As the teen pregnancy rate dropped overall in the 1990s by 21 percent (26 percent for black teenagers and 15 percent for whites) to levels not seen since the 1970s, the rate for Hispanic teens dropped only a total of 7 percent (and actually rose for Mexican-American girls specifically), according to figures released in 2001 by the Centers for Disease Control.

p. 46 *The authors attribute*   This "gender convergence" was nearly complete in questions about creating artistic works, raising a family, obtaining recognition from colleagues, having administrative responsibility for the work of others, and being very well-off financially (*American Freshman* 1997, 9).

p. 47 *Today, even though the double standard*   In her 1999 book *Slut! Growing Up Female with a Bad Reputation*, Leora Tannenbaum documents that the double standard was very much alive for junior high and high school girls.

p. 52 *About the same number*   According to web site tabulations I made from the coded PREMARX question data from the National Opinion Research Center's annual General Survey, from the 18 to 34 age group, sorted by gender. For the latest year for which statistics are available, 1996, 13.7 percent of the men and 18.5 percent of the women surveyed agreed that premarital sex was "always wrong." Even closer percentages of men and women agreed that premarital sex was "almost always wrong" (6.9 percent of men and 8.5 percent of women); "wrong only sometimes" (23.7 percent of men and 26.5 percent of women); and "not wrong at all" (55.7 percent of men and 46.5 percent of women). These data are compared with the results from a similarly worded question, labeled PREMARS1.

p. 54 *This has been a gradual change*   The men's rates have remained more constant, falling gradually from 18 to 17.5 from those born between 1933 and 1942. All the races have followed these trends, with blacks and Hispanics a cohort ahead (that is, each generation of blacks and Hispanics foreshadowing white rates twenty years later).

p. 54 *These young women were almost*   Of the youngest women, 9.6 percent reported five or more partners by age 18, compared with 5.5 percent of the boomers and 2 percent of the older group.

p. 54 *At least half of women surveyed*   The most common reason, given by 47.5 percent of the women, was affection for a partner, cited by 24.9 percent of men. In a reversal of percentages, the most common reason that men gave was "curiosity/readiness for sex" (at 50.6 percent), while only 24.3 percent of women gave that answer.

p. 55 *The 1995 National Survey of Family Growth*   In the National Survey of Family Growth, 8 percent of the total sample said that their first intercourse was not voluntary, reflecting to some extent the findings of the 1994 University of Chicago National Health and Social Life Survey, which reported that 24.5 percent of girls' first experiences were not wanted but not forced (compared with 7.6 percent of boys), and 4.2 percent forced (compared with 0.3 percent of boys).

p. 55 *During their long period of singlehood*   Young women's numbers of partners are actually similar to those of the boomer women at their age but markedly different from the rates of older generations. The NHSLS reported that by age 20, more than half the women of the youngest group surveyed, those born between 1963 and 1972, already had had two or more sex partners, and 13.3 percent had had five or more. Of the boomers, the women born one cohort earlier, between 1953 and 1962, the number was slightly lower; 48.1 percent had had two or more partners at that age, with 11.5 reporting five or more. Of the older women born between 1943 and 1952, 35.7 percent reported having had two or more partners before age 20, with 8.3 percent reporting five or more. In the oldest generation surveyed, those born between 1933 and 1944, only 16.2 percent said they had had two or more partners at this age, with only 1.1 percent having had five or more (Laumann et al. 1994, 198). The 1995 National Survey of Family Growth had similar results, with women under 40 having the highest numbers of partners (42).

p. 55 *The average number of lifetime partners*   Reporting one life partner were 21 percent of males and 25 percent of females; 19 percent of both reported two, and 14 percent of both reported six to nine. Sixteen percent of males and 12 percent of females reported ten or more. However, it is unclear whether men really do have more partners or whether they just say they do. The phenomenon of men's citing more partners than women is often difficult to explain. Logically, since it "takes two to tango," we would expect men and women to report the same patterns. Considering that this discrepancy is common in major surveys in the United States and Europe, the NHSLS authors noted: "The inconsistency constitutes an important puzzle for which we, like others, have no good answer" (Laumann et al. 1994, 185). But they do offer some possible explanations. One is that men may be having sex more with other men, more than the frequency with which women have sex with one another. The men also may be having sex with people outside the age range surveyed, such as girls under 18. Finally, as a result of differing social expectations, men also tend to exaggerate and women to understate their sexual experience.

p. 55 *This last survey also found*   The 1998 survey was the result of more than six hundred readers responding to a questionnaire printed in the September 1997 issue of *Glamour*. The 1999 survey was of two hundred sexually active 18- to- 35-year-olds.

p. 56 *Reflecting the numbers found*   In Lottes's study of college students at an eastern state university in 1989, 44 percent of females (and 65 percent of males) reported that they had had sex without emotional involvement (Lottes 1993, 657).

p. 56 *There are a few differences*   Of her sample, 44 percent of women and 58 percent of men surveyed reported "one-night stands." But women were still four times likelier than men (44 percent versus 9 percent) to believe that casual sex could lead to a committed relationship (Regan and Dreyer 1999).

p. 58 *Forty percent of both the women*   Women revealed more concern about AIDS in that they were far more likely to become more selective of their partners.

More women than men (but still the vast minority of them) used the strategies of working harder on their current relationship, asking a partner about his or her sex history, becoming monogamous, holding off having sex with a new partner, and using spermicides (Juran 1995, 46).

p. 58 *The same researcher found*   Of the urban bar patrons questioned, the primary behavior response was condom use, reported by 56 percent of respondents in a 1995 study, 35 percent in a 1991 study, and only 4 percent in a 1986 study (Juran 1995, 56).

p. 58 *The most recent and comprehensive*   Of those who began having sex in the 1990s, 54 percent used them, compared with 36.4 percent in the late 1980s, 25.1 percent in the early 1980s, and only 18 percent in the 1970s.

p. 59 *The NHSLS study revealed*   These results are true, despite some mixed messages in the text and with the actual numbers cited in graphs in *The Social Organization of Sexuality*, the academic analysis of the study. The text of the study notes that both men and women had acquired fewer partners by age 20 than did the boomers in the sexual revolution. However, the charts reveal that this was slightly true only for men. This study and others correlate these declines in sexual promiscuity to AIDS.

NOTES TO CHAPTER 3

p. 64 *Sex researchers have also noticed*   In *Sexual Salvation* (1994), feminist psychologist Naomi McCormick notes that "by now, most single heterosexual men have had at least one experience with being asked on a date by a woman" (19).

p. 64 *Fifty-four percent of females*   Another 1991 study of college students found large numbers of women initiating dates (though less often than men did): 54 percent of women reported initiating dates within the last month and 72 percent in the past six months. "This clearly indicates along with earlier data," write authors J. R. McNamara and K. Grossman, "that women are no longer willing to wait and hope that a man will take the lead in initiating a date" (25). They also found similarities between the high anxiety levels of men and women before initiating a date, the only difference being that males rated physical appearance more prominently than women did (McNamara and Grossman 1991, 25).

p. 65 *In Lottes's study*   In her survey, a majority of the males (88 percent) had shared the expenses for a date or had a female pay the entire expense for a date (72 percent). Forty-seven percent of females and 36 percent of males reported that they had shared dating expenses ten or more times (Lottes 1993, 658, 659).

p. 66 *In Lottes's sample*   An additional study (1991) by Charlene Muehlenhard and Marcia McCoy of the University of Kansas revealed that when the females they surveyed detected an underlying double standard of judgment from men, they were less likely to acknowledge their own desire for sex.

p. 71 *According to the* Details *survey*   They have reached that state in similar ways: 77 percent of men and 70 percent of women through oral sex, 76 percent of men and 72 percent of women by manual stimulation by a partner, and 80 percent of men and 74 percent of women through intercourse.

p. 72 *The group of women*   However, women aged 25 to 29 (31.1 percent) had a slightly higher rate than did women in their early thirties (29.1 percent) and late thirties (28.3 percent). The rate was highest for women in their late forties, at 34.3 percent, indicating that orgasm for women was a function of self-knowledge and experience (Laumann et al. 1994, table 3.7, 116).

p. 75 *Reflecting this recent shift*   The numbers remain steady for men from 18 to 44, ranging from 31.6 to 39.6 percent; they then start dropping with older age groups, with only 15.6 percent of men aged 55 to 59 reporting this preference.

p. 77 *When asked to describe*   For women, farther down the list was "cautious," cited by 24 percent, and "self-confident," listed by 23 percent.

p. 77 *Reflecting perhaps*   The *Details* survey counted a small yet significant percentage of self-described heterosexual women who had had sexual contact with other women. Fourteen percent had kissed, 11 percent had caressed, 5 percent had experienced "manual-genital stimulation," and 2 percent had shared oral sex.

p. 84 *Tasha, the most open*   Although men still masturbate in much higher numbers, the two genders share the same motivations. The greatest number do so to relieve sexual tension (63 percent of women and 73 percent of men), to obtain physical pleasure (42 percent of women and 40 percent of men, but many more of the educated women), and to relax (32 percent of women and 26 percent of men). Just as many do it if a partner is not available (32 percent of both women and men) (Laumann et al. 1994, table 3.3, 86). This last reason combats some of the stigma that masturbation is only for people who can't get a partner to "do it the real way." The University of Chicago's National Health and Social Life Survey quotes independent analyses that masturbation does not vary in frequency among women living with a partner and those who have never married. In fact, cohabiting women (the most sexually experienced overall) masturbated slightly more than the others did (Laumann et al. 1994, 83).

NOTES TO CHAPTER 4

p. 90 *But the other 54 percent*   This is nearly the same response given by women surveyed in the 1997 *Details* Sex on Campus study: 58 percent of women said that they had *not* had a one-night stand (Elliott and Brantley 1997, 15).

p. 90 *The National Survey of Family Growth*   I noticed similar proportions, and great variety in sexual experiences, among my staunchly individualistic interview sample, even in the same group of acquaintances or friends. For example, of the four women I interviewed in Santa Barbara, California, two had waited until marriage (one for religious reasons), and two others had had a little experience with casual sex in college but then afterward were strictly monogamous. Among the four law students in Washington, D.C., were a Vietnamese woman from a strict Catholic family who never had had sex or a relationship, a religious Lutheran woman who had had sex in two committed relationships, and two others who had had several casual sex encounters. Of the three women in their early twenties at Texas Women's University, one planned on remaining a virgin until marriage because of religion; another was waiting until she was in a stable relationship; and another had had sex in a long-term relationship three years earlier. The prevalence of virgins among my sample matches the national statistics. Among the seventy-two women I interviewed in my core group aged 17 to 36, fourteen had been virgins in their twenties, and six were currently virgins.

p. 94 *Certainly those most vocally favoring*   Two 1999 polls, the first to measure abstinence in sex education, concluded that one in three districts uses an abstinence-only curriculum that permits discussion of contraception only in regard to its failure rates (Wilgoren 1999). From 1997 to 1999, joined by the states' matching funds, the federal government funded 698 new abstinence-only programs and 21 media campaigns, costing about $500 million in public funds (Smith 1999).

p. 95 *Despite the genders' views*   In the UCLA Higher Education Research Institute survey *The American Freshman: National Norms for Fall 1998,* 53.6 percent of men and 27.7 percent of women agreed that "sex is OK if people like each other."

NOTES TO CHAPTER 5

p. 114 *Indeed, family priorities*   According to the 1996 UCLA Higher Education Research Institute annual survey of college freshmen, 72.1 percent of women considered raising a family as "essential or very important." This is significantly higher than the 1974 figure of only 56.8 percent and is closer to the 1968 record high of 77.8 percent. (The survey first asked this question in 1969.) Men's rating of family as such a priority reached an all-time high in 1996, accounting for 72.3 percent of the sample, compared with a low of 53.3 percent in 1974 and 66.5 percent in 1969.

p. 114 *And even though more women*   In 1996, 62.3 percent said they said that they aspired to be "an authority in my field" (one of many such career ambition indicators listed), which was between the low of 54.3 percent in 1971 and the high of 72.1 percent in 1977. (Of course, this does not mean that women have retreated from having a career, as more women than ever are in college and in a position to make such career decisions.) Meanwhile, men have also made more manageable career goals, compared with the late 1970s and 1980s. In 1996, about 66.2 percent rated reaching this authority as a priority, compared with 1966, when 70.3 percent gave this response, and their all-time high of 78.1 percent in 1987.

p. 117 *According to the 2000 Virginia Slims*   In a nationwide cross section of 2,177 women and a control group of 826 men, 18 years and older, interviewed between May 15 and July 22, 1999. Sponsored by Philip Morris USA and conducted by Roper Starch Worldwide, the Virginia Slims Opinion Poll, first taken in 1970, is considered the most definitive source of information on the history of women's opinions and their changing role in society.

p. 118 *Building on boomer patterns*   Between 1970 and 1990, the number of married-couple families with children declined by almost 1 million, and their share of households dropped 14 percentage points (*Household and Family Characteristics* 1995, viii). In the 1990 Virginia Slims/Roper Organization Opinion Poll, the majority of men (58 percent) and women (52 percent) said that two children would make the ideal family. In contrast, in a survey taken by Gallup in 1941, about 70 percent of Americans thought that three or more children made the ideal family.

p. 122 *Although people are still having*   In 1998, when the University of Chicago's General Social Survey asked adults about the morality of sexual relations with someone other than a marriage partner, 78 percent said it was always wrong. In 1973, 69 percent gave that answer.

p. 123 *The same study also found*   Men spend 2.3 hours per day caring for their children, up by a half hour since 1977, according to the National Study of the Changing Workforce, by the Families and Work Institute, a nonprofit research group based in New York.

p. 125 *Many women are grateful*   In 1998, 27.7 percent of children under 18 lived in a single-parent home, an increase from 5 percent in 1960. About 84.1 percent lived with their mother (*Marital Status* 1998).

p. 130 *Yet women's personal changes*   In the 2000 Virginia Slims Opinion Poll, responding to a question asking why marriages may be weaker, very few (just 6 percent of the women and 8 percent of the men) blamed the women's movement. The majority of responses (to an open-ended question) focused on the lack of commitment, "issues that pertain to both sexes equally." The most common responses, given by at least 40 percent of men and women, were a lack of communication, respect, and not taking marriage seriously (62).

NOTES TO CHAPTER 6

p. 133 *The average age*   Comparison of data from 1983 to 1998, table 6 of the 1983 *Marital Status and Living Arrangements* and table 7 of the 1998 version. The increase of 44 percent is for never-married women aged 15 and older living alone.

p. 133 *When asked whether people*   These numbers were more consistent for older singles, however. Women aged 18 to 24 were more eager than the men in their age group to get married, with 93 percent wanting to marry, compared with 88 percent of the men; see the 1993 survey of 1,057 respondents conducted by Guido Stempel III, a journalism professor at Ohio University, in conjunction with the Scripps Howard News Service.

p. 133 *Physical well-being is also*   Quoting Dr. Joan S. Tucker, a psychologist at Brandeis University, describing a recent study by the Rand Center for the Study of Aging in Santa Monica, California. The center determined that men who married were in poorer physical condition than were their counterparts who stayed single. Nonetheless, the married men outlived their single brethren by three to four years.

p. 135 *But today, cohabitation*   Fifty-six percent of all marriages between 1990 and 1994 were preceded by cohabitation. From 1965 to 1974, that figure was about 10 percent; see the study by the Institute for Social Research at the University of Michigan published in the summer of 2000 in the *Annual Review of Sociology* (Nagourney 2000).

p. 142 *In reality, the teenage birthrate*   In 1997, the U.S. birthrate reached a record low of 14.5 births per 1,000 population; see U.S. Department of Health and Human Services, "Births: Final Data for 1997," vol. 47, no. 18, press release dated April 29, 1999.

p. 149 *A more traditional and*   The most often cited estimate, from a 1989 survey by the National Council for Adoption, is that each year nearly 25,000 babies in the United States are adopted by nonrelatives. In 1970, by contrast, some 75,000 babies were put up for adoption. In general, before 1973, 9 percent of all children born to never-married mothers were given up for adoption, compared with 4 percent between 1973 and 1981 and 2 percent between 1981 and 1989.

NOTES TO CHAPTER 8

p. 175 *Women's most dramatic employment gains*   The statistics for specific fields reveal the inroads. In 1993, the percentage of women architects was 18.6 percent, compared with only 4.3 percent in 1975; in 1993, 22.8 percent of lawyers and judges were women, compared with only 7.1 percent in 1975 (Frye 1996, 39, quoting Bureau of Labor Statistics 1994). In 1990, 35.3 percent of managers were white women, and 6.9 percent were women of color (Frye 1996, 39, quoting Institute for Women's Policy Research 1995).

p. 176 *In the 1980s*   In the next two decades, women's involvement in the labor force accelerated for many reasons. One was that the women's movement encouraged women to work, for either personal satisfaction or independence. This contradicted widespread public beliefs from 1950s Freudian psychiatry that ambitious or career-oriented women were emotionally stunted. The economy also expanded, providing jobs for most of those who sought them. Women also obtained more education, which qualified them for better jobs. Birthrates were declining, both reflecting and contributing to women's participation in the workforce. The first federal laws against sex discrimination in employment, the Equal Pay Act of 1963 and the Civil Rights Act of 1964, were passed. The Pregnancy Discrimination Act of 1978 and the Equal Opportunity Commission's Guidelines on Sexual Harassment in 1980 began to shift the law's focus toward those forms of discrimination faced specifically by women. And with the declining industrial economy, most of the jobs that have opened up in the past several decades are in the service sector, work that men and women can perform equally well. In contrast, the number of jobs offering family wages requiring physical strength and performed traditionally by men—in agriculture, mining, and manufacturing—has dropped.

p. 176 *Gender differences are still*   For example, more than a quarter of women but only 3 percent of men work in administrative support jobs. The gender differences are most striking in the relatively higher paying and traditionally male trades, the precision production, craft, and repair occupations; in 1994, for example, 2 percent of electricians and 1 percent of carpenters were women (Herz and Wootton 1996, 57, quoting Bureau of Labor Statistics).

p. 176 *White women have gained*   A 1991 study by Marilyn Power, an economist and professor at Sarah Lawrence College, showed that even though their career status has improved from being limited to domestic jobs, black women still trail white women in dead-end service jobs, which include practical nurses, waitresses, hospital attendants, and building and kitchen workers. But black women are less concentrated in both domestic work and other service jobs. In 1960, 37.5 percent of employed black women were private household workers, the lowest-paying job, compared with 3.5 percent of employed white women. By 1989, only 3.5 percent of black women were domestic workers, compared with 1.3 percent of employed white women. In 1960, 60 percent of all employed black women were service workers, compared with 20.3 percent of employed white women. In 1989, 27.3 percent of employed black women were in service occupations, compared with 16.1 percent of employed white women (Kleiman 1991).

p. 176 *Half of these households*   This shift is a result of wide-ranging structural and social change, with varying explanations, from less-educated men not being able to support families because of a loss of industrial jobs, to men's psychological flight from commitment, to a drop in government social services, to more women's deciding to live on their own. In 1978, sociologist Diana Pearce called attention to this phenomenon she called the "feminization of poverty."

p. 176 *In 1998, the U.S. Census Bureau*   In 1997, a record 89.6 percent of women aged 25 to 29 had finished high school, compared with 86 percent of the men. In addition, women also led men with college completion rates: 29 percent for women compared with 26 percent for men. In these years, young women of all races have made notable progress, especially black women in finishing high school. In 1970, only 32.5 percent of black women aged 25 to 29 had finished twelve or more years of school, compared with 87.6 percent in 1997. Hispanic women have been slower to catch up, with only 66.3 percent in that age group finishing high school in 1997. In contrast, that year 90 percent of white women aged 25 to 29 had finished high school, compared with 55 percent in 1970. These discrepancies continue with college. In this age group, 30.4 percent of white women, 17 percent of black women, and only 11.3 percent of Hispanics had graduated from college (*Educational Attainment* 1998, 1–5).

p. 177 *The women college graduates*   Twelve percent of college-educated men, versus 7.3 percent of college-educated women, had a same-sex partner. But when asked if they had "desire, attract or appeal" for the same sex, 12.8 percent of college-educated women agreed, compared with only 9.4 percent of college-educated men (Laumann et al. 1994, 305).

p. 180 *Despite the rhetoric*   Antiwar organizers popularized the slogan "girls say yes to guys who say no." When women protested these demands, they were shot down. A notorious remark allegedly made by Stokely Carmichael of the Student Nonviolent Coordinating Committee was that "the only position for women in the SNCC is prone."

p. 183 *That is, in the 1990s*   See an excerpt of Roiphe's book in *Cosmopolitan* and George Will's column "Sex Amidst Semi-Colons" in *Newsweek*. These charges of "date-rape hype" first appeared in an article in the October 1990 *Playboy* by Stephanie Guttman, "Date Rape: Does Anyone Really Know What It Is?"

NOTES TO CHAPTER 9

p. 194 *By all accounts*   Fifty-one percent of Jews are college graduates, compared with 31 percent who are not religious, 25 percent of white mainline Protestants, and 16 percent of white evangelical Christians. One example of education's effect is the use of birth control, which is correlated most positively with education and is used much more often during first intercourse by Jews and the nonreligious than by these other groups (*Diminishing Divide* 1996, 36).

p. 194 *As a group,*   A survey published in Roof's 1993 book found "a cultural fault line" between those born before and after World War II in measures of strength of religious identity, the importance of arriving at one's own beliefs, whether religious attendance is necessary to being a "good" Christian or Jew, and in views of whether the rules of morality within churches or synagogues are too restrictive. For example, 56 percent of baby boomers, as opposed to 41 percent of earlier generations, saw church attendance as unnecessary. The boomers' influences in the 1960s were numerous. Although only a small percentage of Americans actually participated in antiestablishment movements, individualistic philosophies of that era became absorbed into the mainstream, in a process that is still continuing. As young people questioned the establishment in civil rights and antiwar protests, the scrutiny of religious institutions was a natural follow-up. Another factor was the younger generation's greater affluence. Whereas the older generation had been preoccupied more with survival, 1960s youth had the chance to explore more advanced "hierarchies of needs." They had greater expectations to find spiritual meaning beyond material possessions, which they could more easily take for granted.

p. 201 *"Church leaders cannot"*　William D'Antonio summed up two studies. The first was commissioned in 1979 by Joan Fee and her colleagues at the Center for the Study of American Pluralism, and its results were published in 1981 as *Young Catholics in the United States and Canada*. The 1993 study was commissioned by Catholics for a Free Choice (CFFC) and conducted by KRC Research and Consulting of New York (1994, 33–34).

NOTES TO CHAPTER 10

p. 222 *Also, read in private*　Focus groups of women named confidentiality as a major attraction of sex information from women's magazines (see Deborah Treise's 1997 Kaiser Foundation report).

p. 224 *Although the editors would not*　The median age of the *Mademoiselle* reader was 28, compared with 29 for *Glamour* and 31 for *Cosmopolitan*. *Mademoiselle* readers have median income of $39,000, compared with *Glamour*'s $41,000 and *Cosmo*'s $37,000. Forty-nine percent of *Mademoiselle*'s readers attended college, fewer than *Glamour*'s 50 percent and ahead of *Cosmo*'s 46 percent. *Mademoiselle*, with a circulation of 1.2 million, called itself "the young women's magazine." It generally had a younger feel, a transition from *Seventeen*. It relied heavily on advice, with six columns—on love, men, sex, friends, money, and work. In 1994, when editor in chief Elizabeth Crow made it more mainstream, covering the tracks of the more risqué year-long reign of British editor Gabe Doppelt, who used the most emaciated of the waif models and ran such features as renting a porn movie or examining the legalization of marijuana (Carmody 1994).

p. 229 *This narcissism and superficiality*　An example is the much-publicized decision of the Kroger grocery chain in early 2000 to display *Cosmo* behind blinders in its thousands of stores because of the racy teasers on the cover (Navratil 2000).

NOTE TO THE CONCLUSION

p. 234 *For example, women still*　Of those aged 18 to 24 surveyed by the 1994 National Health and Social Life Survey at the University of Chicago, 70.2 percent of men said that they "always had an orgasm" with their partners, but only 21.5 percent of women that age gave that response. For men aged 25 to 29, the percentage was 72.8, and for women, it was 31.1 (Laumann et al. 1994, 116–77).

Bibliography

Altman, Lawrence K. 1997. "AIDS Deaths Drop 19 Percent in U.S., Continuing a Heartening Trend." *New York Times*, 15 July, A10.

The American Freshman: National Norms for Fall 1998. 1999. By Linda J. Sax et al. Los Angeles: Higher Education Research Institute of the University of California.

The American Freshman: Thirty Year Trends. 1997. By Alexander W. Astin et al. Los Angeles: Higher Education Research Institute of the University of California.

Angier, Natalie. 1998. "Men. Are Women Better Off with Them, or without Them?" *New York Times*, 21 June, Women's Health sec., 10.

Baber, Asa. 1995. "A New Kind of Rush" [on fraternities under fire]. In "Men" column, *Playboy*, February, 32.

Bachu, Amara. 1993. "Fertility of American Women: June 1992." Washington, DC: U.S. Bureau of the Census, July.

Baker, Russell. 1993. "Sexwise It's the Pits." *New York Times*, 17 April, 21.

Bakos, Susan Crain. 1990. *What Men Really Want.* New York: St. Martin's Press.

Baldwin, J. D., S. Whitely, and J. I. Baldwin. 1992. "The Effect of Ethnic Group on Sexual Activities Related to Conception and STDs." *Journal of Sex Research* 29, no. 2: 189–205.

Ballenger, Josephine. 1992. "Uncovering Abortion: Sisterhood Is Cautious." *Columbia Journalism Review*, March/April, 16.

Bawden, Jennifer. 2000. *Get a Life Then Get a Man.* New York: Plume.

Beauvoir, Simone de. 1952. *The Second Sex.* Trans. and ed. H. M. Parshly. New York: Knopf.

Belcastro, Philip A. 1985. "Sexual Behavior Differences between Black and White Students." *Journal of Sex Research* 21, no. 1 (February): 56–67.

Belkin, Lisa. 1998. "Now Accepting Applications for My Baby." *New York Times*, 5 April, 59.

Bell, R. R., and K. Coughey. 1980. "Premarital Sexual Experience among College Females." *Family Relations* 29: 353–57.

Bellah, Robert N., et al. 1996. *Habits of the Heart: Individualism and Commitment in American Life.* Berkeley and Los Angeles: University of California Press.

Bennett, Amanda, and Anita Sharpe. 1996. "AIDS Fight Is Skewed by Federal Campaign Exaggerating Risks." *Wall Street Journal*, 1 May, A1, A8.

Berke, Richard L. 1998. "Chasing the Polls on Gay Rights." *New York Times*, 2 August, Perspectives sec., 3.

Bibby, Patricia. 1997. "MTV's Sex Education: Straight Talk and Giggles." *Chicago Tribune*, 24 September, sec. 5, 7.

Bishop, P. D., and A. Lipsitz. 1990. "Sexual Behavior among College Students in the AIDS Era: A Comparative Study." *Journal of Psychology and Human Sexuality* 3: 35–52.

Blume, Judy. 1975. *Forever*. New York: Bradbury Press.

Boone, Sharon. 1999. "200 Men's & Women's Private Sex Styles." *Glamour*, November, 210–13.

Bouris, Karen. 1993. *The First Time: Women Speak Out about 'Losing Their Virginity.'* Berkeley, CA: Conari Press.

Bowman, Karilyn. 1999. "Living Happily Ever After: Marriage under the Microscope." *The Public Perspective: A Roper Center Review of Public Opinion and Polling*, April/May.

Brady, Lois Smith. 1996. "Why Marriage Is Hot Again." *Redbook*, September, 122–24, 148.

Brotman, Barbara. 1997. "Bedtime Stories." *Chicago Tribune*, 13 July, sec. 13, 1.

Brown, Helen Gurley. 1962. *Sex and the Single Girl*. New York: Bernard Geis.

——. 1970. *Sex and the New Single Girl*. New York: Bernard Geis.

——. 2000. *I'm Wild Again: Snippets from My Life and a Few Brazen Thoughts*. New York: St. Martin's Press.

Brown, Rita Mae. 1976. *Plain Brown Wrapper*. Oakland, CA: Diana Press.

Bureau of Labor Statistics. 1997. "Developments in Women's Labor Force Participation." By Howard V. Hayghe, pp. 41–46, *Monthly Labor Review*. Washington, DC: U.S. Government Printing Office, September.

——. 2000. *Employment and Unemployment. Estimates from the 1999 Current Population Survey*. Washington, DC: U.S. Government Printing Office, January.

Butler, Patrick. 1998. "Miss America Brings Her AIDS Message to Truman." *Lerner Newspapers*, 1 July, 1, 5.

Cagle, Jess. 1995. "A Special Report: The Gay '90s." *Entertainment Weekly*, 8 September, 312.

Carlson, Karen J., Stephanie A. Eisenstat, and Terra Ziporyn. 1996. *The Harvard Guide to Women's Health*. Cambridge, MA: Harvard University Press.

Carmody, Deirdre. 1994. "New Makeover for Mademoiselle." *New York Times*, 21 March, C6.

Cassell, Carol. 1984. *Swept Away: Why Women Fear Their Own Sexuality*. New York: Simon & Schuster.

Childers, Kim Walsh, Debbie Treise, and Alyse Gotthoffer. 1997. "Sexual Health Coverage: Women's, Men's, Teen and Other Specialty Magazines." Menlo Park, CA: Henry J. Kaiser Family Foundation, April 18. (Also an abbreviated supplement to the May/June 1997 *Columbia Journalism Review*.)

Clair, Roxanne. 1999. "Making School Safe for Queer Kids." *Curve*, September, 18–19.

Clark, Russell D., and Elaine Hatfield. 1989. "Gender Differences in Receptivity to Sexual Offers." *Journal of Psychology and Human Sexuality* 2: 39–55.

Cooper, Mike. 1998. "U.S. Says Abortions up for First Time This Decade." *Reuters* report, 3 December.

Costello, Cynthia, and Barbara Kivimae Krimgold, eds. 1996. *The American Woman 1996–1997: Women and Work.* New York: Norton.

Cotter, Katie. 1997. "Dating a Man." *The Advocate,* 18 February, 41.

Crichton, Sarah. 1993. "Sexual Correctness: Has It Gone Too Far?" *Newsweek,* 25 October, 52–64.

Czape, Chandra. 1999. "Sex Ethics Column." *Glamour,* March, 82.

D'Antonio, William. 1994. "The Young and the Restless." *Conscience* 15 (published by Catholics for a Free Choice, Washington, DC), no. 3 (Autumn): 33–40.

Daum, Megan. 1996. "Safe-Sex Lies." *New York Times Magazine,* 21 January, 32–33.

Davidson, K., and N. Moore. 1994. "Masturbation and Premarital Sexual Intercourse among College Women: Making Choices for Sexual Fulfillment." *Journal of Sex and Marital Therapy* 20, no. 3 (Fall).

Davis, Clive M., et al. 1996. "Characteristics of Vibrator Use among Women." *Journal of Sex Research* 33, no. 4: 313–20.

Davis, Flora. 1991. *Moving the Mountain: The Women's Movement in America since 1960.* New York: Simon & Schuster.

Del Castillo, Adelaida R. 1978. "Malintzin Tenepal: A Preliminary Look into a New Perspective." In *Essays on La Mujer,* ed. Rosaura Sanchez and Rosa Martinez Cruz, pp. 124–49. Los Angeles: University of California, Chicano Studies Center Publications.

D'Emilio, John, and Estelle B. Freedman. 1988. *Intimate Matters: A History of Sexuality in America.* New York: Harper & Row.

The Diminishing Divide: American Churches, American Politics. 1996. Washington, DC: Pew Research Center for the People and the Press, June 25.

Dixon, Jim. 1995. "Men Q&A column." *Mademoiselle,* August, 68.

Dobson, James. 1975. *What Wives Wish Their Husbands Knew about Women.* Wheaton, IL: Tyndale House.

Douglass, Marcia, and Lisa Douglass. 1997. *Are We Having Fun Yet? The Intelligent Woman's Guide to Sex.* New York: Hyperion.

Duff, Christina. 1996. "More than Friends: The Tie That Binds Is Glittering Anew." *Wall Street Journal,* 3 April, 1, 10.

Educational Attainment in the United States: March 1998 (updated). 1998. By Jennifer C. Day and Andrea E. Curry. Washington, DC: U.S. Bureau of the Census, December.

Edut, Ophira, ed. 1998. *Adios, Barbie.* Seattle: Seal Press.

Edwards, Gavin. 1992. "Age of Confusion: Missing Out on the Sexual Revolution." *Details,* August, 36.

Ehrenreich, Barbara. 1990. *The Worst Years of Our Lives.* New York: Pantheon Books.

Ehrenreich, Barbara, Elizabeth Hess, and Gloria Jacobs. 1986. *Re-making Love: The Feminization of Sex*. New York: Anchor Books.

Elder, Janet. 1997. "Poll Finds Women Are the Health-Savvier Sex, and the Warier." *New York Times*, 22 June, 8.

Elliott, Leland, and Cynthia Brantley. 1997. *Sex on Campus: The Naked Truth about the Real Sex Lives of College Students* (includes results of the *Details* magazine's College Sex Survey). New York: Random House.

"The Entertainers." 1999. *Entertainment Weekly*, 1 January, 14–46.

Faderman, Lillian. 1991. *Odd Girls and Twilight Lovers: A History of Lesbian Life in Twentieth Century America*. New York: Columbia University Press.

Fein, Ellen, and Sherrie Schneider. 1995. *The Rules: Time-Tested Secrets for Capturing the Heart of Mr. Right*. New York: Warner Books.

Felder, Leonard. 1994. "Sex Speak." *New Woman*, September, 111.

Ferguson, Marjorie. 1983. *Forever Feminine: Women's Magazines and Cult of Femininity*. London: Heinemann.

"Fewer College Freshmen Endorsing Casual Sex, Survey Finds." 1997. *Chicago Tribune*, 13 January, 4.

Fielding, Bridget. 1998. *Bridget Jones's Diary*. New York: Viking Press.

Fillion, Kate. 1996. "This Is the Sexual Revolution" (Young Women and Sex in the 1990s). *Saturday Night*, February, 36–41.

Findlen, Barbara, ed. 1995. *Listen Up: Voices from the Next Feminist Generation*. Seattle: Seal Press.

Finley, B., C. E. Starnes, and F. B. Alvarez. 1985. "Recent Changes in Sex Role Ideology among Divorced Men and Women: Some Possible Causes and Implications." *Sex Roles* 12: 637–53.

Firebaugh, Glenn. 1990. "Components of Change in Gender Role Attitudes, 1972–1988." Paper presented to the Population Association of Toronto, May.

Flanders, Laura. 1994. "The 'Stolen Feminism' Hoax." *EXTRA*, September/October, 6–9.

Forrest, Jacqueline Darroch, and Richard R. Fordyce. 1993. "Women's Contraceptive Attitudes and Use in 1992." *Family Planning Perspectives* 25, no. 4 (July/August): 175–79.

Forsyth, Sandra. 1995. "Will I Lose Him If I Don't Move in with Him?" *Mademoiselle*, March, 46–50.

———. 1997. "Living Together Is Hell." *Mademoiselle,* January, 132–34.

Fowlkes, Martha R. 1994. "Single Worlds and Homosexual Lifestyles: Patterns of Sexuality and Intimacy." In *Sexuality across the Life Course*, ed. Alice S. Rossi, pp. 151–84. Chicago: University of Chicago Press.

Frankel, Valerie. 1996. "Almost Sex (on 'Outercourse')." *Mademoiselle*, October, 149–53.

Friday, Nancy. 1991. *Women on Top*. New York: Simon & Schuster.

Friedan, Betty. 1963. *The Feminine Mystique*. New York: Norton.

Frye, Jocelyn C. 1996. "Affirmative Action: Understanding the Past and Present." In *The American Woman 1996–1997: Women and Work*, ed. Cynthia Costello and Barbara Kivimae Krimgold, pp. 32–43. New York: Norton.

Gamson, Joshua. 1996. "Do Ask, Do Tell." *Utne Reader* (reprinted from the fall 1995 *American Prospect*), January/February, 81.

Garrity, Terry, with John Garrity. 1984. *Story of "J": The Author of* The Sensuous Woman *Tells the Bitter Price of Her Crazy Success*. New York: Morrow.

Gibbs, Nancy G. 1993. "Bringing up Father." *Time*, 28 June, 52–61.

Gilbert, Neil. 1991. "The Campus Rape Scare." *Wall Street Journal*, 27 June, 10.

Glaser, Gabrielle. 1994. "The New Chastity." *Mademoiselle*, March, 119–21, 165, 171.

Glenn, Norval. 1987. "Social Trends in the United States: Evidence from Sample Surveys." *Public Opinion Quarterly* 51 (Winter): S109–S126.

Gody, Celia, Linda Andrews, and Christina Harter. 1990. *The Thirty-Five Million: A Preliminary Report on the Status of Young Women*. Washington, DC: Institute for Women's Policy Research, Young Women's Project.

Goodman, Ellen. 1995. "The Final Chapter: Senate Will No Longer Be Able to Dismiss Boorish Behavior." *Chicago Tribune*, 12 September, sec. 1, 15.

Grauerholtz, Elizabeth, and Richard T. Serpe. 1985. "Initiation and Response: The Dynamics of Sexual Interaction." *Sex Roles* 12: 1041–59.

Greeley, Andrew M., William C. McCready, and Kathleen McCourt. 1976. *Catholic Schools in a Declining Church*. Kansas City. Sheed & Ward.

Guttmann, Stephanie. 1990. "Date Rape: Does Anyone Really Know What It Is?" *Playboy*, October, 48–56.

Harris, Lynn. 1997. "Casual Sex: Why Confident Women Are Saying No." *Glamour*, September, 314–15, 335–36.

Harrison, Kathryn. 1997. *The Kiss*. New York: Random House.

Hellman, Peter. 1993. "Crying Rape: The Politics of Date Rape on "Campus." *New York Times*, 8 March, 33–37.

Herrmann, Brenda. 1993. "Sex? Cool Your Jets!: 'Wings' Star Practices What She Preaches (Yep, She's a Virgin)." *Chicago Tribune*, 9 March, KidNews sec., cover.

Herz, Diane E., and Barbara Wootton. 1996. "Women in the Workforce: An Overview." In *The American Woman 1996–1997: Women and Work*, ed. Cynthia Costello and Barbara Kivimae Krimgold, pp. 44–78. New York: Norton.

Hite, Shere. 1976. *The Hite Report*. New York: Dell.

———. 1994. *The Hite Report on the Family: Growing Up under Patriarchy*. London: Bloomsbury.

Holden, Stephen. 1999. "A New Rule: The Beautiful Are the Bad.' *New York Times*, 28 February, A13.

Holmes, Anna. 2000. "Masturbation: The Double Standard." *Glamour*, March, 172–76.

Holmes, Steven A. 1996. "Black-White Marriages on the Rise." *New York Times*, 4 July, A10.

Household and Family Characteristics (March 1994). 1995. By Steve Rawlings and Arlene Saluter. Washington, DC: U.S. Bureau of the Census, September.

Household and Family Characteristics (March 1998). 1998. By Lynne M. Casper and Ken Bryson. Washington, DC: U.S. Bureau of the Census, October.

Hung, Mindy. 1998. "Waiting to Be Un-Zipped." *Salon*, 4 November, available online @ www.salon.com.

Hutton, Julia. 1992. *Good Sex: Real Stories from Real People*. San Francisco: Cleis.

Iovine, Julie V. 1999. "Castle First, Prince Later: Marketing to Ms." *New York Times*, 21 October, B1.

"J." 1969. *The Sensuous Woman*. New York: Lyle Stuart.

Jacobs, A. J. 1999. "Let's Talk about Sex (on "Sex and the City")." *Entertainment Weekly*, 5 June, 32–34.

Jacobs, A. J., and Jessica Shaw. 1999. "Virgin Spring." *Entertainment Weekly*, 2 April, 10, 11.

Jacoby, Susan. 1993. "Accidentally Pregnant." *Glamour*, August, 259.

Janus, Samuel S., and Cynthia L. Janus. 1993. *The Janus Report on Sexual Behavior*. New York: Wiley.

Jesser, Clinton J. 1978. "Male Responses to Direct Verbal Sexual Initiatives of Females." *Journal of Sex Research* 14: 118–28.

Jewel, Dan. 1998. "A Question of Honor." *People*, 16 June, 149–51.

Juran, Shelly. 1989. "Sexual Behavior Changes as a Result of a Concern about AIDS: Gays, Straights, Females and Males. *Journal of Psychology and Human Sexuality* 2: 61–77.

———. 1991. "Sexual Behavior Changes among Heterosexual, Lesbian and Gay Bar Patrons as Assessed by Questionnaire over an 18-Month Period." *Journal of Psychology and Human Sexuality* 4: 111–21.

———. 1995. "The 90s: Gender Differences in AIDS-Related Sexual Concerns and Behaviors." *Journal of Psychology and Human Sexuality* 7, 3.

Kaiser Family Foundation. 1996. Survey on Americans and AIDS/HIV. Menlo Park, CA: Henry J. Kaiser Family Foundation, June 26.

Kaiser Family Foundation. 1996. Survey on Teens and Sex. 1996. Menlo Park, CA: Henry J. Kaiser Family Foundation, June.

Kallen, David J., and Judith J. Stephenson. 1982. "Talking about Sex Revisited." *Journal of Youth and Adolescence* 11, no. 1, 15.

Kamen, Paula. 1991. *Feminist Fatale: Voices from the "Twentysomething" Generation Explore the Future of the Women's Movement*. New York: Donald I. Fine.

———. 1996. "Acquaintance Rape: Revolution and Reaction." In *"Bad Girls/Good Girls": Women, Sex and Power in the Nineties*, ed. Nan Bauer Maglin and Donna Perry, pp. 137–49. New Brunswick, NJ: Rutgers University Press.

Kass, Leon R. 1997. "Courtship's End." *Chicago Tribune Magazine*, 9 February, 20.

Keller, J. F., S. S. Elliott, and E. Gunberg. 1982. "Premarital Sexual Intercourse among Single College Students: A Discrimination Analysis." *Sex Roles* 8: 21–32.

Kelley, Kathryn, Elaine Pilchowicz, and Donn Byrne. 1981. "Responses of Males to Female-Initiated Dates." *Bulletin of the Psychonomic Society* 17: 195–96.

Kerrill, Tamara. 1997. "It's Getting Crowded." *Chicago Sun-Times*, 1 June, 16.

Khazzoom, Loolwa. 1999. "Sexual Liberation." *Moxie* (Summer): 34–35.

Kinsey, Alfred C., Wardell B. Pomeroy, Clyde E. Martin, and Paul H. Gebbhard. 1953. *Sexual Behavior in the Human Female*. Philadelphia: Saunders.

Kleiman, Carol. 1991. "Black Women Still Likely to Get Stuck at Low-End Jobs." *Washington Post*, 14 July.

Knecht, G. Bruce. 1997. "Hard Copy: Magazine Advertisers Demand Prior Notice of 'Offensive' Articles." *Wall Street Journal*, 30 April, 1.

Koedt, Ann. 1970. "The Myth of the Vaginal Orgasm." *Notes from the Second Year: Women's Liberation*, ed. Shulamith Firestone and Ann Koedt, pp. 37–43.

Konigsberg, Eric. 1998. "Sex Ed." *Spin*, June, 96–104.

Korman, S. K. 1983. "Nontraditional Dating Behavior: Date-Initiation and Date Expense–Sharing among Feminists and Nonfeminists. *Family Relations* 32: 575–81.

Koss, Mary, Christine A. Gidycz, and Nadine Wisnicski. 1987. "The Scope of Rape: Incidence and Prevalence of Sexual Aggression and Victimization in a National Sample of Higher Education Students." *Journal of Consulting and Clinical Psychology* 55, 162–70.

Kuczynski, Alex Rodriguez. 1999. "Enough about Feminism. Should I Wear Lipstick?" *New York Times*, 28 March, Perspectives sec., 4.

Laumann, Edward O., John H. Gagnon, Robert T. Michael, and Stuart Michaels. 1994. *The Social Organization of Sexuality: Sexual Practices in the United States*. Chicago: University of Chicago Press.

Laumann, Edward O., Anthony Paik, and Raymond C. Rosen. 1999. "Sexual Dysfunction in the United States." *Journal of the American Medical Association* 281: 537–44.

Lawrance, Kelli-an, David Taylor, and E. Sandra Byers. 1996. "Differences in Men's and Women's Global, Sexual, and Ideal-Sexual Expressiveness and Instrumentality." *Sex Roles* 34, no. 5/6: 337–57.

Lawson, A. 1988. *Adultery*. New York: Basic Books.

Leary, Mark R., and William E. Snell Jr. 1988. "The Relationship of Instrumentality and Expressiveness to Sexual Behavior in Males and Females." *Sex Roles* 18, no. 9/10: 509–22.

Lehrman, Karen. 1997. *The Lipstick Proviso: Women, Sex and Power in the Real World*. New York: Doubleday.

Levin, Lance. 1998. "Did Someone Say Orgasm Survey?" *Glamour*, July, 172–75.

Lewin, Tamar. 1997. "Fearing Disease, Teens Alter Sexual Practices." *New York Times*, 5 April, 7.

———. 1998a. "Debate Distant for Many Having Abortions." *New York Times*, 17 January, A1, A7.

———. 1998b. "Men Assuming Bigger Share at Home, New Survey Says." *New York Times*, 15 April, A16.

Lind, Michael. 1998. "The Beige and the Black." *New York Times Magazine*, 16 August, 38–39.

Lipsky, David. 1995. "Sex on Campus!!! The Latex Generation." *Rolling Stone*, 23 March, 80–85 ff.

Locker, Sari. 1995. *Mindblowing Sex in the Real World: Hot Tips for Doing It in an Age of Anxiety*. New York: HarperCollins.

Lottes, Ilsa. 1993. "Nontraditional Gender Roles and the Sexual Experiences of Heterosexual College Students." *Sex Roles* 29, no. 9/10: 645–69.

"Love Rules: The 1994 Details Survey on Romance and the State of Our Unions." 1994. *Details*, May, 107–13.

MacDonald, N., et al. 1990. "High Risk STD/HIV Behavior among College Students." *Journal of the American Medical Association* 263, 23: 3155–59.

Madigan, Charles. 1998. "Courtship without the Court." *Chicago Tribune*, 29 March, Perspectives sec., 1, 6.

Mansbach, Toby. 1998. "How Many Men Have You Slept With?" *Glamour*, March, 242–45.

Marin, Rick. 1999. "Those New Teen-Age Movies Fogged My Glasses." *New York Times*, 22 March, B9.

Marital Status and Living Arrangements (March 1994). 1996. By Arlene F. Saluter. Washington, DC: U.S. Bureau of the Census, February.

Marital Status and Living Arrangements (March 1998). 1998. By Terry A. Lugaila. Washington, DC: U.S. Bureau of the Census, October 29.

"Married Sex Sizzles." 1995. *EDK Forecast*. New York: EDK Associates, 5 March, 6.

McCarthy, Mary. 1963. *The Group*. New York: Harcourt, Brace and World.

McCarthy, Tara. 1997. *Been There, Haven't Done That: A Virgin's Memoir*. New York: Warner Books.

McCormick, Naomi B. 1994. *Sexual Salvation: Affirming Women's Sexual Rights and Pleasures*. Westport, CT: Praeger.

McCracken, Ellen. 1993. *Decoding Women's Magazines*. New York: St. Martin's Press.

McGavin, Patrick Z. 1996. "Single Minded." *Chicago Tribune*, 17 November, sec. 13, 1–2.

McGuire, Elizabeth. 1998. "Still Seeking a Perfect Balance." *New York Times*, 11 August, A9.

McMahon, Kathryn. 1990. "The Cosmopolitan Ideology and the Management of Desire." *Journal of Sex Research* 27, no. 3 (August): 381–96.

McNamara, J. Regis, and Kandee Grossman. 1991. "Initiation of Dates and Anxiety among College Men and Women. *Psychological Reports* 69: 252–54.

Michael, Robert T., et al. 1994. *Sex in America*. Boston: Little, Brown.

Miles, Rosalind. 1988. *A Woman's History of the World*. New York: Harper & Row.

Moore, Myreah, and Jodie Gould. 2000. *Date like a Man: To Get the Man You Want and Have Fun Doing It!* New York: HarperCollins.

Muehlenhard, Charlene L., and Marcia L. McCoy. 1991. "Double Standard/ Double Bind: The Sexual Double Standard and Women's Communication about Sex." *Psychology of Women Quarterly* 15, no. 3 (September): 447–61.

Muehlenhard, Charlene L., and Richard M. McFall. 1981. "Dating Initiation from a Woman's Perspective." *Behavioral Therapy* 12: 682–91.

Muehlenhard, Charlene L., and Teresa J. Scardino. 1985. "What Will He Think? Men's Impressions of Women Who Initiate Dates and Achieve Academically." *Journal of Counseling Psychology* 32: 560–69.

Murray, Thomas E. 1985. "The Language of Singles Bars." *American Speech* 60: 17–30.

Nagourney, Eric. 2000. "Study Finds Families Bypassing Marriage." *New York Times*, 15 February, D8.

National Survey of Family Growth (1995). 1997. Series 23, no. 19. Hyattsville, MD: U.S. Department of Health and Human Services, Centers for Disease Control and Prevention, National Center for Health Statistics, May.

Navratil, Wendy. 2000. "Read All about It." *Chicago Tribune*, 2 February, sec. 8, 1, 7.

Nelson, Blake. 1993. "Straight, No Chaser." *Details*, December, 74, 78.

Nelson, Mariah Burton. 1994. *The Stronger Women Get, the More Men Love Football*. New York: Harcourt, Brace.

Nelson, Sara. 1996. "'He Practically Lives with Me': A Look at the Downside of Casual Cohabitation" (sexual ethics column). *Glamour*, May, 150.

Obejas, Achy. 1993. "The Gay Gap." *Chicago Tribune*, 25 April, sec. 5, 1, 6.

Ogden, Gina. 1999. *Women Who Love Sex: An Inquiry into the Expanding Spirit of Women's Erotic Experience*. Cambridge, MA: Womenspirit Press.

O'Sullivan, Lucia F., and E. Sandra Byers. 1992. "College Students' Incorporation of Initiator and Restrictor Roles In Sexual Dating Interactions." *Journal of Sex Research* 29, no. 9 (August): 435–46.

———. 1993. "Eroding Stereotypes: College Women's Attempts to Influence Reluctant Male Sexual Partners." *Journal of Sex Research* 30: 270–82.

Paglia, Camille. 1992. "The Rape Debate, Continued." In her *Sex, Art, and American Culture*, pp. 55–74. New York: Vintage Books.

Pagnozzi, Amy. 1992. "Virgins with Attitude." *Glamour*, April, 234–37, 293–97.

Petchesky, Rosalind. 1990. "Giving Women a Real Choice; Abortion Issue." *The Nation,* 28 May, 732.

Pinsky, Drew, and Adam Carolla, with Marshall Fine. 1998. *The Dr. Drew and Adam Book: A Survival Guide to Life and Love.* New York: Dell.

Plotnikoff, David. 1999. "Sites Click with Young Women." *Chicago Tribune,* 1 February, sec. 4, 8.

Pogrebin, Robin. 1996. "Lesbian Publications Struggle for Survival in a Niche Dominated by Gay Males." *New York Times,* 23 December, C7.

Popenoe, David. 1993. "American Family Decline, 1960–1990: A Review and Appraisal." *Journal of Marriage and Family* 55 (August): 527–55.

Radakovich, Anka. 1994. *The Wild Girls Club: Tales from below the Belt.* New York: Crown Books.

Regan, Pamela, and C. Dreyer. 1999. "Lust? Love? Status? Young Adults' Motives for Engaging in Casual Sex." *Journal of Psychology and Human Sexuality* 11: 1–24.

Reinisch, June M., with Ruth Beasley. 1990. *The Kinsey Institute New Report on Sex: What You Must Know to Be Sexually Literate.* New York: St. Martin's Press.

Reiss, I. L. 1967. *The Social Context of Premarital Sexual Permissiveness.* New York: Rinehart and Winston.

———. 1986. *Journey into Sexuality: An Exploratory Voyage.* Englewood Cliffs, NJ: Prentice-Hall.

Rensin, David. 1994. "20 Questions for Heather Locklear." *Playboy,* September, 136–39.

Roberts, Tara. 1994. "Am I the Last Virgin?" *Essence,* June, 79–80, 117–18.

Robinson, I. E., and D. Jedlicka. 1982. "Changes in Sexual Attitudes and Behavior of College Students from 1965–1980: A Research Note." *Journal of Marriage and the Family* 44: 237–40.

Roche, J. P. 1986. "Premarital Sex: Attitudes and Behavior by Dating Stage." *Adolescence* 21: 107–21.

Roiphe, Katie. 1993a. "Date Rape's Other Victim." *New York Times Magazine,* 13 June, 26–30, 40, 68.

———. 1993b. *The Morning After: Sex, Fear, and Feminism on Campus.* Boston: Little, Brown.

———. 1994. "Date Rape: State of Siege." *Cosmopolitan,* January, 148–51.

———. 1997. *Last Night in Paradise.* Boston: Little, Brown.

Roof, Wade Clark. 1993. *A Generation of Seekers: The Spiritual Journey of the Baby Boom Generation.* San Francisco: HarperSanFrancisco.

Rossi, Alice S., ed. 1994. *Sexuality across the Life Course.* Chicago: University of Chicago Press.

Rowe, Chip. 1995. "The Safe Generation" (campus survey on political correctness). *Playboy,* June, 75–78, 152–53.

Sacks, Raina. 1990. "Sex on Campus." *InView,* March/April, 16.

Savage, Dan. 1998. *Savage Love: Straight Answers from America's Most Popular Sex Columnist*. New York: Dutton/Plume.

Seaman, Barbara. 1972. *Free and Female: The New Sexual Role of Women*. Greenwich, CT: Fawcett Crest.

Seelye, Katharine Q. 1995. "Gay Sister of Gingrich Will Lobby." *New York Times*, 3 June, A9.

Seggel, Heather. 1998. "Hating Loveline." *Bitch Magazine* 3, no. 1, 6–9.

Shalit, Wendy. 1999. *A Return to Modesty*. New York: Free Press.

Sheehy, Gail. 1976. *Passages*. New York: Dutton.

Sheffield, Rob. 1994. "Pearl Jams." *Details*, July, 64.

Sherwin, R., and S. Corbett. 1985. "Campus Sexual Norms and Dating Relationships. A Trend Analysis. *Journal of Sex Research* 21: 258–74.

Shreve, Jenn. 1998. "The Lady Is Not a Tramp." *Salon*, 11 February 1998, available online @ www.salon.com.

Sidel, Ruth. 1991. *On Her Own: Growing Up in the Shadow of the American Dream*. New York: Penguin.

Simon, Rita J., and Jean M. Landis. 1989. "Women's and Men's Attitudes about a Woman's Place and Role." *Public Opinion Quarterly* 53 (Summer): 265–76.

Sjoo, Monica, and Barbara Mor. 1987. *The Great Cosmic Mother*. San Francisco: Harper & Row.

Smith, Lynne. 1999. "Sex Education Centering on Abstinence Is Growing in Popularity." *Los Angeles Times*, 5 September.

Smith, Tom W. 1990. "The Sexual Revolution?" *Public Opinion Quarterly* 54 (Fall): 415–35.

———. 1994a. "Attitudes toward Sexual Permissiveness: Trends, Correlates, and Behavioral Connections." In *Sexuality across the Life Course*, ed. Alice S. Rossi, pp. 63–97. Chicago: University of Chicago Press.

———. 1994b. *The Demography of Sexual Behavior*. Menlo Park, CA: Henry J. Kaiser Family Foundation.

Solinger, Rickie. 1992. *Wake Up Little Susie: Single Pregnancy and Race before Roe v. Wade*. New York: Routledge.

Sommers, Christina Hoff. 1994. *Who Stole Feminism? How Women Have Betrayed Women*. New York: Simon & Schuster.

Sprecher, Susan. 1989. "Premarital Sexual Standards for Different Categories of Individuals." *Journal of Sex Research* 26, no. 2 (May): 232–48.

Sprecher, Susan, and Pamela C. Regan. 1996. "College Virgins: How Men and Women Perceive Their Sexual Status." *Journal of Sex Research* 33, no. 10: 3–15.

Starr Report. 1998. By Independent Counsel Kenneth W. Starr on his investigation of President Clinton, made public on 11 September. *New York Times*, 12 September 1998, B1–B24.

Stein, Sharman. 1995. "Marriage in the '90s: Ties Seem a Bit Likelier to Bind." *Chicago Tribune*, 1 August, sec. 4, 1.

Steinfels, Peter. 1991. "Debating Intermarriage and Jewish Survival." *New York Times*, 18 October, 1.

Stepp, Laura Sessions. 1999. "Parents Are Alarmed by an Unsettling New Fad in Middle Schools: Oral Sex." *Washington Post*, 8 July, A1.

Sullivan, Marion. 1999. "The Importance of Reaching the Post-Roe Generation: The Face and Future of the Reproductive Rights Movement." Pro Choice Public Education Project's web site available online @ www.protectchoice.org.

Tager, Joshua. 2000. "Gay. Not Gay." *Glamour*, January, 86–87.

Talese, Gay. 1980. *Thy Neighbor's Wife*. New York: Doubleday.

"The Tampon Taboo—The Period Goes Public." 1995. *EDK Forecast*. New York: EDK Associates, 5 March, 4–5.

Tannenbaum, Leora. 1999. *Slut! Growing Up in America with a Bad Reputation*. New York: Seven Stories Press.

Teegardin, Carol. 1993. "Is Parton Practising Reverse Sexism?" *Calgary Herald*, 13 March, F17.

Tharps, Lori L. 1999. "Women on Top: In TV, Film, and Music, Chicks Ruled the Roost." *Entertainment Weekly 1999 Year-End Special*, 70.

Thompson, Sharon. 1995. *Going All the Way: Teenage Girls' Tales of Sex, Romance and Pregnancy*. New York: Hill & Wang.

Treise, Deborah. 1997. "A Series of Focus Groups: Women, Men and Teens on Magazines as a Resource on Sexual Health." Menlo Park, CA: Henry J. Kaiser Family Foundation, April 18.

Twenge, Jean M. 1997a. "Attitudes toward Women, 1970–1995: A Meta-Analysis." *Psychology of Women Quarterly* 21: 35–51.

———. 1997b. "Changes in Masculine and Feminine Traits over Time: A Meta-Analysis." *Sex Roles* 36, no. 5/6: 305–25.

Vance, Debra-Ann. 1998. "Honor Club Ignores Pregnant A Student." *Cincinnati Post*, 15 April, available online @ kypost.com.

Vanzant, Iyanla, with Almasi Wilcots. 1999. *Don't Give It Away*. New York: Fireside.

Villarosa, Linda, ed. 1994. *Body and Soul: The Black Women's Guide to Physical Health and Emotional Well Being*. New York: HarperCollins.

Virginia Slims Opinion Poll 2000: Voices of Women. 2000. Commissioned by Philip Morris USA and conducted by Roper Starch Worldwide Inc. 8th ed. of survey, first conducted in 1970. Released February.

Vobejda, Barbara, and D'Vera Cohn. 1994. "Feds Note Big Rise in Stay Home Dads." *Washington Post*, 20 May, 3.

Wallis, Claudia. 1989. "Onward Women!" *Time*, 4 December, 82.

Warren, James. 1993. "Glamour's Jack Kliger." *Chicago Tribune*, 30 May, Tempo sec., 2.

Warshaw, Robin. 1988. *I Never Called It Rape*. New York: Harper & Row.

Weinberg, Martin S., Ilsa L. Lottes, and Liahna E. Gordon. 1997. "Social

Class Background, Sexual Attitudes and Sexual Behavior in a Heterosexual Undergraduate Sample." *Archives of Sexual Behavior* 26, no. 6 (December): 625.

Weinberg, Martin S., and C. J. Williams. 1980. "Sexual Embourgeoisement? Social Class and Sexual Activity: 1938 1970." *American Sociology Review* 45: 33–38.

Werner, Erica. 1997. "The Cult of Virginity." *Ms.*, March/April, 40–43.

Westheimer, Ruth. 1994. Syndicated advice column. *Chicago Tribune*, 25 July, 10.

Whitley, Bernard E. 1988. "The Relation of Gender-Role Orientation to Sexual Experience among College Students." *Sex Roles* 19, no. 9/10: 619–38.

Wilgoren, Jodi. 1999. "Abstinence Is Focus of U.S. Sex Education." *New York Times*, 15 December, A16.

Wilkinson, Kathleen. 1999. "Why Aren't There More Lesbian Features?" *Curve*, November, 24–26, 33.

Will, George. 1993. "Sex amidst Semi-Colons." *Newsweek*, 4 October, 92.

Wilson, Stephan M., and Nilufer P. Medora. 1990. "Gender Comparisons of College Students' Attitudes toward Sexual Behavior." *Adolescence* 25, no. 99 (Fall): 615–27.

Wolfe, Linda. 1981. *Women and Sex in the 80s: The Cosmo Report*. Bantam Books.

———. 1995. "Hot Monogamy." *Mirabella*, March, 127.

Wyatt, Edward. 1999. "Women Gain the Doctoral Chase." *New York Times*, 4 November, A17.

Wylie, Philip. 1942. *Generation of Vipers*. New York: Farrar & Rinehart.

Young, Toby. 1997. "Are You There God? . . . I Have a Few Thoughts on the Internet." *Spy*, November, 49–54.

Index

About the Author

Paula Kamen is a Chicago-based journalist, lecturer, playwright, and the author of what is widely noted as the first postboomer feminist book, *Feminist Fatale: Voices from the "Twentysomething" Generation Explore the Future of the "Women's Movement"* (1991). Her writing on feminism and young women has appeared in the *New York Times, Washington Post, Might, Ms., In These Times,* and the *Chicago Tribune.* Kamen has contributed essays to about a dozen anthologies, including *Next: Young American Writers on the New Generation* (1994), *Bad Girls/Good Girls: Women, Sex and Power in the Nineties* (1996), and *Shiny Adidas Track Suits and the Death of Camp: The Best of* Might *Magazine* (1998).

Since 1994, Kamen has been a visiting research scholar with Northwestern University's gender studies program. She is a 1989 graduate of the University of Illinois.

Photo by: J. B. Spector